Reimagining Textuality

Reimagining Textuality

Textual Studies in the Late Age of Print

Edited by

Elizabeth Bergmann Loizeaux
and
Neil Fraistat

THE UNIVERSITY OF WISCONSIN PRESS

The University of Wisconsin Press
1930 Monroe Street
Madison, Wisconsin 53711

www.wisc.edu/wisconsinpress/

3 Henrietta Street
London WC2E 8LU, England

Copyright © 2002
The Board of Regents of the University of Wisconsin System
All rights reserved

5   4   3   2   1

Printed in the United States of America

Library of Congress Cataloging-in-Publication Data
Reimagining textuality : textual studies in the late age
  of print / [edited by] Elizabeth B. Loizeaux and Neil Fraistat.
      270 pp.   cm.
   Includes bibliographical references and index.
   ISBN 0-299-17380-1 (cloth: alk. paper)
   ISBN 0-299-17384-4 (pbk.: alk. paper)
      1. Discourse analysis.   2. Editing.   3. Communication—Audio-visual
   aids.   4. Communication and culture.   I. Loizeaux, Elizabeth Bergmann.
   II. Fraistat, Neil, 1952–
   P302 .R454 2002
   302.2'02'08—dc21   2001001946

Publication of this book has been made possible in part by the generous support
of the Anonymous Fund of the University of Wisconsin–Madison.

Contents

Acknowledgments	vii
Introduction: Textual Studies in the Late Age of Print *Neil Fraistat and Elizabeth Bergmann Loizeaux*	3
Prologue: Compu[e]ting Editorial Fu[ea]tures *Jerome J. McGann*	17

Textuality and the Reproduction of Texts

The Philosophical Discourse of [Textuality]? *David Greetham*	31
Production, Invention, and Reproduction: Genetic vs. Textual Criticism *Daniel Ferrer*	48
Editing Bodies *Joseph Grigely*	60
Response: Shoptalk—Working Conditions and Marginal Gains *Rachel Blau DuPlessis*	85

Textuality and the Visual

Graphicality: Multimedia Fables for "Textual" Critics *Morris Eaves*	99
Taking Textual Time *Mary Ann Caws*	123

Intimations of Immateriality: Graphical Form, Textual Sense, and the Electronic Environment 152
Johanna Drucker

Response: Every Which Way but Loose 178
Charles Bernstein

Textuality and Culture

The Muse Learns to Tape 189
Tim Hunt

From Text to Work: Postcolonial Textuality 211
Henry Schwarz

Testing the Wires 225
Stuart Moulthrop

Response: Text Culture Grammatology 241
Gregory L. Ulmer

Contributors 253
Index 257

Acknowledgments

The making of *Reimagining Textuality* emphatically confirms what its individual essays contend: that writing and publishing are fundamentally social, collaborative affairs. We would like to thank George Bornstein, for setting this volume in motion and for his generous help and support along the way, and Marjorie Perloff, for offering sage and very practical advice at a crucial point in the manuscript's evolution. Our colleagues and friends, Jonathan Auerbach and Ted Leinwand, responded with their usual speed and acumen to an early draft of the introduction.

At the University of Wisconsin Press, we are grateful for the support of Raphael Kadushin and the attentive copyediting of Jane McGary.

Our greatest debt, of course, is to the contributors for their enthusiasm and their willingness to test the limits.

Finally, we would like to thank our families—especially Bill and Emma Loizeaux and Shawn and Ann Cleveland Fraistat—for the warm generosity and high spirits with which they supported our labors on this book.

Reimagining Textuality

Neil Fraistat and Elizabeth Bergmann Loizeaux

Introduction
Textual Studies in the Late Age of Print

As we began writing this introduction, two articles appeared in the *New York Times* with striking relevance for our volume. The first announced a decision by the Judiciary Committee of the U.S. House of Representatives to post Kenneth Starr's report on President Clinton on the Internet before the committee members even had a chance to read it. The second was an essay by Walter Murch on his re-editing of Orson Welles's last Hollywood feature film, *Touch of Evil*. Both reports raise interesting questions about textuality at the close of the twentieth century. In the first instance, we are led to ask what it might mean to have a political culture mediated by the World Wide Web: a culture in which the Starr report can become a major textual event, not only distributed to millions of users but also transformed—as the term "users" rather than "readers" suggests—sliced, diced, and recontextualized in an unimaginable number of ways, then redistributed by hundreds of websites. Such textual proliferation and mutation and the concomitant instant globalization of texts are characteristic of the late age of print, an age we see as a transitional moment in the conditions of textuality, analogous in importance to the change from manuscript to print.

Walter Murch's work on Welles's cult classic, *Touch of Evil* (1958), brings to the fore another pressing set of questions. Welles was notorious for the amount of time he spent editing his films, and his slow labor on what was intended as a B picture spooked Universal Studios into taking the project away from him, shooting more footage, and re-editing the whole. The extent of these alterations was not widely known until recently, when a rediscovered fifty-eight-page memo from Welles to Universal made clear that, in the words of Murch, "the film never accurately reflected Welles's intentions" (*New York Times,* 6 September 1998). In creating his version of the film, Murch returned to the negative of the 1958 version as his base text and—following the instructions in Welles's memo, as well as he could construe them—made about fifty changes, several of them substantial, in an effort to create "a better version of the same film, which is to say, more in line with the director's vision, more self-consistent, more resonant, more confidently modulated, clearer. In other words, more as it should have been in the first place." Murch, however, concedes that whether "the film is now the way Welles would have wanted it had he been given a free hand, we will never know." This uncertainty is heightened by Welles's own memo, written after he had seen the initial cut, which states: "The purpose of this memo is not to discuss every change I think should be made in the final version. I am passing on to you a reaction based not on my conviction as to what my picture ought to be, but only what here strikes me as significantly mistaken in your picture" (quoted by Murch).

Yet the textual history of *Touch of Evil* is even more complicated than Welles's distinction between "my picture" and "your picture" suggests. There are at least five distinct versions: the unfinished version that Welles filmed but only partially edited, which he calls "my picture"; "your picture," the initial cut of the film prepared by Universal and shown to Welles, in which four new scenes had been added to "clarify" the plot line; the film actually released to theaters—a version Welles never saw—which not only adds the four scenes that Welles did not film but also cuts fifteen minutes of material that Welles did film; a 1987 video release of the film that appears to be a hybrid mix of the initial cut and the released version; and Murch's 1998 attempt to return to Welles's intentions. Ironically, it has been Universal's released version that has been most influential in film history, championed by such auteurs as Jean-Luc Godard, François Truffaut, and the rest of the French New Wave, who thought they were celebrating Welles's work alone. Murch's return to a version based on Welles's intentions thus alters some of the film's distinctive features that have been important in its reception history and that have influenced other directors.

The complicated textual history of *Touch of Evil* leads us to ask how the tools and practices of textual scholarship might illuminate its text. What would it mean, for example, to do a textual edition of *Touch of Evil*—or of any film? Could there be meaningful textual editions of television shows, gardens, maps, or buildings—or, for that matter, of human bodies? How might the forms and methods of textual scholarship be adapted to serve nonliterary texts in the late age of print?

Such questions require contextualization. Until recently, the gap between textual scholarship and postmodern theory and criticism was nowhere wider than in their divergent concepts of text and textuality. There is no need to rehearse here how structuralism and poststructuralism since the late 1960s have altered our sense of textuality by reading as "texts" a broad range of cultural phenomena. Whereas the philologically derived focus of textual scholarship has been on text as a literary object, the semiotically inflected focus of postmodern theory and criticism, derived from Roland Barthes and Jacques Derrida, has been on text as a function of signifying practices. In the 1980s, however—prompted largely by the seminal work of D. F. McKenzie and, especially, Jerome J. McGann—textual scholarship began moving in interdisciplinary directions, reconceiving its idea of text as words on a printed page while bringing its own disciplinary insights to fields and cultural phenomena beyond its accustomed purview.[1] From the cross-pollination of postmodernism and textual scholarship has arisen the hybrid field of textual studies.

As a discipline, textual studies provides a broad umbrella for a host of subfields concerned with the production, distribution, reproduction, consumption, reception, archiving, editing, and sociology of texts. Although the field is far-flung, its most compelling energies are directed toward reimagining the methods, objects, and goals of textual scholarship. On one hand, scholars are exploring textuality beyond the printed word and assembled book, treating for the first time as the object of textual scholarship (subject to being edited and archived) other cultural products that postmodern theory has been reading as texts. On the other hand, partly as a result of this exploration, they are interpreting the book itself and the various forms of print textuality and manuscripts as cultural products. Thus, through textual studies, not only are the methods and concerns of textual scholarship being made available to other fields, but those methods and concerns themselves are dialectically shaping and being shaped by other kinds of textuality beyond the book—as the essays in this volume illustrate. Chief among these kinds is electronic textuality, which is creating new forms of textuality and making possible new ways of reproducing, editing, and archiving texts. With its multimedia and networked capabilities, electronic textuality foregrounds the role played by the visual and aural elements of textuality, as well as the social and material ontologies of texts.

As it has moved beyond the book, textual studies has brought into focus the materiality of the book itself. The work of Jerome McGann, in particular, has created the grounds for what might be termed a "poetics of the book," in which the material and linguistic elements of a book are seen as interacting under the horizon of its production, transmission, and reception.[2] Especially useful has been McGann's distinction between a book's bibliographical codes—such elements as page format, paper, typefaces, price, advertising mechanisms, and distribution venues—and its linguistic codes, which include not only all the linguistic text proper, but also the set of surrounding paratexts (e.g., prefaces, dedications, footnotes).[3] Beyond relating books to their own sociohistorical moment in new ways, McGann's bibliographic code has activated for critics material elements long thought extraneous to the central business of interpretation—for example, the size, shape, cover design, color, typeface, illustrations, and decorations of a book. If such distinctions, then, require us to recognize that words in books always come embodied and in the company of other kinds of material signs, they also require us to recognize the multiplicity and significance of those signs.[4] Is it a function of our logocentrism—as several essays in this collection suggest—that we have designated a code for the word and lumped everything else under "bibliographic"?

In practice, material bibliographic codes most often mean the visual elements of a text, the critical pursuit of which has illuminated the problem of extending "text" beyond the word. Insofar as "biblio-" retains its origin in the production of words, by extending it to the visual we risk perpetuating a long history of Western attitudes toward the image as subordinate to the word. Although McGann and others have attempted to liberate the suppressed image, the "bibliographic" as a category subsumes the visual under the linguistic; by bringing images within the rubric historically defined by language, this assumes that images are amenable to language-derived interpretive strategies, thereby participating in what Murray Kreiger contentiously describes as "the ultimate imperialistic move by literature and literary criticism to subject to its terms all the arts and all the arts of discourse alike."[5] Semiotics, which has done so much to allow us to see sign systems in relation to one another and to make interdisciplinary work possible, nonetheless tends to homogenize difference so that everything appears to behave like language.

Textual studies is not alone in this interdisciplinary dilemma. The new art history, which came into force in the 1980s, propelled (like textual studies) by the heady possibilities of applying the methods of literary analysis to nonverbal signs, almost immediately began to question itself.[6] W. J. T. Mitchell posits that the postmodern "linguistic turn," which helped to produce both textual studies and the new art history, is already giving way to a "pictorial turn" that began with the advent of photography.[7] If this is true, we urgently need better understanding of the visual elements of textuality: what images are, and how they mean. For textual studies, there are local corrections, such as replacing or supplementing "bibliographic" with "iconic" or "graphical" (the term Morris Eaves uses in his essay on Blake in this volume) to designate the visual aspects of texts—but these changes evade the central issues. The challenge is not simply to replace the hegemony of the word with that of the image, but rather to articulate the verbal and visual together. Textual studies must learn to carry the full weight of its claims to interdisciplinarity.

Nowhere are these claims more strenuously tested than in the realm of electronic textuality, in which image, word, and sound cohabit promiscuously. Hyperbolic arguments are routinely made both for and against the idea that electronic textuality is a radical break with past forms of textuality, and it is often historicized as the fault line between the modern and the postmodern. Yet, as Espen Aarseth notes, "The ideological forces surrounding new technology produce a rhetoric of novelty, differentiation, and freedom that works to obscure the more profound structural kinships between superficially heterogenous media."[8] Textual studies needs to map these kinships, theorizing new media in terms of the old, and vice versa. For example, from the perspective of electronic technology, the book can now be seen as a supple technological wonder in itself, a highly adaptive machine providing an array of elegant options for presenting complex orders of information. Although hypertext—especially the larger hypertext that is the World Wide Web—promises a new kind of nonhierarchical, nonlinear, decentered textuality, the fact remains that print textuality too can have many of those characteristics. Moreover, the most common organizational strategy on the "decentered" Web is the hierarchical list itself, and most users prefer to visit links from meta-lists rather than to follow links within documents in search of information.[9] Similarly, although textual editors have been turning increasingly to the digital environs of the World Wide Web and the CD-ROM for advantages they offer in terms of accessibility, searchability, extensibility, interactivity, and storage capacity, the Standard Generalized Mark-up Language (SGML) in which data for these editions and archives are usually encoded is so hierarchically organized that it has trouble accounting for the complex structures of imaginative works of literature and art, as Jerome McGann elaborates in his essay in this volume. Arguments over the "true" nature of electronic textuality must at least account for the interplay of these counter-tendencies, even as they acknowledge the blurred edges of distinctions between electronic and print textuality.

In contrast to print texts, which always have a local habitation and a name, the ontology of electronic texts is fluid and dynamic: not just dependent on a confluence of interacting hardware and software, but also never quite the same on any two computers. Electronic texts also have a kind of verticality in their linguistic code that is absent in print: beneath the alphanumeric language of the electronic text proper are layers of alphanumeric codes, from the system software of the computer to the word-processing programs or software packages in which the linguistic text was generated and through which it is being read. Such layering opens up the possibility of an aesthetics not just of the ultimate presentation on screen, but within the writing of the mediating code itself. Various programmers are known to have distinctive styles and flourishes that act as their "signatures" but are invisible to anyone without access to the code itself, and such signatures can be manifested at any or all levels of the alphanumeric text. The textual relations among these multiple layers of signification still await theorizing, as does the larger question they help to frame: Where are we to locate the materiality of electronic texts?

Such a question becomes even more vexed when one recognizes the plurality of electronic textuality, which goes beyond hypertexts proper to include search engines, databases, interactive games and robots, e-mail, websites of untold variety, and the digital communities of MOOs and MUDs. The variety of digital forms and formats; the sheer number of participating authors, editors, wizards, producers, consumers, chatters, and users; the collaborative space they all share on the World Wide Web, itself an ever-changing nexus of juridical, institutional, national, transnational, and economic interests—all these make clear why, as Kathryn Sutherland has pointed out, electronic textuality "furthers the impossibility of textual, literary, and cultural critics assuming and defending the separateness of their activities: electronic representation enacts the inclusiveness of text."[10]

To talk about texts and textuality, then, is ultimately to talk about culture, the ground on which we and our texts inhabit the textual condition. We live in a transitional moment in which literacy is giving way to what Greg Ulmer calls "electracy," and human subjectivities are being transformed as much by *how* we read as by *what* we read. The very "inclusiveness of text" of which Sutherland speaks, then, places rigorous demands on the scope and methods of textual studies as a critical practice.

In spite of these demands, textual studies is still largely a language-based and print-centered discipline whose methods meet resistance and sometimes even incoherence whenever visual images or sound and not words are the dominant mode of expression—for example, when the medium of the book is exchanged for the multimedia formats of films, performance art, or digital texts. Thus, the "first-generation" exuberance of a McKenzie, calling for a bibliography that would in effect encompass all conceivable texts, has necessarily given way to a "second-generation" self-consciousness about the array of resistances posed by nonlinguistic texts and about the limitations of existing textual scholarship for confronting them. It is in the spirit of this second generation or second wave of textual studies that the essays in this volume have their being. The authors are conscious that the process of reimagining textuality is continual, both fraught with difficulties and vibrant with possibilities.

As should now be apparent, the issues faced by textual studies range far beyond what can be covered in any single collection of essays. *Reimagining Textuality* focuses on three dynamic interdisciplinary fields in which textual scholarship and postmodern theory and criticism are beginning to talk to each other about text and textuality in especially innovative and suggestive ways: textual editing, verbal-visual studies, and cultural studies. The book starts within the community of textual scholarship and editorial theory with the prologue and a section on textual reproduction. It extends into verbal-visual, postcolonial, and cultural studies with essays by scholars— some already grounded in textual scholarship, some not—who have been asked to test the methods and concerns of textual studies in those fields. We begin with "Compu[e]ting Editorial Fu[ea]tures," a prologue by Jerome J. McGann, whose work on the "textual condition" made possible much of what follows. The new understanding of textuality that McGann proposed in a series of books in the late 1980s and 1990s helped to open up textual criticism to postmodern theory; his meditation here on the practical difficulties and theoretical implications of putting such conceptions of textuality into practice in both editing and critical writing underscores the necessity for continued reimagining of the modes and methods through which we reproduce scholarly texts, especially as we work through the implications and possibilities of electronic textuality.

The essays in the first section, "Textuality and the Reproduction of Texts," introduce current issues in textual scholarship, demonstrating the contributions made by postmodern theory over the past fifteen years to editorial theory and practice. All three reimagine textuality by resisting what David Greetham calls the "Platonizing impulse" of modern textual criticism, and what Joseph Grigely calls "Romantic idealism": the imagining of some ideal text toward which editors labor. Institutionally sanctioned by the Modern Language Association's Committee on Scholarly Editions and theoretically articulated by W. W. Greg and Fredson Bowers, this imagining has guided editorial activity since the mid-twentieth century. In his historically and philosophically wide-ranging overview of textual criticism, "The Philosophical Discourse of [Textuality]?," Greetham argues instead for a concept of textuality that substitutes timeliness for timelessness, locality for generality, particularization for universalism, and a "rhetoric" of text for a "grammar" or "logic" of text. This postmodern model, he suggests, returns to the premodern, to the medieval.

Arguing the merits of genetic criticism (founded in the study of drafts) and of process rather than product, Daniel Ferrer in "Production, Invention, and Reproduction" would crack open the concept of "textual production": such production consists not just of the various printed versions of a text but also of the drafts that stretch back behind it. Textuality, then, concerns as much "the process of writing," "a movement," as it does the thing one reads on the screen or holds in the hand. The drafts—the *avant-texte*—are "open fields" whose "injunctions" to the reader are multiple (a scenario, for example, is an injunction to "tell a story in different words"; marginal comments might say more explicitly, "change this"). In their dialectic of invention and repetition, drafts demonstrate in immediate terms that the author is made in the process of production, and that authorial intent is fluid and provisional.

Joseph Grigely, a conceptual artist and textual theorist, sets textual criticism in conversation with body criticism, genetics, and taxidermy in his essay, "Editing Bodies." He extends Ferrer's analysis of the "traditional representation of textual transmission as genealogy" and what comes with it—women figured as a source of pollution in the pure male line (Ferrer)—and adds an editorial vocabulary that shares the concepts of difference and deviance with the science of eugenics, with which it developed historically. Grigely's "peregrinations" among tabloids, postcards, ads, pop art, and high art engage the categories (the "fantasies," in Ferrer's terms) under which bodies and texts are altered and reproduced: the beautiful, the normal, the natural. "By its very nature, editing is a transgressive practice," writes Grigely. "What is ironic about this is that art cannot exist by any other means."

Rachel DuPlessis's response to these three essays, "Shoptalk," reminds us that on the other side of the theorizing—on the other side of the social processes to which texts are subject, about which Greetham, Ferrer, and Grigely speak so differently and provocatively—are social needs and difficult questions regarding which works get reproduced and edited in the first place, and to what ends. As DuPlessis puts it, "The expansion of the canon has necessitated a pragmatic look around." However one wants to define "text," readers still need something to read, "some reasonable, decent edition" of, say, Charlotte Smith. Under the light of DuPlessis's musings as poet, feminist critic, and editor, new editorial theory—for all its celebration of difference and variety—risks developing into a critic-centered study practiced on the work of established authors; its intention to acknowledge and present multiple versions, though admirable, is often simply not practical, even in electronic media. Whose work gets reproduced in expensive multi-version editions? What kinds of production are most fruitful for genetic criticism? Who benefits? These are the questions that DuPlessis would have us keep in view.

The essays in the next section, "Textuality and the Visual," grapple with the materiality of the text, in particular the visual component so problematic for McGann. In doing so, they revisit "time" and "space"—that "venerable opposition," as Morris Eaves in "Graphicality" calls it, articulated by Gotthold Lessing in the eighteenth century to categorize the verbal (temporal) and visual (spatial). Continuing DuPlessis's concern with canon formation, Eaves demonstrates how Blake's "intercanonical" work that straddles the verbal and the visual impeded his entry into either canon, despite proponents on both sides. Although Swinburne "rescued" Blake for posterity, he did so by sponsoring him into the canon of words and thereby abetting the persistent misunderstanding of his work: "This decorative work is after all the mere husk and shell" of the poems, he wrote. The gendered aspects of textual transmission, broached by Ferrer and DuPlessis, surface again as Eaves persuasively argues that Swinburne's recuperative effort to present the essential (verbal) Blake rests on Western suspicion of the image as female, bodily, childish, excessive: something to be outgrown or shed as Blake's reputation matured.

Opening out difficulties like those that confounded Blake's readers and editors and nearly consigned him to oblivion, Mary Ann Caws in "Taking Textual Time" turns, as does DuPlessis, to the reader/beholder's share. She asks us to "worry" for the moment about time in its local dimension, about pace as well as space, about the demands made on readers by complex, antilinear, verbal/visual/aural texts. Taking Shusaku Arakawa and Madeline Gins's project *The Mechanism of Meaning* as her example, Caws, like Grigely, explores issues highlighted by extending the concept of text beyond the conventional objects of textual criticism. Whereas Ferrer sees the injunctions texts give their readers as fairly legible, Caws thinks they are not, particularly when those texts make heavy use of the visual: "We are complex readers; we have not learned, most of us, to be complex viewers." She wonders whether we can slow ourselves down enough to learn to look, to adjust ourselves to the varying paces demanded by verbal-visual texts.

Turning from material to seemingly immaterial verbal-visual texts, Johanna Drucker in "Intimations of Immateriality" brings her experience as book artist and theorist to bear on philosophical and practical issues of electronic textuality, a topic that gathers force through the volume in McGann's prologue and the essays by Greetham, Ferrer, and Eaves. "What portion," she wants to know, "of the actual message and meaning a text communicates is challenged, intensified, or lost in this electronic environment?" To answer that, she begins at the level of the letter, asking, "What constitutes the information of a text?" Drucker refutes from a different angle the Platonic concept of textuality that Greetham also rejected: the materiality of a text is significant, even "within its (mis)perceived condition as immaterial in the electronic environment." The spatial and temporal freedoms of the electronic environment, she suggests, may unsettle "fixed relations of materiality" and offer "possibilities for reconceptualization of language as information in the traditional media as well as in hypertext and electronic formats."

Charles Bernstein's response to these three essays, "Every Which Way but Loose," underscores the difficulty of reading verbal-visual texts: "For who among us has not secretly read our paperback, graphics-expurgated, Blake with the glee of a schoolchild high on Cliff notes, even after many professions of born-again faith in the only truth of his visualized hypermedia?" He celebrates the challenges these texts pose to what he calls "the 'humanist' ideology dominant within the university and also in the mass media." Returning our attention to the "ideal," he sees a relation between fear of electronic media and an "intensively anti-materialist, which is to say idealist, assertion of cultural authority and legitimacy." For Bernstein, accepting multiple versions of a work means accepting the nature of writing itself as transformation and translation (what Grigely calls "transgression"). The relation between versions, then, "is not a moral one of right and wrong but an ethical one of reciprocity." Implicitly here, and explicitly in his admiration for "explorers of hypertext" and the "radically paratactic explorations" of modernist and contemporary poets, he calls for "works that require the active participation and critical reflection of viewers and readers." His conclusion to the essay, a response to Arakawa and Gins and to Caws on Arakawa and Gins, both demonstrates and demands the reciprocity he admires.

The final section of the book, "Textuality and Culture," pursues intersections between textual studies and the similarly nascent fields of cultural studies and postcolonial studies. Tim Hunt's opening essay, "The Muse Learns to Tape," attends to the dynamic between the oral and the literate in jazz and its development in rock-and-roll (Jelly Roll Morton and the Grateful Dead, for example). Hunt explores whether the tendency toward formal and structural articulation and stability that accompanies the transformation of the oral/performative/improvisational into text is "inherent in the nature of textuality itself," or whether it changes with and reflects "particular textual media." Like Drucker, he is interested in what can be learned about textuality by studying the transformation of one mode into another. Like Greetham, he insists on a "textual rhetoric" "of which our models for written productions are specific instances."

Continuing Hunt's interest in production and transformation, Henry Schwarz returns to Barthes and poststructuralism to "open a conceptual space between European textual theory and cultural practice in postcolonial India." Directly addressing Barthes's essay "From Work to Text," whose terms underlie many of the discussions in this collection, he argues that "far from displacing the material solidity of the work onto the ineffable transient text that can be interpreted variously and without limits, Barthes hypermaterializes the text." In a complex and nuanced argument, Schwarz suggests the parallels between Barthes's and Althusser's structures of production: as human labor for Althusser has value only when it produces something that can be exchanged, so Barthes insists that the writing body "does not know meaning as such but acts as a transport and a limit for the passing on of language." The text in that sense gives rise to the work. The "aleatory materialism" of Barthes and Althusser has, argues Schwarz, "resonances with other forms of textual productivity beyond Europe," especially in the decolonizing world "where Marxism was prominent as theory and practice for most of the twentieth century, and where the relations of text and production . . . pose vital questions for urban intellectuals attempting to communicate with differently literate, rural audiences."

Stuart Moulthrop's "Testing the Wires" returns to electronic textuality, particularly the World Wide Web, and recognizes a danger to what Rachel DuPlessis identified in regard to new concepts of textuality in general: that electronic textuality may develop "in a purely esoteric or inward direction." Like DuPlessis, he asserts that "our needs are increasingly practical." The problem is not just in textual practices or in theory, but more fundamentally in social institutions, including academic institutions in which (quoting Mark Taylor and Esa Saarinen) "expert language is a prison for knowledge and understanding." Turning to the possibilities offered by the Web, Moulthrop asks whether it can "pass the test of social application." He answers that "the early indications seem negative," in large part because the Web is strongly dominated by the interests of global capitalism; however, a way forward might be suggested by Martin Spinelli's vision of "a public identified as producers, not consumers." This is, indeed, as Moulthrop concludes, a test, not only of our willingness to engage but also of our ability to articulate our textual lives with the matrix of social forces to which they are connected.

Gregory Ulmer's response to this section—which also broadly sums up the whole volume and looks beyond it—proposes that we are poised on the edge of a great cultural shift akin to that from orality to literacy, a shift to "electracy." This change, says Ulmer, will be accompanied by new structures of thought and new kinds of identity; it will require new models of textuality that are drawn not from the book but from the verbal-visual-aural in some yet unimagined way. For Ulmer, W. J. T. Mitchell is right: we are experiencing a "pictorial turn" that will revolutionize our way of being in the world. Like Caws, Ulmer believes we do not yet know how to look at texts; more important, like Moulthrop, he thinks we must become not merely savvy (visually literate) consumers of the new kind of texts the computer makes possible, but active producers of them. "If ever our society needed its textual theorists," he concludes, "now is the time."

As is perhaps most evident in the title of DuPlessis's response "Shoptalk," a workshop atmosphere prevails in this book, as it should. The essays here come out of the contributors' daily engagements with issues that are coalescing under the rubric of textual studies. Different voices—often informal, all distinct—approach the issues raised by new forms and understandings of textuality within different specializations. We asked the contributors to be provocative, even polemical, and to press the limits they saw from the perspectives of their particular interests. They are testing how plastic the concept of "text" is, what issues it raises, and how far it can be extended and still be useful. Personal anecdotes abound, as do explicit questions and the playing out of possibilities as perhaps no more than possibilities.

In all these essays, the predominance of metaphors and the search for models suggest the probing nature of the efforts to reimagine textuality in the late age of print—a trying out and trying on. Their variety reflects the current state of our discipline: in Gregory Ulmer's account, what happened in the 1970s when poststructuralist theory (and, one might add, feminist criticism) opened the literary canon and extended the field of inquiry to other cultural artifacts. This variety is, as Ulmer suggests, unified by the concept of text. From McGann's musings on a rejected essay, through Grigely's experiences in the supermarket check-out line, to Tim Hunt's memories of the San Francisco music scene of the 1970s, the points from which many of these essays depart suggest the extent to which textual issues pervade our daily lives and underlie pressing questions of our culture. Within the academy, departments of language and literature are developing interdisciplinary courses in textual studies; rethinking introductory courses for graduate study in those same terms; forming cross-disciplinary "collectives" to develop the possibilities of electronic textuality and theorize its significance; and pondering the new forms of subjectivity that the late age of print both promises and threatens to bring into being. We hope this book, in its variety and openness, will be suggestive for all these ongoing reimaginings of textuality.

Notes

1. See McKenzie, *Bibliography and the Sociology of Texts* (London: British Library, 1986) and McGann's *A Critique of Modern Textual Criticism* (Chicago: University of Chicago Press, 1983) and his *The Textual Condition* (Princeton: Princeton University Press, 1991).

2. One implication of a poetics of the book is that it calls for a refocusing of lit-

erary history. Closely allied with New Historicism in this regard, textual studies is shaping a literary history focused on reception, on production practices and limitations, and on social conceptions of what a book is and does. Eaves's essay on Blake in this volume demonstrates both the necessity for such a history and its explanatory powers.

Two other essays suggest the ways textual studies is also reconfiguring our traditional historical categories. Greetham provocatively aligns the postmodern and the medieval, a coupling reinforced by Drucker's return to medieval graphical structures of knowledge to suggest the significance of spatial arrangements, that tenet of postmodern textuality. In addition, these two scholars, here and elsewhere, set some terms for rethinking high modernism and its relation to postmodernism. Seeing in high modernism the origins of concepts of text and author that recent textual criticism seeks to supplant, Greetham would "grant, as a medium for discussion, Clement Greenberg's assertion that the paradigm of modernism is an opaque, non-referential, noncontextualized essentialism" (*Palimpsest: Editorial Theory in the Humanities,* ed. George Bornstein and Ralph G. Williams [Ann Arbor: University of Michigan Press, 1993], 19). This is precisely the definition Drucker rejects in *The Visible Word* (Chicago: University of Chicago Press, 1994) as untenable because it ignores, as art and literary history have in its wake, the importance of typographic innovation in high modernist verbal and visual art. Pursuing the implications of McGann's "bibliographic codes," recent work on such modernist poets as Yeats and Pound suggests that Drucker is right, and in her essay here she sees such postmodern poets as Loss Pequeño Glazier, Jim Rosenberg, and Charles Bernstein continuing in electronic form the very experiments with verbal-visual textuality that characterize the high moderns.

3. McGann, *The Textual Condition,* 12–14.

4. The richly suggestive essays in George Bornstein and Theresa Tinkle's collection *The Iconic Page in Manuscript, Print, and Digital Culture* (Ann Arbor: University of Michigan Press, 1998) demonstrate how materialist readings are already transforming our understanding of literary history as well as of individual authors and works. See especially Michael Camille's "Sensations of the Page: Imaging Technologies and Medieval Illuminated Manuscripts" (33–54), which usefully reminds us that texts appeal not just to the eyes but to the "entire sensorium," in Bornstein and Tinkle's felicitous phrase (2).

5. Murray Kreiger, *Ekphrasis: The Illusion of the Natural Sign* (Baltimore: Johns Hopkins University Press, 1992), 26.

6. See, for example, Norman Bryson, "Intertextuality and Visual Poetics" in a special issue of *Style* on "Visual Poetics," edited by Mieke Bal (22, no. 2 [summer 1988]: 183–93).

7. W. J. T. Mitchell, "The Pictorial Turn," in *Picture Theory: Essays on Verbal and Visual Representation* (Chicago: University of Chicago Press, 1994), 11–34.

8. Espen Aarseth, *Cybertext: Perspectives on Ergodic Literature* (Baltimore: Johns Hopkins University Press, 1997), 14.

9. For an argument that the surface structure and the deep structure of the Web may be at odds and that, although hypertextuality may in and of itself be decentral-

izing, the Web as a hypertext collection works against this decentralization in important ways, see Neil Fraistat, Steven E. Jones, and Carl Stahmer, "The Canon, the Web, and the Digitization of Romanticism," *Romanticism on the Net* 10 (May 1998), http://users.ox.ac.uk/~scat0385/rcron.html.

10. Kathryn Sutherland, introduction, in *Electronic Text: Investigations in Method and Theory* (Oxford: Clarendon Press, 1997), 3.

Jerome J. McGann

Prologue
Compu[e]ting Editorial Fu[ea]tures

A short time ago, I was asked informally to submit something to the distinguished journal *Computers and the Humanities*. I was pleased to send a new piece that was nearing completion.

Don't turn off your set. It is true that anecdotes, especially personal ones, often make dismal invitations in the discourse of scholarship. But this one is, I hope, peculiarly apt in the context of this collection of original (in both senses of the word) essays about "textual studies in the late age of print."

The problem with my essay arrived in two waves. When I sent it for consideration, I noted to the editors that it called for a half-dozen color reproductions "illustrating" the final section. I asked if this would this present any difficulties. None at all, a return letter assured me, though I would have to pay the costs involved, which came to several thousand dollars.

Since I couldn't afford that expense, I made a double decision. First, I would remove the last part of the essay and modify the earlier parts to accommodate the change. The essay was in any case organized in modular units, so the revision would not be too difficult. But because that last section contained what was for me the most intellectually challenging material in the piece, I knew that I would have to find another way to "publish" it. That was not very difficult, either: I would simply post the whole essay on my Web page, including links to digital files of the color images that could not be included in the printed essay.[1] (There is a benevolent irony here. Those images were originally digital files created in Adobe Photoshop. Had they been reproduced in *Computers and the Humanities,* the print texts would have been, as Frank O'Hara might have said, "a step away from them.")

Several months passed before the reader's report arrived with its second wave of problems. It was an excellent report—searching, intelligent, and even (always pleasing) full of favorable remarks. Making revisions in light of the critique was going to improve the essay, so I felt—and still feel—grateful to this anonymous reader.

But the reviewer saw a "major weakness" in the essay: "its somewhat unclear structure." The point was elaborated in this way:

> There is no initial overview, and no final summary. . . . The thematic composition suffers from a lot of back and forth, and it contains a combination of project report and theoretical argument which makes the paper too long, confusing and hard to follow. The statement of goals for the paper (or for the Rossetti Archive) is clear enough, but it is not always clear that the material discussed is relevant to these goals, and there is no clear evaluation of the results in terms of the goals.[2]

I weighed these comments for some time before realizing that they could not be dealt with through any kind of "revision" process. The reader's difficulties signaled a gap between an essay that was being looked for and the one that had actually been written. More important, this gap seemed to me an index of a wider division of thought about how to address certain key conceptual issues that attend many current projects involving "computer" and "humanities" scholarship. The problem with printing the images represents an elementary version of this larger question.

I

Let me begin with this problem of printing the images. Within the community of scholars who work on and with electronic textuality—theorizing and building the tools and then reflecting on the events—a division has emerged in the area of electronic editions that goes, as Robert Frost once wrote, "out far and in deep." In its simplest form, the question is: Should a scholarly edition be organized as an "image-based" edition, or should it concentrate its computerized resources on tools for searching, analyzing, and collating alphanumeric data? As Julia Flanders observes in a good recent essay[3] on this question in *Computers and the Humanities,* this problem has two facets:

> One involves the practical design of scholarly electronic editions. This is the issue of how visual evidence functions within the intellectual economy of the edition and how it interacts with the other kinds of information the edition offers . . . [i.e.] the role of transcribed text, of metadata, of text encoding, of references, of computational features such as algorithms for collating variants or manipulating the text. (301)

The second question, more far-reaching, involves "the way editions produce textual knowledge" and, hence, the role that digital imaging can play in the design and development of these scholarly instruments.

Working with images, particularly full-color images, in a paper-based medium has always been problematic. It is not easy to produce these images in print, and it is always expensive, as my experience with *Computers and the Humanities* showed. On the other hand, reproducing, storing, and manipulating color images in electronic media is relatively simple and inexpensive. (Some might say "all too simple.") When I learned that my digitized images could not be included in the essay in *Computers and the Humanities,* I decided to load the complete essay with its color images for Web access. The whole process took only a couple of hours.

This event constructs an allegory about the respective limits and powers of paper-based texts and electronic texts. At first glance, we see the far greater flexibility and power of the computerized environment, which can accommodate and interrelate many types of information-bearing media: textual, of course, but visual (still and moving pictures) and audial as well. On reflection, though, our view shifts; however easily I was able to upload my essay for World Wide Web access, its Internet availability also disconnects it and makes it invisible in important ways. Simply put, the audience of the Web is vast, whereas *Computers and the Humanities* targets and focuses its readership. The disadvantage of publishing my essay on my website is that from that point, it does not readily enter the network of scholarly discourse for which it was written.

We might point out that soon (alas, a relative word) these scholarly journals will be stored and disseminated in some electronic "Web-based" form. Besides, the "network of scholarly discourse" in this field is fairly restricted, so the Internet location of the essay can be found with relative ease. A moment's reflection, though, brings us back to sad reality. First, the transition of scholarly journals from print to electronic form is not happening quickly, even in a field like "computers and humanities"—and despite the fact that an electronic journal offers vastly augmented capabilities for scholars and their work. Second, even among scholars interested in electronic textuality in the humanities, materials posted on the Internet tend to escape notice, engagement, and citation.

Both these points carry some significant consequences. The first emerges when we consider the debate about whether scholarly editions should be alphanumeric or image-based. In addressing this question, Flanders insists— rightly, in my view—that computerized editions should be designed to "provide textual information as high-quality data which can be analysed and processed" (Flanders, 301). She understands that a computerized version of the traditional "facsimile" edition can be an important undertaking; but ultimately, even such works, including their paper-based forebears, are looking for critical and analytic treatment. In this connection, it helps to recall that the history of the scholarly edition has been written in two forms: the critical edition, on one hand, and the facsimile edition (or its "diplomatic" variant) on the other. That history tells us in the simplest way that "text" conveys itself in two coding systems, one linguistic and the other graphic (or, more precisely, bibliographic).

Prima facie, then, the optimal scholarly edition would combine the resources of facsimile and critical editing. Such a combination has been impossible in paper-based instruments, for obvious reasons. Computerized tools are leading us—some of us, anyhow—to revisit the question of whether such an optimal scholarly edition might now be achievable. The simplest hypermedia construction, for example, already represents a minimal instance of combining facsimile and critical resources. Electronic tools make it easy to search and analyze vast bodies of electronic objects. The objects can be physically dispersed, and they can be of various kinds (pictorial, audial, alphanumeric). So far, however, unless this data is alphanumeric, the search and analysis capacities of electronic tools function only at gross levels. That fact has led to the rapid development of SGML projects and the deployment of SGML's TEI offspring in "computers and humanities" scholarship. It also leads Flanders to conclude that "the most significant future trend in electronic editing" is not with image-based editions but with alphanumeric ones (Flanders, 301).[4]

I think this statement is probably true, and I think the opposite is also true. Everything depends on what is meant by "the most significant future trend."

The "future" of electronic editions that are coded alphanumerically, or that deploy such coding as part of their work, has already been sketched. It *has* its "trend," so to speak, because it has its practitioners. We see it in certain determinative editions like Willard McCarty's *Onomasticon,* Peter Robinson's *Canterbury Tales,* or Hoyt Duggan's *Piers Plowman,* as well as in certain tools that manipulate alphanumeric text for what are at present simply game-playing operations, like *Batmemes* and *Anagram Insanity.*[5] The Rossetti Archive itself, which has been associated with image-based editing models, is fully SGML-encoded. It is clear that the models being developed in projects of these kinds have already marked out a "future trend" that will be played out in important ways. Text encoding will continue to grow in wisdom, age, and grace—not only hierarchical schemes (like SGML/TEI) but nonhierarchical ones as well (the Wittgenstein Project's MECS scheme is the first serious effort in this direction).[6]

What is the future of image-based editing? That is much less clear, for the simple reason that we do not yet have the means to search and analyze digital images in ways that correspond to what we can do with alphanumeric data. Yet everyone agrees, as Flanders's essay reminds us, that an ideal computerized edition would deploy and coordinate structured electronic searches of both image and alphanumeric data. We will secure those means only if we insist on doing so, despite the evident obstacles. In this case, we have to construct a future that has not yet been shaped and defined as clearly as the other future preferred by Flanders. It is moot which is the more "significant": the future we think we know, or the future we know we need. Both are significant; indeed, they depend on and create each other.

At this point, the allegorical import of my experience with *Computers and the Humanities* begins to be relevant. The problematic images exemplified some experiments I had made with image-editing tools. I was demonstrating how they might be used for certain kinds of critical and interpretive operations. Because *Computers and the Humanities* is a paper-based journal, however, it is organized a priori, and at the most basic levels, *not* to be able to take up materials of these kinds. The expense of reproducing the images is merely an index of the recalcitrance of the paper format, which in this case is itself an index of a future we think we know, rather than a future we know we need. Even had I the cash to pay for printing the color images, the paper-based format would have delivered only a denatured version of the material. An electronic *Computers and the Humanities* is what my essay actually needed. Not only could such an instrument easily have shown the actual digital files (rather than paper reproductions), it actually could have reconstituted the processes by which those files were generated. It could have restaged the initial set of experiments. It could even have given the reader/user the means to replay the same experiments, or to set up new ones for comparative analytic purposes.

What I am describing here is not some longed-for but unseen future. The technological means for doing what I just described are readily available. Indeed, it would be easier (in terms of what one would have to learn), and probably much less expensive, to start up an electronic journal with those capacities than to try to found a corresponding scholarly print journal.

What is "the most significant future trend in electronic editing?" It all depends on how one imagines the future. What is "the future" of that subset of the future, text encoding? I strongly suspect that nonhierarchical models will overtake this field, and that hierarchical markup models will become subordinated "moments," as Kant would say, within nonhierarchical schemes. This will happen for one simple reason: the texts that most interest humanities scholars do not appear to be organized primarily in hierarchized forms. We *need* nonhierarchical schemes, though at present this is exactly what we do not have. We need them because so much of our attention focuses on "imaginative" works. Imitations of life, they reproduce themselves in correspondingly mysterious and (apparently) unpredictable ways. They continually make us aware of the inadequacy of hierarchized markup models.[7]

In this frame of reference, "the most significant future trend in electronic editing" may well lie with projects committed to goals that are necessary but as yet difficult to locate. Projects like the Rossetti Archive are undertaken precisely because they involve imperative scholarly needs that we do not yet know how to meet—in this case, the need to find ways to search and analyze digital images. Here necessity must be the mother of invention, and the undertaking of the project establishes its own set of demands: that its needs be met. In the course of building the Rossetti Archive, and well after we had committed ourselves to SGML-based markup, we came to realize how inadequate that form of encoding was to the actual needs of our project. The Archive will realize itself and its SGML future, which I have no reason to deplore. But that future, in my view, is far less significant than the one promised by two other current scholarly undertakings that involve nonhierarchical demands and materials. Not without reason has the MECS program for nonhierarchized markup been the pursuit of Wittgenstein scholars; and now lying at the horizon of our attention is the Peirce Project, with its stunning corpus of "existential graph" manuscripts. The "iconic indeterminacy" of these documents—the phrase is Mary Keeler's—will not submit easily to hierarchized markup schemes, and they also need search and analysis procedures that can include various kinds of images.[8] Something new will have to be developed if these works are to be produced in a computerized format that aspires to something more than facsimile reproduction.

II

There is another problem—or another opportunity. After more than thirty years of unfulfilled expectations, humanities computing took off in 1993. Why this abrupt change occurred is less important, at least for this particular place and moment, than are some of its consequences. The World Wild West (sometimes called the World Wide Web) has summoned millions of people, including many humanities scholars, to explore the resources of this strange but promising land.

That is an American set of metaphors, and the images are importantly inapt. What we have is not so much a new world as a new set of tools, designed and built for certain purposes by certain people, which have caught the attention of a very different set of people with very different interests. The computer pioneers among humanities scholars (in North America, at any rate) were almost all practitioners of what German philology used to call "the lower criticism": linguists, enumerative and analytic bibliographers, lexicographers, textual logicians. They were the first in their discipline to glimpse the untraveled world whose margin keeps fading forever as we move toward it.

In the 1990s, these new tools have fallen into the hands of many other kinds of humanities and literary scholars. Most are students, both graduate and undergraduate. At the University of Virginia (UVA) and the Institute for Advanced Technology in the Humanities, I have watched scores of these young people get hired for various projects on a work-study basis. Almost none has had any interest or training in editing, philology, or textual studies. They quickly learn what they need or want to know about these great elementary forms of our discipline and then pursue their own interests. All this takes place in a high-energy feedback loop, so that in five years at UVA we have witnessed an extraordinary transformation in humanities education. Now, when I advertise for a work-study student for the Rossetti Archive, every applicant already possesses a wide range of computer and even programming skills. These are not people I have met before. The ones I see are all literary scholars.

I mention this situation because it relates to the opening anecdote about the rejection of my essay by *Computers and the Humanities*. The skillful reader of that essay rightly pointed out that it lacked certain orderly procedures she or he expected in a scholarly presentation. Part of the essay was speculative, part was simple report; sometimes the exposition was theoretical, sometimes highly factual. The essay did not keep these different kinds of material separate but instead kept moving "back and forth" (as the reader wrote) so that it became "confusing and hard to follow." Perhaps most exasperating, the essay had "no initial overview, and no final summary . . . and . . . no clear evaluation of . . . results." The reader was quite right about all this.

Nonetheless, I cannot see that the essay would be improved if I tried to reframe it along the lines suggested by the reader. I *can* see how changes of those kinds would obscure the principal thrust of the essay. How does one summarize work that is constantly undergoing change—not merely quantitative change, such as additions to the material corpus, but methodological change at various levels of the work's structure? How does one evaluate results that, even as they are achieved, generate new problems and possibilities? And how does one present this kind of situation without shifting "back and forth" from speculative to practical considerations, from reports on concrete research activities to discussion of theoretical matters? The "back and forth" dialectic of the essay is a simplified representation of what has been going on day by day in the building of the Rossetti Archive.

I am not saying that this is the way all projects of this kind ought to proceed. It *is* the way we have been proceeding, deliberately. Our heuristic goal is to publish, in four installments, a hypermedia archive of all of D. G. Rossetti's textual and pictorial works that will be open to structured search and analysis, including collation, of its materials. Our ultimate goal is to study how to model archival instruments of this kind. Building the Archive is important, but studying the model we are building is far more important.

The primacy we give to this investigative process explains why we have found the presence of new students so crucial. The truth of the matter is that none of us knows what can or might come out of our engagement with these new tools, or how they might be exploited. We know some things, but much remains an obscure object of desire (in a sense Buñuel did not intend). And what we already know often gets in the way of what we might learn. Does anyone really believe that we will not find ways to access the information in digital images so that they lay themselves open to structured search and analysis? No one can do that now, but it will certainly happen.

It will happen in the old-fashioned way, through application and study. As the event approaches, to occur who knows where or when, the studies that pursue it metastasize like cancer. But this is not a growth we want to eradicate. Students come to the Institute and get hired on a project, say the Blake Archive. They help to build it, but in the process they are traitorously spying on the work and stealing away with novel ideas. Some of those get poured back into the project, but the project is an old wineskin and cannot hold the new vintage. I am not inventing this narrative, any more than I invented my initial anecdote. The Blake Archive had a spy, a young scholar named Matt Kirschenbaum, who became the project manager of that archive. But his secret life gradually leaked out. He is the author of a Ph.D. thesis completed in the UVA English department on the theory of the visual design of information. It is a remarkable work—the first thesis to be completed in our department that has no paper-based existence. It is entirely digital and on-line.[9] And there are spies all over the Rossetti Archive.

"Great!" some literary scholars may respond. "Let a thousand flowers bloom. But let them bloom in media studies, in information technology, among librarians and archivists. We have poetry to think about, and our concern is with books. Whatever circuitries come with this brave new world, we will still have the books to deal with."

What I relate here is only one person's story, so I cannot expect to persuade the reader to believe what I have found to be true: that these tools are opening the books handed down to us in startlingly new and informative ways. They are utterly transforming editing and textual scholarship, which are the foundation of all literary interpretation and cultural studies. The Rossetti Archive and works like it were not undertaken to study computer hardware or software but rather poems, stories, translations, pictures, and photographs, as well as the vehicular forms in which they live and move and have their being. I am continually amazed by the unforeseen results this work seems to discover, almost randomly. The last section of the essay I wanted to publish in *Computers and the Humanities*—the part with the digital images—centered on some experiments I was carrying out with those images. The experiments involved deforming the image of a recognized and highly overdetermined object, in this case Rossetti's famous painting *The Blessed Damozel*.

What became an experiment had begun as recreation with a friend, fooling around with the graphics software of Adobe Photoshop. As we played with random deformations, I began to see the painting in entirely new ways. The deformations, I have since come to realize, were breaking down the rhetorical authority of the "finished" picture and allowing certain of its concealed features to emerge. I showed this work to Lisa Samuels, a poet and graduate student who was writing her thesis with me. I knew it would interest her because her thesis was concerned with the problem of how to develop lucid explanations of poetic style, and she had been exploring the use of textual deformations as an instrument of stylistic analysis. Since that time, we have written an essay together titled "Deformance and Interpretation."[10]

But why did I include that material in my *Computers and the Humanities* essay, whose subject was (according to the essay's subtitle) "The Theoretical Goals of the *Rossetti Archive*"? However interesting it might be in its own right, surely that material had nothing to do with that topic, as the reader pointed out. But from another perspective—*my* perspective—it had everything to do with the Archive and its goals. As I have said, building the Archive is important, but studying the process and extrapolating its results are what drives the work. Those results often have nothing at all to do with the Archive, and least of all with computers or their software. People who work *in* the humanities *with* computers must stay aware of that.

In conclusion, let me say this. I have spent much of my working life as an editor and textual theorist, but it took this encounter with electronic instruments to overthrow what I thought I knew about books—what they are and how they work. I know, in part, why this has happened: because computers are stupid. The idea of the computer is simple and profound, and I know—I've been told—there are very smart machines out there. They are not the ones I work with now or ever will work with. All the computers I know are dull and unimaginative. To make them do anything at all, we must supply incredibly precise and, above all, unambiguous instructions. We must not write poems to them—though we can, I know for a fact, make them reveal things about poems that people find interesting. Trying to be computer-precise about things like poems and paintings and books, things immensely more complicated than computers, is a merciless experience. It forces us to look at our thinking, and our ideas, with unaccustomed rigor. In the event, it may lead us toward "imagining what we don't know."

By the way, that was the title of the genuine rejected article.

Notes

1. The URL for the essay is: http://jefferson.village.virginia.edu/~jjm2f/chum.html.

2. The Rossetti Archive is a short title for The Complete Writings and Pictures of Dante Gabriel Rossetti: A Hypermedia Research Archive. This project has been under development at the University of Virginia's Institute for Advanced Technology in the Humanities since 1993. The first installment (of four) was published online (http://jefferson.village.virginia.edu/rossetti/) in spring 2000 by the University of Virginia's Institute for Advanced Technology in the Humanities.

3. Julia Flanders, "Trusting the Electronic Edition," *Computers and the Humanities* 31 (1998): 301–10.

4. SGML is Standard Generalized Markup Language, a system for marking up alphanumeric text so that information can be organized in the text for structured searches and analyses. TEI is the Text Encoding Initiative, a project that uses the model of SGML as the basis for a markup structure designed specifically for the kinds of textual documents commonly used by academics, and especially by humanities scholars. Both SGML and TEI conceive texts as hierarchical structures.

5. All these resources can be investigated through an elementary Web search.

6. For good discussions of TEI and MECS and problems of text markup, see Allen Renear, "Text Ontology from Below: The Contribution of Computing Practice to New Theories of Textuality," lecture abstract (address: http://www.cs.ucc.ie/renearTalk.html) as well as his "Out of Praxis: Three (Meta)Theories of Textuality," in *Electronic Text: Investigations in Method and Theory,* ed. Kathryn Sutherland (Oxford: Clarendon Press, 1997), 107–26. See also Allen Renear, Elli Mylonas, and David Durand, "Refining Our Notion of What Text Really Is: The Problem of Overlapping Hierarchies," *Research in Humanities Computing* 4 (1996): 263–80. Other perspectives come from David T. Barnard, Ron Hayter, Maria Karababa, George Logan, and John McFadden, "SGML-Based Markup for Literary Texts: Two Problems and Some Solutions," *Computers and the Humanities* 22 (1988): 265–76. The scholars working on the Wittgenstein Project have attempted a different approach to text markup in order to evade some of the limitations of TEI/SGML. See Claus Huitfeldt, "Multi-Dimensional Texts in a One-Dimensional Medium," in *Wittgenstein and Contemporary Theories of Language,* ed. Paul Henry and Arild Utaker (Bergen, Norway: The University of Bergen, 1992), 142–61, reprinted in *Computers and the Humanities* 28 (1994): 235–41.

7. Here is an example of a typical kind of problem. There is a large corpus of extant proof material relating to Rossetti's 1870 volume, *Poems.* Most of these are integral proofs, more or less intact, but many are different kinds of proof and/or manuscript assemblages put together by Rossetti and/or other persons, with or without

Rossetti's cooperation or knowledge. These heteroglot and wildly nonhierarchical assemblages do not easily submit to an SGML design, least of all to a TEI structure. By manipulating certain standard markup fields, however, one can "trick" the markup system into organizing documents of these kinds so that they lay themselves open to structured search and analysis. Rather, I should say that one can trick the system so that the marked-up document parses against the DTD. Theoretically, then, the SGML software should be able to process these documents. What is theoretically correct, however, often turns out to be highly problematic in practice. The SGML limitations here have forced us to modify our plans for implementing our full text markup resources.

8. See Mary Keeler, "Iconic Indeterminacy and Human Creativity in C. S. Peirce's Manuscripts," in *The Iconic Page in Manuscript, Print, and Digital Culture,* ed. George Bornstein and Theresa Tinkle (Ann Arbor: University of Michigan Press, 1998), 157–94.

9. See Kirschenbaum's website for further information on his work: http://www.glue.umd.edu/~mgk/.

10. Jerome McGann and Lisa Samuels, "Deformance and Interpretation," *New Literary History* 30, no.1 (winter 1999): 25–26.

TEXTUALITY AND
THE REPRODUCTION OF TEXTS

David Greetham

The Philosophical Discourse of [Textuality]?

Is there a philosophical discourse of textuality? I think so, and the existence of this collection of essays implies that others do as well. My title—a cooption of Jürgen Habermas's title of his passionate defense of Enlightenment rationality and modernity, *The Philosophical Discourse of Modernity*—is doubly variant.[1] First, by substituting "textuality" for "modernity" I apparently reinforce the widely held assumption that textual criticism is a distinctly "modern" (i.e., postmedieval) enterprise, and I suggest that the Great Divide between modernity and *medievalismus* is firmly in place, as far as textual study is concerned.[2] Alterity lives![3] But second, by posing Habermas's declarative statement (*there is* a philosophical discourse of modernity) as an interrogative (*is there* a philosophical discourse of textuality?), I question not only the congruence of modernity and textuality, but also the possibility of demarcating a single philosophy—especially in the modern sense of the proper purview of a rational philosophy—under which textual study can be examined. In this essay, I adopt Stephen Toulmin's prescription for modern philosophy as the substitution of (*a*) logic for rhetoric, (*b*) the universal for the particular, (*c*) the general for the local, and (*d*) the timeless for the timely: in other words, as Platonic rather than Aristotelian.[4]

I will demonstrate, as Toulmin does for philosophy, that the conjugation or synonymy of "modernity" and "textuality" is itself deeply problematic; it has led to a "grammar" (or "logic") of text rather than a "rhetoric," a universalism rather than particularization, a generality rather than a locality, and a search for timelessness (what textuists have come to call the "definitive edition") in place of timeliness; and these characteristics have become a cultural liability for textual practitioners as the dominance of the modern has waned.[5] For example, under the auspices of grammaticality over rhetoric, we have been all too eager to construe a *subject* (authoriality, intention, the originary moment) from the *remaniements* of the *predicate* (documents, affects, or what is referred to in this volume as "[re]production").[6] Under the auspices of the Platonized ideality of the modern, we have devoted ourselves to the construction of such universal, general, and timeless conceits as "ideal copy," "ideal text," and the superhistorical, non-context-bound "text that never was."

This is a large agenda for an introductory essay; in the main narrative, I can do no more than sketch the rough outlines of my argument, which should be understood as a heuristic experiment in postmodernist rhetoric, not as an evenhanded and comprehensive *summa*. I have deliberately selected the anecdotal, the particular, and the timely as a provocative "probe" into modernity and textuality, fully conscious of the inevitable critique: "All this talk of a 'heuristic probe,' as if a probe could be anything but heuristic."[7]

For the purposes of my rhetoric at this moment, I can therefore claim that it is no accident that Habermas's declarative statement appeals to modernity as an enabling discourse, and that it is no accident that, among conservative textual critics, Lawrence Rainey[8] has invoked the fulfillment of the Enlightenment discourse observable in Habermas's conflicts with, say, Derrida and Lyotard, as the positivist, (old)-historicist, and "philological" rock on which contemporary textuality should be refounded.[9]

Richard Rorty mocks the attempts of "weak textualists" to don the trappings of philosophy as an empowering discourse, "to think that literature can take the place of philosophy by *mimicking* philosophy—by being, of all things, *epistemological.* Epistemology still looks classy to weak textualists."[10] In the same way, I will argue that the delimiting of textuality as the apotheosis of modernity in general, and of the rationalist project of the Enlightenment in particular, is not only a weak argument (and a cultural liability); it also misrepresents both the history of textuality as a multivocal discourse and the anti-epistemological, other-than-rational modes of production and representation that textuality has always had available. Far from "mistakenly think[ing] to impress the populace by wrapping [our]-selves in the shabby togas stripped from the local senators,"[11] I will contend that textuality, when viewed from the longer perspective that both the Renaissance and the Enlightenment sought to suppress, is already empowered with a multitude of discourses, of which modernity is only one, and a "shabby" one at that.

I have dealt with some of the specific components—legal, taxonomic, biological, forensic, and annotational—of this thesis in various recent writings.[12] My intention here is to "reimagine" the production alternatives as well as the rival histories and agendas of textuality for our current cultural moment, with the caveat that, in order to see this moment as something other than just a fulfillment of the Renaissance/Enlightenment scriptures, it will be necessary to cast a very wide chronological and discursive net, for which the *explicatio* and fuller *descriptio* can be found in the works just noted.

Quite properly, after all this invocation of the timely and the local, I begin with my own current moment, the moment of inscription (if that is still the right word for the electronic evanescence of composition on-screen) of this essay. I am using a Windows environment in which simulacra of *folders* and *disks* and *printers* and *scissors* and *text-pages* and *glue* and *magnifying glasses* and a even a humanoid *coach* infest the upper taskbar of my screen. These simulacra are *icons,* and their iconicity seems to depend on their textual transparency: they appear to dispense with (programmatic) language in order to provide an immediacy of comprehension and access. Of course, even this apparent immediacy and transparency have to be learned; scissors and magnifying glasses are familiar objects in some cultures and cultural moments, but less so in others. The icon does not do away with language as text; it simply transforms it into a different grammatical system. I confess that I came to Windows only grudgingly, after putting up a resistance based on my comfort and familiarity with the DOS-based language, which seemed to be more like "real" language, and thus more honest, more direct, more "textual" than those flying windows. As Sherry Turkle has documented, DOS users often liked to think of themselves as being in closer contact with the "guts" of the machine than they would have been in an iconic system.[13] Having to enter long strings of alphanumeric "commands" on the keyboard seemed more "sincere," paradoxically more "transparent," than clicking an icon with a mouse. I remember that when our technician installed an early version of Windows on my office computer, he waxed enthusiastic about the fact that he had not had to "touch the keyboard at all" to accomplish the tasks of installation. "So what?" I thought. "What's the big deal in *not* touching a keyboard? Isn't that where the real action is?" And so, when he left the office, I reassuringly shut down Windows, went back into my good old DOS system, and felt the comforting click of keys. I was still in command. As Turkle argues, and as I have since come to understand, such ontological comfort—a desire to be in direct communion with the vehicle of text production—was illusory. Yes, "Windows" is perhaps an unfortunate misnomer: far from providing textual transparency, far from enabling the textual producer to "see" through a glass, Windows as a system and each individual window and the icon that calls it up render the textual glass even darker, less transparent: the alphanumeric codes that DOS would have used are hidden, obscured, elided, by that click of the mouse. But even if Windows (and the Macintosh operating system that it emulates) is a textual con game, it is obviously one that our culture of text producers is eager to play: my word-processing system when I wrote the first draft of this essay (Corel WordPerfect 7 for Windows 95) was initially not even available in a DOS version. My then-five-year-old son, brought up in a mouse-clicking textual universe in which he is completely at home phenomenologically, would doubtless react to DOS with the same astonishment that must have greeted Cardinal della Rovere's insistence that his print copy of Appian's *Civil Wars* be transcribed back into manuscript (a "real" text) before the book could be placed on his codicologically austere shelves.

Turkle's insistence that DOS aficionados were deluding themselves in thinking that punching a keyboard was a textually transparent and unmediated operation is part of her general concern with the reconfiguration of the textuality of identity in electronic environments. If the agent of text production misconstrues his or her prerogative and empowerment in operating the vehicle for text production, what hope is there that the interpreters of such text production (textual critics, scholarly editors, even "literary" critics) will "comprehend" that agency and its transparency, or lack thereof? What possibility that *text* as icon or as vehicle can be satisfactorily imagined, never mind *re*imagined, in a way that will prove semantically, practically, or epistemologically illuminating for our cultural moment, or any other?

An emblem: my friend and colleague Gerhard Joseph is one of the most percipient and sophisticated nonpractitioner textuists I know. (By "nonpractitioner" I mean only that he does not count himself as editor or textual critic in his own text production, but he is as much a textuist in the sense of an interrogator of texts as any formal "editor.") He has written a dense, provocative, and highly engaging book, *Tennyson and the Text,* taking his title from the weaving figure of text in "The Lady of Shalott" and artfully demonstrating how that figure can be used as a device for confronting Tennyson's textuality as a whole.[14] It looks like a strange match—the poststructuralist deconstructor of texts and the conservative, positivist, Victorian nationalist poet—but it is a match that has proved very productive.[15] Joseph's *Tennyson and the Text* relies on, or at least takes off from, Roland Barthes's construal of text as "tissue" or "network," the weave or pattern of the *textile,* especially as that weave can be continually unwoven or rewoven and resists a formal, teleological, and definitive meaning. Barthes thus famously contrasts *text* ("a methodological field," "subversive," "paradoxical," "dilatory," "plural," "a weave of signifiers," a "network") with *work* (which "can be held in the hand," "the object of a literal science, of philology," "caught up in a process of filiation" and "an organism").[16] That dialectic is inverted (I would even say "deconstructed") in G. Thomas Tanselle's redefinition of the two terms in almost exactly the *opposite* configuration. For Tanselle, it is *work* that is ineffable and beyond our grasp, and *text* that is concrete and specific and determined.[17] *Tennyson and the Text* is on secure etymological ground in portraying text as tissue and network, for this strand of meaning (and its connection with the woven pattern of *textile,* etymologically coterminous) has been present in English since the very earliest occurrences of the word in Middle English.[18] Gerhard Joseph as a textuist is philologically sound.

But after the publication of this book, there came a chance encounter in a corridor at the City University of New York, when he and I were discussing my textual brief for a guest appearance in his doctoral seminar, "Alternative Worlds and the Technological Horizon." Yes, I would address the intertextuality of hypertext, and I might even show some of the digital morphs I had "written" for a presentation at a conference on "Digital Resources in the Humanities" at Oxford in the summer of 1996. So "network" and "tissue" would indeed be one of the strands, but so would the other, alternative meaning of "text": the text as *textus,* the authority, the original, the center, the revealed truth.[19] There was a pause. "What?" said my host and reweaver of Tennyson. "You're saying there's *another* meaning to 'text' beside 'network' and 'tissue'?" It wasn't quite scales falling from his eyes, but I could see that this recognition of the unnamed, unthought-of "other" (especially if that "other" brought with it the very authority and determinability that the Barthesian "network" denied) had suddenly confronted him not just with a dialectic that had been culturally suppressed, but with a whole range of other models for (Tennysonian) textuality of which *Tennyson and the Text* had been innocent. Ever the critic quick on his feet (or the artful dodger), Joseph then gave "three sequential mini-texts or *lexias* for the price of a seamless one" at the annual meeting of the Modern Language Association within a few weeks of our conversation, addressing both aspects of transparency and objectivity, and tissue and network. The revelation in the corridor opened up rather than closing off the text-critical options with which Joseph could now play.

But what did the encounter teach me as textuist? First, it demonstrated just how culturally conditioned our textual choices might be: for the producer of *Tennyson and the Text,* "text" had to be Barthesian and tissue, whereas the *textus* as authority and revealed truth of Scripture (and thus "scriptures" in general) was unthinkable for that moment. Second, it showed just how successful the Enlightenment and poststructuralism together (despite their very different ideological agendas) had been in cordoning off the critical, textile sense of "text" for a hermeneutic nonphilological intellectual medium (and thereby our having to assume, just as de Man and "strict and pure" bibliographers alike had assumed, that philology was "prehermeneutic," non-critical, and thus positivist).[20] Third, it provided an opportunity to "reimagine textuality," an opportunity that I will run with in the rest of this essay.

There is one further irony, even paradox. The "reimagination" I will construe as our postmodernist discourse of textuality will indeed turn out to be a reaction against the rationalism, objectivity, and *grands recits* of the Enlightenment and modernity; however, in one of those cultural loops or reinvestments that characterize both iterability and alterity, we will find that postmodernist textuality is one of the elements of a general "return to the Middle Ages" that Umberto Eco observes in present culture.[21] Postmodernism as medieval? Contemporary textuality as anti-modernist? These are large claims, and they might make some contributors to this volume distinctly uncomfortable. Hasn't the death of the author (to say nothing of the death of God) liberated us from the constraints of a theocratic universe and a rigid social and philosophical system, as well as from the claims of the Renaissance and Enlightenment? Wasn't the Middle Ages a period of textual certitudes, or at least of hope for such certitudes? Is not the history of medieval textuality (from Isidore's *Etymologiae* with its agenda for a transparent and universal link between text and meaning[22] to Scholasticism and the similarly universalist agenda of the Encyclopedists to "comprehend" all phenomena[23]) the most egregious example of a longing for a *grand recit*? And finally—however uneasy we may now feel about Renaissance subjectivity, Cartesian dialectic, and Enlightenment rationalism—were not all these components of modernity advances over the epistemological aridity, structural insularity, and unthinking authoritarianism of the medieval Christian West? Well, yes and no; or in Abelard's phrase, sic et non.[24]

I do not go so far as to claim that Abelard's work *Sic et non* is a "negative dialectics" in the mode of Adorno, or that the fracturing of textuality that was inherent in the method known as *sic et non* is somehow a response to Habermas *avant la lettre*.[25] It is important, however, to remember that Scholastic dialectic presupposed the potential viability (and thus rhetorical authority) of both parts of the evidentiary formula—thesis and antithesis—without the positivist cop-out, or rhetorical failure of nerve, that characterizes both Hegelian and Marxist dialectics. That is, although textual *synthesis* was indeed the trope under which the Scholastic agenda and medieval textuality as a whole might have operated (specifically, to find the *grand recit* that would provide a typological unification of pagan Classical texts with the revealed truth of Judeo-Christian texts), the fulfillment of these Scriptures and their conjoining into a full discourse of textuality was in practice forever deferred. It was forever placed under the graphic mark of *différance,* to be given a totalized, "modernist" utterance only outside the limitations of human history, *after* the full text of history had been "always already written" and comprehended typologically. Because the synthesis was (unlike those of Hegel and Marx) post-historical and post-empirical, the most that the alert textuist-hermeneuticist-dialectician could look to find was the *traces* or *signatures* of a now cloudy transparency of meaning: "For now we see through a glass, darkly; but then face to face" (I Cor. 13:11). Windows indeed; and windows that, like those on my screen, paradoxically only seem to have transparency of iconic meaning while in fact hiding the operations of the text.

For the Renaissance—or, in its self-nomination rather than its Enlightenment reinscription, the "Revival of Learning"—these operations had become stable rather than fluid and fluctuating. As W. Speed Hill has observed, for the Revival of Learning, and perhaps particularly for the Reformation and the Elizabethan religious settlement, Scripture had been stabilized in the sense that its author had already withdrawn from his work, thereby making the textuality of Scripture amenable to human reason.[26] Though not yet simply the clock-maker, God had, in authorial terms, ceased revising his work, which had thus achieved an ontological and thus potentially hermeneutic perfection, if only we could approach it with the right interpretive tools. In Hooker's *Laws of Ecclesiastical Polity,* we are already halfway to the Enlightenment conviction that laws in general are discoverable and the universe permanently in place. Far from sympathizing with and continuing the medieval deferred dialectic in the Abelardian sense of *sic et non,* Hooker is emblematic of the textuality of empirical transparency, which was to lead to the empiricism (and the endorsement of a "plain style") of the British Royal Society, and to the belief that the laws of physics, biology, economics, politics, and even human nature were as tractable and discoverable through patient and replicable observation as were the laws of ecclesiastical polity. The constitutionalism of the American and French revolutions, with its inscription of texts that were constructed to cover all the eventualities of social behavior and governmental prerogative, was as symptomatic of this shift (within the agenda of modernity) from the *différance,* traces, and negative dialectics of medieval textuality as were Newton's laws of motion, Adam Smith's economics, the secure classification of Linnaean taxonomy, and the political determinism of the Glorious Revolution of 1688.

But how do these historical *données* (the "givens" of both an Enlightenment, progressivist view of human development and of a postmodernist, diffusionist, and nonteleological view) impinge on the "reimagining" of textuality that is the project of this volume? Can it really be that, in reveling in the postmodernist breakdown of the *grands recits* of Christianity, Marxism, Newtonian physics, and the Enlightenment, we have constructed or fallen unwittingly into another even greater *recit*—one that does not simply take us out of the Enlightenment project but fulfills a project that preceded modernity?

Again, *sic et non.* There is one recursive characteristic of postmodernist textuality that does reinscribe us firmly within an earlier model, and that is the interrogation of the singularity and ontologically circumscribed nature of *text.* It is a rhetorical trope of the recent historiography of textuality that modernist criticism, despite its apparent denial of the historicized author as a dangerous fallacy, required the unifying cognitive consciousness of authoriality to resolve the tensions, ambiguities, ironies, and so on that motivated modernist *explication de texte.* Moreover, this formalist concentration on "the text itself" was deeply implicated in the actual graphic ("clear-text") construction as well as the ideology of the great period of modernist editing, which was dominated by Greg–Bowers copy-text theory and most conspicuous in the monumental editions "sealed" by the MLA's Center for Editions of American Authors and its successor, the Center for (later Committee on) Scholarly Editions. The pristine transparency of those clear-text editions—in which "the text itself" asserts its logistic and phenomenological superiority over the record of variance embedded in the deliberately invisible, or occluded, apparatus—sought to render culturally impotent the margins of discourse, whether bibliographical or political, and to separate the Platonized *textus* of "the text that never was" from the accreted social detritus that too often accompanied the text proper in this fallen world. The corollary of this segment of recent historiography is that the fractured, fragmentary, versionist, and "extra-textual" editorial enterprise of postmodernism denies the firm structuralist bipolarity between the "text itself" and its margins. Indeed, the very term "editing," insofar as it is associated with modernist, Platonist eclecticism, has become something of a slur under postmodernism: McGann argues that Greg–Bowers "critical editing" is an impropriety in its attempt to deny the socialization of text, and he insists that his hypermedia Rossetti Archive is an "archive," not an "edition"; and Randall McLeod declares that "editions suck. Somebody should tell the editors."[27]

This shift from modernist text to postmodernist text is more or less that between the two main strands of the etymological *text:* from the *textus* to the *textile.* If this is so, and if postmodernism celebrates the continual weaving of text and its dispersal over the entire field of human activity and its "traces," then I contend that, in this aspect of reimagined textuality, we have indeed become medievalists again and have cast off the securities of the modernist distinction between text and margin.[28]

In this reimagined universe of textuality, postmodernism collapses the "text itself" and its accoutrements, for it is no longer possible to discern exactly where "text" ends and "commentary" begins.²⁹ The irony of this seepage between *textus* and *textile* is that eventually there is no *outside,* since "text" becomes inclusive of all its variants and its belated critiques: *"Il n'y a pas dehors de texte."* Such a territorial impasse can be seen by modernist textuists as a counsel of despair³⁰ that makes "editing" (especially in the sense of "cutting" or "pruning" or "cleaning" ³¹) no longer possible. Exactly: we cannot prune or cut or clean because we can no longer be sure what initial/ideal/originary *shape* we are looking for in hacking at the raw marble of text, by gradually removing all that is extraneous to its pure form. And so, if both Michelangelo's formula for a text in the plastic arts (simply to remove from the block everything that is "extraneous" to the sculpture that resides within it, by "hacking," *per forza di levare,* with a claw chisel³²) and the "passionate" formula of Stephen Dedalus ("If a man hacking in fury at a block of wood . . . make there an image of a cow, is that image a work of art? If not, why not?"³³) for separating text from textile are called in doubt by the lack of a self-delimiting *outside,* a firm edge or boundary to the patterns discoverable, then what Tanselle has described as a bibliography that "moves outside books and . . . becomes a pattern of life" is, by default, the only possible medium for full textual analysis.³⁴

As medieval textuists from Isidore to Abelard to Aquinas might say, "So what?" Of course mundane texts can have no perceptible edges to us, because we cannot stand sufficiently outside them; we cannot get a purchase on their always already written strands of meaning. The medieval concept of text is always already written and universal because its author, God, stands outside the constraints of time (the Crucifixion is thus *always* happening, before and after as well as during the actual historicized event), and also because the total narrative that is the creation on both syntagmatic and paradigmatic axes must cohere, but it can do so only beyond our ability to observe the totality of that coherence. Fortunately for us dull sublunary textuists, the author has been gracious enough to sign his work—indeed, to embed "signatures" in the Book of Creation in a fully bibliographical sense.³⁵ That is, the signatures serve to demarcate "gatherings" of text, sequentia or quires or quaternions or collectanea or florilegia (depending on the semantics of bibliographical *formula,* i.e., "little form"). The medieval book—with its spatial ambiguities and collocations between text and margin, and its linear inconclusiveness (the seeming adventitious binding of "separate" works into a single, but often temporary, bibliographical unit)—is difficult, even impossible, to decode using modernist principles of external unity and singularity of utterance; just so, the universal (i.e., "medieval") text of phenomena will be susceptible to analysis only with tools other than those promoted by modernism and its tropes (tension, paradox, irony, and so on, all resolvable under the singularity of the "well-wrought urn").

There is already some sign that modernist scruples about the *propriety* of textual evidence are being challenged. As I have written elsewhere, the influence of *annaliste* history on both New Historicism and *l'histoire du livre* has promoted an explosion of the bibliographical phenomena of textual evidence, often to the discomfort of those to whom the intrinsic/extrinsic, internal/external, textual/nontextual dialectic is an important epistemological tool—indeed, a precision instrument for textual surgery.[36] Make this tool blunt or its practitioners indecisive, and we have lost far more in particularity and "local knowledge" than we can possibly have gained in contemplating the whole world.[37] But when D. F. McKenzie uses landscape as a "text" for bibliographical construal, or when McGann uses "Reagan's Farewell" as an exemplary "text" on "how to read a book," or when Joseph Grigely uses the human body as a "text" to comment on eclecticism and idealism (in this volume and elsewhere), all are being eminently postmodern in breaking down the *grand recit* of modernist textuality.[38] And they are being eminently medieval as well. Landscape, politics, and the body: these are all perfectly susceptible to textual analysis according to a medieval hermeneutic of textuality; indeed, it would be impious to declare that they are "nontextual" and thus not part of either (or both) the *textus* and the *textile*.[39]

There are, of course, enormous differences in rationale and expectations between the medieval and postmodernist discourses of textuality. Although both might look for Derridean "traces," and both would accept *différance* as a necessary hermeneutic and phenomenological condition, they would do so for very different reasons. I hope I am not seen as merely playing into the "romance" of postmodernism by linking its textuality to the medieval. The return to the Middle Ages that Eco describes is not a nostalgic yearning for a lost immediacy that both Marx and the Victorian medievalists (Morris, Tennyson, Rossetti) mourned. Even though much of the hypertextual manifestation of postmodernist textuality (Dungeons and Dragons leading to MOOs[40]) seems to carry some freight of nostalgia, and even though there have been acute attempts to link the bibliographical phenomena of hypertext to medieval habits of reading, my argument differs from these critiques.[41] In my brief to provide a historical and conceptual frame for the "reimagining" of textuality that this volume addresses, it does not really matter to me whether we accept Eco's cultural diagnosis; and, therefore, it does not really matter whether we might eventually imagine the line from humanism to the Enlightenment to modernity as a "middle" age of cultural variance away from the *normative* phenomena of the premodern and the postmodern, although there are good bibliographical grounds for doing so.[42] As a (quondam) medievalist, I might feel some delicious cultural *Schaden-*

freude to see the Renaissance, the Enlightenment, and modernity (all those movements that conspired to degrade and devalue the premodern as an unfortunate episode, a "middle" age that we must overleap and get beyond) lose their status as the fulfillment of the textual scriptures and be reduced to a backformed "middle" ages; but though the symmetry of premodern and postmodern is obviously seductive, my exposition of textuality does not depend on such seductions. In fact, I might just as easily draw my evidence against modernist textuality from the "uncanny" Pergamanians of the Classical period, or from the cultural dispersal of manuscript transmission described by Harold Love, Arthur Marotti, D. F. McKenzie, and others.[43]

My point is rather that there will always be the opportunity, even the necessity, for a battle of the books between "modern-ists" and "pre-/postmodern-ists" and what they represent about textual authority, variance, resolution, and teleology, just as there have been almost continuous battles between *antiqui* and *moderni*. Despite the increasingly convoluted rearguard actions of scholars like Tanselle to hold onto the modern and its textual protocols, we have moved through an epistemic shift in which the values prized by modernist textuality, and especially modernist editing, either are regarded with suspicion or are deemed inimical to currently favored means of textual production. Just as Mark Twain claimed that New York and religion could not cohabit (because those living in the close quarters of urban life were not susceptible to superstition), so it may have been phenomenologically and practically easier for modernist textuality to thrive in the period of the printed book, and it may now be more difficult for this same textuality to inhabit electronic hypertext.[44] Perhaps; except that postmodernist textuality can certainly be seen in various bibliographical artifacts of the printed book, from Sterne's *Tristram Shandy* to Derrida's *Glas*; and I have already demonstrated how modernist principles of coherence and control can be just as present (maybe, given the technical complexity, even more so) in hypermedia textual reproduction as in the print codex. Indeed, the masculinist, phallogocentric, positivist features of hypertext and hypermedia may be even more dangerous to feminist, fluid, postmodernist textuality precisely because the controls and constraints *are* hidden—by those opaque Windows.[45] We may *think* that we are doing postmodern textuality at the very moment that we are being done by modernist, just as the *moderni* of one cultural moment are the *antiqui* of another.

There is no way out of this double bind, nor should there be. When the previously unthinkable becomes the *donnée* of the current moment, it is in a sense still (or equally) unthinkable, for it has now been fully consumed and digested by its cultural practitioners in what Jauss called "culinary reading," unexamined because normative, and therefore *invisible*.[46] This is, after all, Althusser's prescription for an ideology: that it should be internalized to the point that it becomes invisible.[47] I do not believe that postmodernist textuality has yet been so fully consumed that it has disappeared from view, or from interrogation. Indeed, the very publication of this collection suggests that current textuality has not achieved the sort of invisibility that characterized the high modernism of the CEAA and CSE editions in the 1960s and 1970s. Eventually, however, the critical indeterminacies that animate this book will probably be resolved into textual *données,* and we will need another medievalization, another redrawing of the lines of descent and argument and critical filiation. It is only through the invocation of some Middle Ages that we keep ourselves modern.

Notes

1. Jürgen Habermas, *The Philosophical Discourse of Modernity,* trans. Frederick Lawrence (Cambridge, Mass.: MIT Press, 1987). This collection of essays takes aim at the various prophets and exponents of the postmodern, from Nietzsche seen as the "entry" into postmodernity to Heidegger's "undermining of Western Rationalism" to Derrida's "critique of phonocentrism" to Foucault's "critique of reason." Habermas finds all these postmodernist positions inadequate in different ways, and in his final essay, "The Normative Content of Modernity," he declares: "The radical critique of reason exacts a high price for taking leave of modernity. In the first place, these discourses can and want to give no account of their own position. Negative dialectics, genealogy, and deconstruction alike avoid those categories in accord with which modern knowledge has been differentiated—by no means accidentally—and on the basis of which we today understand texts" (336). This "genre" theory of discourse as increasingly fine taxonomic calibrations (textual predicates) from which the subject and thus intention can be drawn is similar to E. D. Hirsch's endorsement of Husserl's transcendental (rather than Heidegger's historicized) phenomenology and is explored more fully for its textual implications in the "intention" and "reading" chapters of my *Theories of the Text* (Oxford: Clarendon Press, 1999).

2. See, for example, Tim William Machan's *Textual Criticism and Middle English Texts* (Charlottesville: University Press of Virginia, 1994), the thesis of which is that the use of "modern" (i.e., humanist and Enlightenment) models of authoriality, intentionality, and textuality is inappropriate to the very different "premodern" protocols of medieval text production.

3. For an examination of the differing national responses (by Paul Zumthor, Eugene Vance, Hans-Robert Jauss, John Burrow, and others) to the "insuperable gulf" or *l'éloignement du moyen âge* instantiated in the concept of "alterity," see the special issue of *New Literary History* 10 (1979).

4. Stephen Toulmin, *Cosmopolis: The Hidden Agenda of Modernity* (Chicago: University of Chicago Press, 1990).

5. Habermas's original German title is *Der philosophische Diskurs der Moderne* (i.e., "the modern," as both a period and a particular disposition, emphasizing the Enlightenment virtues of reason, clarity, and transparency) rather than, say, *Modernismus* or *Modernität.* The English-language distinctions among "the modern,"

"modernity," and "modernism" do not quite parallel the German, and I will use "modernity" and "the modern" in this essay to denote both the postmedieval period as a whole and specific currents within that development, especially the "modernism" of the West in the early and mid-twentieth century.

6. See Paul de Man's critique of such modernist enterprises, "The Resistance to Theory," in his *The Resistance to Theory* (Minneapolis: University of Minnesota Press, 1986); and see my critique of de Man's argument (in that essay and in his paired essay, "The Return to Philology," ibid.), "The Resistance to Philology," in *The Margins of the Text,* ed. D. C. Greetham (Ann Arbor: University of Michigan Press, 1997), 9–24.

7. *The Listener,* 28 September 1967, 386/2 (see *OED2,* "heuristic" A.a.), of McLuhan's style.

8. Lawrence Rainey, "Cultural Authority and the Crisis of Editorial Theory," paper presented at the Society for Textual Scholarship conference, New York City, 17 April 1993. See my response in "Textual Theory and the Territorial Metaphor," the introduction to *Theories of the Text.*

9. On Habermas versus Derrida, see note 1. On Lyotard, particularly with regard to social enfranchisement or constraint of electronic media, see Charles Ess, "The Political Computer: Hypertext, Democracy, and Habermas," in *Hyper/Text/Theory,* ed. George Landow (Baltimore: Johns Hopkins University Press, 1994), 225–67, and references therein.

10. Richard Rorty, "Nineteenth-Century Idealism and Twentieth-Century Textualism," in his *Consequences of Pragmatism* (Minneapolis: University of Minnesota Press, 1982), 156.

11. Rorty, ibid.

12. See my "Contemporary Critical Theory: From Modernism to Postmodernism," in *Palimpsest: Editorial Theory in the Humanities,* ed. George Bornstein and Ralph Williams (Ann Arbor: University of Michigan Press, 1993), 9–28; "[Textual] Criticism and Deconstruction," *Studies in Bibliography* 44 (1991): 1–30; "Postduction: 'Glosynge Is a Glorious Thyng, Certayn'" in *Editing the Middle English Text,* ed. Douglas Moffat and Vincent McCarren (Ann Arbor: University of Michigan Press, 1997), 287–302; "Resistance to Philology" in *Margins of the Text;* "Textual Forensics," *PMLA* 111 (1996): 32–51; "Phylum-Tree-Rhizome," *Huntington Library Quarterly* 58, no.1 (1996): 99–126, special issue on *Reading from the Margins: Textual Studies, Chaucer, and Medieval Literature,* ed. Seth Lerer; "The Telephone Directory and Dr. Seuss: Scholarly Editing after *Feist v. Rural Telephone,*" *Studies in the Literary Imagination* 29 (1996): 53–74, special issue on *Editing the Literary Imagination,* ed. Tom Quirk. The present essay is in many ways the culmination of this recent work for a wider audience.

13. Sherry Turkle, *Life on the Screen: Identity in the Age of the Internet* (New York: Simon and Schuster, 1995), 23.

14. Gerhard Joseph, *Tennyson and the Text: The Weaver's Shuttle* (Cambridge: Cambridge University Press, 1992).

15. Joseph artfully divides his book into "Victorian Warp: Perception" and "Victorian Woof: Representative Men and Mystified Women," with an "Interweave" on "My Lady('s) Shuttle: The Alienation of Work into Text."

16. Roland Barthes, "From Work to Text," in *Image Music Text,* trans. Stephen Heath (New York: Hill and Wang, 1977), 155–64.

17. G. Thomas Tanselle, "Textual Criticism and Deconstruction," *Studies in Bibliography* 43 (1990):1–33. See also Paul Eggert, "Document and Text: The 'Life' of a Literary Work and the Capacities of Editing," *TEXT* 7 (1994): 1–24; and Joseph Grigely, "The Textual Event," in *Devils and Angels: Textual Editing and Literary Theory,* ed. Philip Cohen (Charlottesville: University Press of Virginia, 1991), 167–94, for further commentary on the *text/work* relation.

18. See *OED2* headnote/etymology: "that which is woven, web, texture." See the examples cited in my "[Textual] Criticism and Deconstruction," *Studies in Bibliography* 44 (1991): 1–30.

19. See *OED2* headnote *text* "the Scriptures, the Gospel"; 1b "an original or authority"; 2b "in the original form and order, as distinguished from a commentary, marginal or other, or from annotations . . . the authoritative or formal part"; 2c "the original matter"; 3a "the very words and sentences of Holy Scripture"; 4a "a short passage from the Scriptures, esp. one quoted as authoritative"; 4b "a short passage from some book or writer considered as authoritative; a received maxim or axiom." I would demonstrate this fixed, scriptural sense of "text" in a digital environment by showing the "authority" that the technical morphist has, while hidden by those Windows again, in controlling pixellation, compression ratio, and so on.

20. This is a dense scenario and cannot be articulated fully in the space of this essay. My contention is that, paradoxically, both the rationalism of the Enlightenment and the "uncanny" criticism of deconstruction argued that philology must, of its very nature, be objectivist and positivist. As coopted by the analytical bibliographers of the Anglo-American school (from Pollard to Greg and Bowers), textual *criticism* lost most of its critical faculties in order to become an empiricist exemplar of the history of technology. As intellectually ghettoized by the deconstructors, these positivist claims for textual criticism were taken all too seriously, and poststructuralists like de Man failed to perceive that the activities of bibliographers and textuists could not be neatly ignored as "pre-hermeneutic." See my "Resistance to Philology" and "Uncanny Texts and the Science of Textuality," Symposium on Rationality, Trinity College, Hartford, April 1997.

21. Umberto Eco, "The Return to the Middle Ages," in *Travels in Hyperreality,* trans. William Weaver (New York: Harcourt Brace, 1986). For the textual historian, it is (in Eco's terminology) the formal shift from a "systematic" textuality to an "additive and compositive" one that best illustrates the conflation of premodern and postmodern aesthetics.

22. See *Isidori Hispalensis Episcopi etymologiarum sive originum libri XX,* ed. W. M. Lindsay (Oxford: Clarendon Press, 1911). Isidore sought to arrange the text of the entire phenomenological universe around the transcendental principle of etymology, by which all of nature could be properly construed if only the (Latin) terms of identity could be made transparent. That is, he used a DOS-based system.

23. The Encyclopedist movement as a whole, particularly as it became a populist *summa* for Scholastic thought, was an attempt to chart the "properties of things," as is suggested by the title of the most "populist" of all the medieval encyclopedias, Bartholomaeus Anglicus's *De proprietatibus rerum,* translated into Middle English

by John Trevisa at the end of the fourteenth century (*On the Properties of Things: John Trevisa's Translation of Bartholomaeus Anglicus* De proprietatibus rerum, ed. M. C. Seymour et al. [Oxford: Clarendon Press, 1975–88]).

24. The modified nominalism of Abelard's *Sic et non* (included in Migne's *Patrologia Latina,* 178) proposes a system of "methodical doubt," confronting 150 theological questions, each both supported and opposed by authority and specific canonical utterance. Although the avowed aim of this dialectic was to subject theological "texts" to the rigor of logical analysis and resolution (by making the postulates of faith susceptible to scientific rather than contemplative scrutiny), the very arrangement of the contradictory but authoritative texts in opposed pairs created a systemics that phenomenologically emphasized the disjunct over the synthesis.

25. The deeper cynicism of Adorno's *Negative Dialectics* (trans. E. B. Ashton [New York: Continuum, 1992]) moves the irrational to another stage of development, resisting affirmative thought in any mode.

26. W. Speed Hill, "Text as Scripture, Scripture as Text: The Case of Richard Hooker," *TEXT* 9 (1996): 93–110.

27. See McGann, "The Complete Writings and Pictures of Dante Gabriel Rossetti: A Hypermedia Research Archive," *TEXT* 7 (1994): 95–105; Randall McLeod, "from *Tranceformations* in the Text of *Orlando Furioso,*" in *New Directions in Textual Studies,* ed. Dave Oliphant and Robin Bradford (Austin: University of Texas Press, Harry Ransom Humanities Research Center, 1990), 60–85. See also Hershel Parker's case against the singular modality of formalist, modernist editing in "'The Text Itself'—Whatever That Is," *TEXT* 3 (1987): 47–54; Derek Pearsall's brief against the modern "critical" edition as a betrayal of medieval textuality, "Editing Medieval Texts: Some Developments and Some Problems," in *Textual Criticism and Literary Interpretation,* ed. Jerome J. McGann (Chicago: University of Chicago Press, 1985), 92–106; Pearsall, "Theory and Practice in Middle English Editing," *TEXT* 7 (1994): 107–26; but see also Lee Patterson's defense of the "modernist" (and specifically New Critical) ideology and methods of the Kane–Donaldson edition of the B version of *Piers Plowman,* "The Logic of Textual Criticism and the Way of Genius: The Kane–Donaldson *Piers Plowman* in Historical Perspective," in *Textual Criticism and Literary Interpretation,* ed. Jerome J. McGann, 55–91, esp. 86–88. For the alternative, German, school of genetic rather than eclectic or idealist editing, see *Contemporary German Editorial Theory,* trans. George Bornstein, Hans Walter Gabler, and Gillian Pierce (Ann Arbor: University of Michigan Press, 1996).

28. For an account of the function of the textual margins from various perspectives (feminist, political, gendered, bibliographical), see the essays collected in *Margins of the Text.*

29. See W. Speed Hill, "Commentary upon Commentary upon Commentary," in *Margins of the Text,* 323–52, for an account of the layering of commentary (which then becomes *text* for the next commentary).

30. See Lee Patterson's claim that, because there can be no clear distinction between "external" and "internal" evidence, editing is inevitably "circular" ("Logic," 60). See also Trevor H. Howard-Hill's modernist dissatisfaction with D. F. McKenzie's *Bibliography and the Sociology of Texts* in Howard-Hill's review, *Library,* 6th ser., 10 (1988): 151–58, and Howard-Hill on McGann's social textual criticism,

"Theory and Praxis in the Social Approach to Editing," *TEXT* 5 (1991): 31–46; Howard-Hill's objections arise mostly because the enlarged view of *text* proposed by both McKenzie and McGann does not easily admit of a secure *boundary* to text.

31. See E. J. Kenney, *The Classical Text: Aspects of Editing in the Age of the Printed Book* (Berkeley: University of California Press, 1974) for an account of humanist/Enlightenment/modern metaphors of *cleansing* and *restoring, passim,* but especially 21–25. The popular usage of "editing" to mean "trimming" or "removing of offensive material" (as in a movie that is "edited for television") may reverse the moral imperative of humanist editing (the omitted parts of the text are not seen as "corruptions" of an authorial text but as potential "corruptions" to the current cultural response), but both rationales depend on some means of adjudicating between the detritus and the "proper" form of the text.

32. *Lettere/contratti* CDLXII; *Carteggio* vol. 4, MLXXXII, quoted in George Bull, *Michelangelo: A Biography* (New York: St. Martin's, 1996), 344.

33. James Joyce, *A Portrait of the Artist as a Young Man* (New York: Viking, 1968), 214.

34. G. Thomas Tanselle, "Historicism and Critical Editing," *Studies in Bibliography* 39 (1986): 18, n.39. There is doubtless an irony in Tanselle's having set up an inclusive agenda of cooption (i.e., Greg–Bowers as a unified field theory to encompass all textual phenomena) only to have that model of inclusivity as a trope raised to an even higher level of experience, that is, the "pattern of life."

35. See Jesse M. Gellrich, *The Idea of the Book in the Middle Ages: Language Theory, Mythology, and Fiction* (Ithaca: Cornell University Press, 1985) for a poststructuralist account of the doctrine of signatures, citing, for example, Hugh of St. Victor's concept of "universal history [as] a book of three stages . . . (*lex naturalis; lex scripta; tempus gratiae*)," with "all of nature [as] God's script—the Book of nature" (34).

36. See the various attempts by G. Thomas Tanselle to incorporate *l'histoire du livre* into the *Weltanschauung* of Greg–Bowers eclecticism; for example, *The History of Books as a Field of Study,* Second Hanes Lecture (Chapel Hill: Hanes Foundation and University of North Carolina Press, 1981).

37. I use "local knowledge" in Paul Oskar Kristeller's sense of textual criticism as having only local and specific validity rather than general and theoretical validity; see his "Textual Scholarship and General Theories of History and Literature," *TEXT* 3 (1987): 1–9.

38. D. F. McKenzie, *Bibliography and the Sociology of Texts* (London: British Library, 1986), esp. 31–32; Jerome J. McGann, "How to Read a Book," in *New Directions in Textual Studies,* esp. 13–14; Joseph Grigely, *Textualterity: Art, Theory, and Textual Criticism* (Ann Arbor: University of Michigan Press, 1996), esp. "Textual Eugenics," 11–50.

39. See Gellrich, *Idea of the Book,* commenting on "the inevitability of the 'idea of the Book' in the Middle Ages as soon as a signifying system—words in Scripture, things in nature—became a metaphor for divinity: the entire preexistent 'totality' of God's plan was potential in the signifying means" (35).

40. See Turkle, *Life on the Screen,* esp. 11–14, "Living in the MUD." It is a cultural commonplace to observe that a large segment of popular computer games and software feature consciously "medieval" characters and ethics, derived out of the ar-

cade video games of an earlier decade and before that from the "fantasy" genre of pulp fiction.

41. See, for example, Arnold Sanders, "Hypertext, Learning, and Memory: Some Implications from Manuscript Tradition," *TEXT* 8 (1995): 125–44, on hypertext "stacks and links" and medieval codicology and bibliographical arrangement, developing arguments from Jay David Bolter's *Writing Space: The Computer, Hypertext, and the History of Writing* (Hillsdale, N.J.: Lawrence Erlbaum, 1991).

42. Increasingly, historians of bibliography are beginning to see the "modern" period and its documentary characteristics as an editorially convenient but chronologically atypical transitional era between the medieval and the postmodern. See my *Textual Scholarship: An Introduction* (New York: Garland, 1992), esp. 74–75; and Donald H. Reiman, "A Happy Medium: Books between 1475 and 1975," paper presented at the conference of the Society for Textual Scholarship, New York, April 1997.

43. See Harold Love, *Scribal Publication in Seventeenth-Century England* (Oxford: Clarendon Press, 1993); Arthur Marotti, "Malleable and Fixed Texts: Manuscript and Printed Miscellanies and the Transmission of Lyric Poetry in the English Renaissance" and "Manuscript, Print, and the English Renaissance Lyric," both in *New Ways of Looking at Old Texts: Papers of the Renaissance English Text Society,* ed. W. Speed Hill (Binghamton: Renaissance English Text Society/Medieval and Renaissance Texts and Studies, 1993), 159–73, 209–21; and D. F. McKenzie, "Speech—Manuscript—Print," in *New Directions in Textual Studies,* 86–109.

44. Such cohabitation or confluence of form and function may, moreover, be a liability. McGann claims that it was the precise "fit" of the print medium of the critical edition with that of its subject—the literary text—that prevented such editions from achieving the necessary distance from the subject; see his "The Rationale of HyperText," *TEXT* 9 (1996): 11–32.

45. Patricia Cockram, a graduate of the City University of New York, has now produced a hypermedia archive of Pound's *Cantos,* in which she demonstrates the "fascistic," "totalitarian" aspects of hypertext, especially in its appearing to provide fluidity of movement (the trains do run on time) while constraining narrative and expression through preconstructed but barely visible hyperlinks.

46. Hans-Robert Jauss, "Literary History as a Challenge to Literary Theory," in *New Directions in Literary History,* ed. Ralph Cohen (Baltimore: Johns Hopkins University Press, 1974), 11–41, esp. 18–19.

47. Louis Althusser, "Ideology and Ideological State Apparatuses (Notes toward an Investigation)," in *Lenin and Philosophy and Other Essays,* trans. Ben Brewster (New York: Monthly Review Press, 1971), 123–73.

Daniel Ferrer

Production, Invention, and Reproduction
Genetic vs. Textual Criticism

Textual critics of all persuasions seem to agree on at least one point: they do not want to be ignored by literary critics. They believe that editors should not be trusted blindly. They want literary critics to look into the way the texts they use have been produced. It seems impossible to disagree with so sensible a request, least of all for genetic critics, who are tempted to recognize in it their own concern with the production of the text, rather than with the textual product. But this may well be a case of false recognition, based on different senses of the word "production"—and on different acceptations of the word "criticism."

That one should look into the editorial procedures followed by the scholars who are responsible for the production of the particular edition one quotes is a perfectly sound piece of advice, but a strangely limited one which lays emphasis on a very narrow section of the production process. Although the scholarly decisions of the editor deserve to be thought about carefully, they can hardly be considered more important than the writerly decisions that were taken at each stage of the elaboration of the work (whether these are conscious or unconscious, collective or individual decisions, deliberate aesthetic gestures, passive acceptance of logical, linguistic, and generic necessities, or routine endorsements of external interference).

Textual critics will insist that the editor's job is precisely to disentangle and to assess the social and authorial decisions that concurred or clashed in the historical production of the text, so that the final arbitration that results in the new edition is largely the consequence of the prior "genetic" work. Editors of the text, however, are concerned only with the final stages of the production process and rarely go beyond the fair copy or the last draft, ignoring the rest of the archive, from the earliest notes and remotest scenarios to the intermediary drafts. If, exceptionally, they look into the primitive stages of the work, it is because they suspect that corruption has crept in as early as that, so that it must be identified there in order to eradicate it and reestablish the purity of the authentic text.[1]

Genetic criticism, in contrast, is concerned with the entire range of documents as evidence of the multiple decisions that were taken along the way, not because they throw light on the proper tenor of the text and help in making new (editorial) decisions, but because the object of genetic criticism is inseparable from the decision-making process itself. The earlier documents, the more inchoate traces, are as interesting as the ultimate corrections; or rather, they are interesting *in relation to* the late variants, the "final" text and all the intermediary stages, because they mark the course of the genetic sequence. Genetic critics believe that interpreters of the text should take an interest in its production (in the broader sense just defined), not out of concern with its exactitude, but because this opens up a whole new dimension to interpretation. Like psychoanalysis, the genetic approach rests on the assumption that it is impossible fully to understand the present state of an utterance without knowing the previous states it has gone through.[2]

Genetic criticism is at the same time a more and a less material pursuit than textual criticism. It is more abstract because its final object is not a printable text but a movement, the process of writing, that can be only approximately reconstituted from existing documents and only imperfectly represented, be it by a narrative, a "genetic" edition, or a hypertextual presentation. It is also more concrete, insofar as it does not go beyond the existing documents toward an ideal text that never existed anywhere, but instead strives to reconstruct, from all the evidence it can muster, a historically attested chain of events.[3]

Reconstructing a chain, however, is more than a mapping of successive stages. Genetic criticism does not simply lay the ground for literary criticism; it is inextricably mixed with it. The genetic approach is a form of literary criticism, but it cannot be separated from the other forms because, if it is to be more than a description, it requires one or more principles of explanation, which are to be found in narratology, sociological or psychoanalytic interpretation, and so on.

Versions: Drafts vs. Editions

In practice, textual critics compare editions, while geneticians compare drafts. Some may consider that there is no essential difference, both being versions of the work, so that we might as well start studying the one that is closest to us and has an immediate social impact. It is true that, in some respects, versions are equivalent, but a radical distinction must be made between them.

It is not *simply* a question of authority (depending on the scholar's point of view, editions can be considered as either more or less authoritative than drafts), for the everyday practice of genetic criticism precisely teaches that authority is anything but a simple question. The difference can hardly be found either in the substance of the versions—the words of the text and the *avant-texte* are often practically the same—so it must be a problem of correlation.

If Flaubert, drafting the outline of "Hérodias," writes the word *ville,* and then goes through six layers of rewriting to change it to *la ville,* and finally changes it back to *ville,* genetic criticism considers that this is not an insignificant event; in spite of appearances to the contrary, the point of arrival is different from the point of departure.[4] The word *ville* of the seventh version is not the same as the word *ville* of the first version, because it retains something of the seven states it has gone through. This may sound irrational—a kind of Borgesian paradox, reminiscent of Pierre Ménard's *Don Quixote*—if one does not keep in mind that the word *ville* is not isolated but inserted in a system, which undergoes a series of transformations and which necessarily retains the traces of the various states of equilibrium or disequilibrium it has gone through.

This manifestation of diachrony in a synchronous system appears very plainly in the general makeup of James Joyce's *Ulysses.* The Early, Middle, and Last styles that marked the evolution of Joyce's writing are juxtaposed in the final work, largely coinciding with the beginning, middle, and end of the book, essential constituents of the aesthetic effect of stylistic diversity that characterizes it.[5] To take a more manageable example, we might turn to a page of the draft of the "Proteus" episode (p. 15 of Buffalo MS. V. A. 3), where we find a number of variations on the words *moon* and *womb* (~~moognmbh/~~ ~~moongb/~~ ~~moongmbwb/~~ ~~moongbm/~~ moongmb/ moongbhmb/ *moongb/* moongmbhb/ moongbh/ moombh).[6] Although these elements finally disappeared completely from the surface of the printed page ("moombh," the provisional choice in this draft, later became "moomb" and was then, probably mistakenly, replaced in the text by the simple "womb"), we can consider, in spite of that superficial disappearance, that they remain active; we can even trace their influence elsewhere in the text;

and we can say that this final "womb" is big with all the variations that preceded it.[7]

It is clear that editorial changes cannot be treated in the same way. For instance, the 1984 edition of *Ulysses* prepared by Hans Walter Gabler with Wolfhard Steppe and Claus Melchior introduced a very important change by reinjecting the word "love" in a crucial passage where the typist had overlooked it: this has affected subsequent readers' perception of this passage and even of the whole book.[8] What would remain of it if the editorial decision was reversed in all later editions?

From a genetic point of view, everything would depend on the reasons for the rejection. If it was found that "love" was really just a misreading by the editor (for "live" or "move," for instance), nothing would remain.[9] But if it was thought advisable not to choose that state for the edition of the final text because it was proved that Joyce had noticed the lack of this word and had endorsed it, then it would still be a very important genetic fact. From the point of view of strict textual criticism, on the other hand, both cases would be equivalent and nothing would remain of the editorial change. Symmetrically, it can be verified that a capital editorial decision, such as the printing of two different versions of *King Lear* instead of a single conflated one, does not prevent the publishing of popular editions of the old text that remain quite unaffected by this editorial earthquake.

This confirms that there is no necessary correlation between editorial versions. Editions are not interdependent in the way that genetic states are, unless we choose to take into account incalculably diffuse interactions, a kind of social butterfly wing effect. In the present state of our means of investigation, these interactions are much less susceptible to scientific analysis than is the difference between the two apparently identical words in Flaubert's drafts.

This is so because every edition refers back to a real or postulated "original" version, all other forms being considered as witnesses of a general process of corruption. However, each genetic state not only depends on all the previous states but also alters their status in a kind of retrospective teleology. Each stage acts as a "rigid designator" (to borrow a concept from analytical philosophy) that identifies the relevant documents in the preexisting archive and turns them into the *avant-texte* leading toward that stage.[10]

Repetition Compulsion: Pragmatics and Psychoanalysis

To investigate this logical and genealogical difference further, we must look into the pragmatic status of the versions. At this point, we will have to reformulate ponderously some basic facts that are so self-evident that they are never stated directly. In his analysis of the status of works of art, Nelson

Goodman carefully discriminates between the case of literary texts and musical scores: for him, it is the execution of the score that constitutes the work, not the score itself, which is only a set of instructions toward the work, whereas such a distinction is not possible for the fictional or poetic text.[11] One might remark, however, that the text, like the musical score, has a prescriptive dimension, even if it confines itself to a single injunction: that it should be repeated, and repeated accurately. In the same way as the musical work comes to exist only when the prescriptions of the score are fulfilled, the text exists—or at least subsists—only if this command is obeyed.

The prescription is so general that it can usually remain implicit, but it is sometimes spelled out. One can think of the part played for centuries by the imprimatur of the Roman Catholic Church, or of the "permission to print" granted by the jury of a thesis, which is an important step in the bestowing of a French Ph.D. But there is a much more common incarnation: the "passed for press" form (*bon à tirer*) signed by the author after the last set of proofs.

Hypertrophied forms of this injunction are to be recognized in the complex combination of notarized contracts, testaments, and codicils with which Châteaubriand tried to ensure the exact reproduction of his *Mémoires d'outre-tombe*; in the eight testaments that Stendhal included in the manuscript of *La Vie de Henri Brulard*; in the weird prayer for faithful transmission that Rousseau inscribed on the manuscript of his *Dialogues* before he deposited it on the altar of Notre-Dame; or in Chaucer's poem *To His Scribe Adam,* enjoining his copyist to reproduce his work with care and fidelity on pain of frightful maledictions. But proclamations, signatures, deeds, prayers, and curses are but tautological hypostatizations of the similar act of language performed by every text.

It is perhaps easier to grasp the injunction under its negative form: one may think, again, of writers' testaments forbidding the publication of part of their work (e.g., Virgil, Mallarmé, Kafka, Saint-John Perse), or, more simply, of the deleatur (the sign used in proof marking to suppress a word or a passage) or the crossing-out. Crossing out a text is a cancellation not necessarily of the text itself but of the underlying injunction. Hence many writers, like Joyce or Flaubert, cross out their drafts once they have been recopied—not because they want to get rid of their contents, but because the injunction to repeat has already been fulfilled. This may also explain why, historically, this type of cancellation (striking through as opposed to scraping or erasing) seems to have appeared in Italy in the thirteenth century in the drafts of legal documents, which had to be kept for records (as we would today keep a photocopy of a title): crossing out turned out to be an easy way of dissociating the semantic content and the illocutionary value of the legal deed.[12]

The complex and often contradictory modulations of this injunction to repeat are the central concern of the textual critic. In this respect, it is interesting to compare textual criticism with psychoanalysis. They both belong to the same scientific paradigm, described by Carlo Ginzburg as an indexical paradigm, and they share common preoccupations.[13] Both are fascinated by errors, to the extent that some textual critics speak of versions as mere "grounds for error" (*supports de faute*)—while psychoanalysis often considers texts as a mere hunting ground for parapraxes and symptoms. But the important point, from a philological point of view, is that errors are failures to repeat. Both psychoanalysis and philology can be described as sciences of repetition. As such, each considers that it has jurisdiction over the other: psychoanalysis has been sharply criticized for its philological failings by Sebastiano Timpanaro, and it will have a field day in its turn when it starts interpreting the rather blatant fantasies underlying the enterprise of textual criticism and many of its formulations.[14] As an almost random sample, one might quote from a widespread manual by Paul Maas:

> The diagram which exhibits the inter-relationship of the witnesses is called the *stemma*. The image is taken from genealogy: the witnesses are related to the original somewhat as the descendants of a man are related to their ancestor. One might perhaps illustrate the transmission of errors along the same lines by treating all females as source of error.[15]

And from Dom Froger, a daring technical innovator in the field:

> Puisque le modèle généalogique est assez inadéquat, ne pourrait-on pas essayer de l'améliorer? . . . On pourrait par exemple y introduire la "mère": ce serait le copiste qui altère le modèle en le transcrivant et modifie le patrimoine héréditaire.[16]

In both cases, there is nothing more than a passing image, but it affords us a glimpse of phobias (fear of woman—and more specifically of the mother—as a source of error and pollution, as the stumbling block in the smooth process of repetition) lurking behind the traditional representation of textual transmission as a genealogy, as a family story.

It should be pointed out that calling attention to such underlying fantasies is not a way of attacking the discipline of textual criticism itself; it is intended simply to suggest the source of some of its rigidities. Every discipline, every scientific pursuit is based on a set of fantasies and ultimately rests, psychoanalysis tells us, on a bunch of sordid secrets. Genetic studies precisely show us that the final result is always qualitatively different from the sum of the preexisting intentions and motivations. But in the field of science (as opposed, perhaps, to the field of art), it is always better to be conscious of those precursors in order to avoid dangerous deviations.[17]

The Open Space of the Manuscript

Whereas textual criticism is concerned with the modalities of the injunction to repeat, genetic criticism, being the study of textual invention, is precisely concerned with what is not repetition.[18] Such a statement must immediately be qualified in many ways: there can be no such thing as pure invention (and if there were, it would lie outside of the scope of any science, of any criticism), so what genetic criticism is actually confronted with is a dialectic of invention and repetition.

Given this fundamental difference, what happens when the genetician becomes an editor of sorts and tries to put the genetic material before the eyes of the public, if only to share the documents that are the basis of the genetic reconstruction of the writing process? The problem is that authors' drafts are highly complex objects. On the one hand, they have some characteristics of a text, and as such they carry the same injunction to repeat: this is the draft as something to be transcribed, by a printer, an amanuensis, or the author himself (but an author's copying is often something very different from a repetition)—or by an editor. But the draft is also a locus of invention, an open space, a field of action where events of writing take place.

The author's manuscript is an open space because it is ruled not by the single prescription to repeat, but by an array of injunctions. Some of those are explicitly present in the margins of the manuscript. For instance, one can read, in so many words, self-injunctions such as "to be verified," "change this," "put this in a different style," "include this somewhere else"—but most of the time, it is the business of the genetician to interpret and formulate these injunctions. For example, a scenario is not an injunction to repeat, but an injunction to tell a story in different words. Notes are injunctions to use elements (with different degrees of tentativeness or of urgency, marked in Proust by the mention *capital* or *capitalissime*), or—as in the case of the Brazilian writer Guimaraes Rosa, who made long lists of things *not* to be used—they can be negative prescriptions. The mandates expressed by Flaubert's exclamation marks in his scenarios or by an interrogation mark in a Joycean draft ("Molly likes left (?) side of her face best") are not so easy to paraphrase. From a genetic perspective, different forms of cancellation make different sense: an erasing, or a slight crossing-out, or a heavy blotting, or, as in the manuscripts of Stendhal, the self-instruction *Ne pas reprendre en dictant* ("not to be taken up when dictating"—which is a subtle way of keeping something, while not allowing it into the next version) are not equivalent, as they would be from a textual point of view, and they are certainly not equivalent to a mere absence. This is why it would be a mistake to try to edit drafts as if they were texts. In a way, when the genetician becomes an editor of drafts, he or she edits not words but the underlying injunctions (which is not the same thing as the utopian endeavor to follow those instructions in order to produce the version intended by the author, differing from any existing version).[19]

The Hypertextual Model

The *avant-texte*, then, is not a text, and it is bound to be mutilated almost beyond recognition when it is forced into the Procrustean bed of a book—but it has many of the characteristics of an electronic hypertext. A hypertext is a nonsequential body of verbal data, but it is also a collection of electronic instructions and commands (the equivalent of the genetic injunctions) keyed to the verbal data, which allow it to be reorganized and reprocessed at will, keeping it in a state of flux. It should be clear that this is only an analogy, I hope more productive than the usual implicit analogy with philological textual history and, more specifically, a reversed Lachmannian stemma. But hypertext, or rather hypermedia, also offers a much more satisfying practical solution than the usual format of the critical edition.

The traditional model of apparatus, presenting one text with a plurality of variants, is totally inadequate to the task: it involves a linearization of something that is not linear; it introduces an artificial hierarchy between elements that are only retrospectively hierarchized; and it causes not only a loss of the energy that nobody who enters into contact with drafts can ignore, but also a sheer loss of information. Some of this information can be retrieved with the help of symbols and diacritics, but a good proportion of it is too subtle to be recoverable by such means (a shade of ink, an intensity of erasure, a balanced position in relation to different word clusters). For instance, when we look at the "Proteus" page mentioned earlier, it becomes obvious that in the storage of elements, their material location is not neutral: the spatial disposition of the writing on the page is a crucial factor for the interrelationships of its various elements.

Genetic work clearly requires facsimiles of the documents, but it is not enough to deliver to the reader a bundle of rough material. It is often necessary to provide a transcription, and in some cases, alternative transcriptions, since any transcription is an interpretation. But the inclusion of transcriptions in the sequence of facsimiles only makes more difficult the insoluble problem of ordering the documents. Genetic files are multidimensional objects, and linear representations, such as books can offer, are necessarily mutilating. There is always a multiplicity of possible genetic orders, and each of them tells a different story. The mere juxtaposition of the manuscripts introduces, under the guise of total neutrality, an unacknowledged bias. The only way of bypassing this sly form of control is to provide a multiplicity of solutions.

Undoubtedly, hypertextual presentation gives the best chance to do justice to the diversity of the material and the multiplicity of the relationships.[20] It offers an unlimited number of paths through the documents; it allows instant juxtaposition of facsimiles, transcriptions, and commentaries (which can be as long as necessary, in various depths of accessibility, so as not to stifle the manuscript themselves); and it welcomes dialogic readings, with unlimited possibilities of reordering, additions of new documents, and changes of readings (which are inevitable for most complex manuscripts).[21]

This does not mean that there is no room for traditional editions and that they will not remain invaluable tools, but it should be realized that they are valid only for a historically limited period (excluding medieval work,[22] and probably future work that will be written directly for electronic media). Moreover, they are adequate only for a very specific and limited form of existence of the work, which genetic criticism would compare (provokingly, but it is necessary to be provoking in order to shake the exclusive hold of the secular textual model) to the ashes remaining when the fire is consumed, or to the footprints on the ground after the dance is over.

An Outside Opinion

Has genetic criticism anything to say about the editing of this limited form of the work (aesthetically and cognitively limited, but historically and sociologically all-important)? A few remarks only.

Copy-text editions and more generally eclectic editions are suspect to genetic criticism: the idea of mixing elements belonging to different versions goes very much against what we discover about the importance of the context, including its most material aspects. Manuscripts prove abundantly the solidarity of all the elements of a version. If an error creeps in, it becomes a context for further additions and transformations and interacts with them. Mixing up the different contextual layers to create a composite text is genetically nonsensical. But if it is to be considered, as Hans Walter Gabler expressed it very well, "a theoretical impossibility, but a pragmatic necessity," then there is no reason not to accept such a necessity. It seems that in such matters, common sense should have the last word.

In the current debate among editors, genetic criticism, in spite of what could be expected, would be on the side of a social approach rather than an intentional approach. The genetician has been trained to consider the notion of intention with great interest (as opposed to New Critics, who ignored it) but with considerable suspicion. The student of manuscript sees an intentionality emerging from the work, but the author's intention appears as a fluctuating, time-bound transaction between a series of writing events and a series of external constraints, providing no firm basis for absolute editorial decisions to be taken.[23] This is true to the point that some of us tend to consider (not out of poststructuralist theoretical prejudice, but as the result of our daily experience with writers' manuscripts) that the text is not produced by the author, but the author is produced by the text.

Although it has been centered until now, to a large extent, on the private sphere of writing, genetic criticism is ready for a broadening of its scope, joining forces with those textual critics who consider textual deviations not as mere "failures to repeat," the deplorable result of a process of dereliction, but as socially motivated *inventions*.

Notes

1. In practice, this is far from being exceptional, and the distinction is blurred. Textual critics, in contact with the manuscripts, often take an interest in the production of the work and provide very useful genetic data, but this remains subordinate, at least in theory, to their central concern, the transmission of the text. Fredson Bowers himself, in his edition of William James, endeavors to reconstruct the evolution of the philosopher's thought (which is not quite the same thing as the dynamics of writing). In some cases, it is clear that some scholars who call themselves textual critics are actually geneticians. The purpose of the restrictive definition adopted here is not to make up a convenient foil for genetic criticism, but to clarify the issues.

2. This is particularly clear in Freud's interpretation of witticisms or of analytic transference. See Tzvetan Todorov, "Freud sur l'énonciation," *Langages* 17 (1970): 34–41. See also *Genesis* 8 (1995), special issue on psychoanalysis and genetic criticism.

3. For a general view of genetic criticism, see *Les Manuscrits des écrivains*, ed. Louis Hay (Paris: CNRS Éditions/Hachette, 1993); and Almuth Grésillon, *Éléments de critique génétique: Lire les manuscrits modernes* (Paris: PUF, 1994), with a glossary and a general bibliography. See also the ten volumes of the collection "Textes et manuscrits" published by CNRS Éditions and the nine issues of the journal *Genesis: Manuscrits, recherche, invention,* published by Éditions Jean-Michel Place.

In English, see Louis Hay, "Does 'Text' Exist?," *Studies in Bibliography* 41 (1988): 64–76; Michel Pierssens, "French Genetic Studies at a Crossroads," *Poetics Today* 11 (1990): 617–25; Frank Bowman, "Genetic Criticism," *Poetics Today* 11 (1990): 627–46; Graham Falconer, "Genetic Criticism," *Comparative Literature* 45 (1993): 1–21; David Hayman, introduction, in *Probes: Genetic Studies in Joyce,* ed. David Hayman and Sam Slote (Amsterdam: Rodopi, 1995), 3–18; the May 1995 issue of *Romanic Review* (86, no. 3); and the June 1996 issue of *Yale French Studies* (no. 89).

4. See Almuth Grésillon, Jean-Louis Lebrave, and C. Fuchs, "Flaubert: Ruminer Hérodias," in *L'Écriture et ses doubles: Genèse et variation textuelle,* ed. Daniel Ferrer and Jean-Louis Lebrave (Paris: CNRS Éditions, 1991).

5. See Michael Groden, *Ulysses in Progress* (Princeton: Princeton University Press, 1977).

6. *The James Joyce Archive,* vol. 12, ed. Michael Groden (New York: Garland, 1978).

7. See Daniel Ferrer, "Between *inventio* and *memoria:* Locations of 'Aeolus,'" in *Joyce in the Hybernian Metropolis: Essays,* ed. Morris Beja (Columbus: Ohio University Press, 1996), 190–97.

8. James Joyce, *Ulysses,* ed. Hans Walter Gabler (New York and London: Garland, 1984).

9. This is a purely fictional hypothesis. A look at the document confirms that the editors' reading is impeccable.

10. See Daniel Ferrer, "La Toque de Clementis: Rétroaction et rémanence dans les processus génétiques," *Genesis: Manuscrits, recherche, invention* 6 (1994): 93–106; translated as "Clementis's Cap: Retroaction and Persistence in the Genetic Process," *Yale French Studies* 89 (June 1996): 223–36.

11. Nelson Goodman, *Languages of Art: An Approach to a Theory of Symbols* (Indianapolis: Bobbs Merrill, 1968).

12. See Armando Petrucci, *Jeux de lettres: Formes et usages de l'inscription en Italie 11–20e siècles,* trans. Monique Aymard (Paris: Éditions EHESS, 1993).

13. See Carlo Ginzburg's "Spie," in his *Miti, emblemi, spie* (Torino: Einaudi, 1986). As Ginzburg points out, textual criticism stands out in this paradigm by its constant effort toward a desubstantialization, based on the distinction between the text and its material support. To a certain extent, genetic criticism, which belongs to the same paradigm, goes in the opposite direction.

14. Timpanaro attacks it from the standpoint of Marxist philosophy, but with the tools of classical philology, in *The Freudian Slip, Psychoanalysis and Textual Criticism,* trans. Kate Soper (London: New Left Books, 1976); first published as *Il lapsus freudiano: Psicanalisi e critica testuale* (Florence: La Nuova Italia, 1974).

15. Paul Maas, *Textual Criticism,* trans. Barbara Plower (Oxford: Clarendon Press, 1958), 20.

16. Dom J. Froger, *La Critique des textes et son automatisation* (Paris: Dunod, 1968), 269–70.

17. As for the fantasies underlying genetic criticism, see, for instance, Jean Bellemin-Noel, "L'Infamilière Curiosité" in *Leçons d'écriture, ce que disent les manuscrits,* ed. Almuth Grésillon and Michael Werner (Paris: Minard, 1985), 345–57.

18. "Invention" in this sense is very different from what philology calls "innovation," which is simply an error (a failure to repeat).

19. This is the position of Thomas Tanselle, as expressed in *A Rationale of Textual Criticism* (Philadelphia: University of Pennsylvania Press, 1989): the manuscript as guide for the reconstruction of one or more versions.

20. But some hypertextual architectures can be much more reductive and compelling than a good printed edition with an intelligent, flexible apparatus.

21. On the possibilities of hypertext for the purpose of genetic criticism, see Jean-Louis Lebrave, "L'Hypertexte et l'avant-texte," in *Texte et ordinateur: Les Mutations du lire-écrire* (La Garenne-Colombes: Espace européen, 1991); Daniel Ferrer, "Hypertextual Representation of Literary Working Papers," *Literary and Linguistic Computing* 10 (1995): 143–45; and Daniel Ferrer and Yvan Leclerc, "Bovary hyper-

texte" the first commercially available hypertextual presentation of genetic material, published by CNRS Éditions as an accompanying tool to Gustave Flaubert, *Plans et scénarios de Madame Bovary,* ed. Yvan Leclerc (Paris: CNRS Éditions, 1995).

22. See Bernard Cerquiligni, *Éloge de la variante: Histoire critique de la philologie* (Paris: Seuil, 1989). This book also presents a fascinating analysis of the ideology underlying traditional philology.

23. See Daniel Ferrer, "Reflections on a Discarded Set of Proofs," in *Probes: Genetic Studies in Joyce,* ed. David Hayman and Sam Slote (Amsterdam: Rodopi, 1995), 49–63.

Joseph Grigely

Editing Bodies

It all started for me in the express checkout lane at Waldbaum's grocery store in Jersey City, New Jersey, late in the summer of 1993. There was a problem with the barcode reader at the cash register, and I got stuck in a long line waiting for the manager to come and fix it. While I was waiting, a rack of tabloids caught my eye. Just above the Milky Way bars, right beside the *Star,* I saw something that was more than just a tabloid: it was *Weekly World News* (fig. 1). The cover story was about a horse born with a human face. His name was Mannie. "Alive and kicking," as *Weekly World News* reported. But Mannie is clearly no mere horse. As the story goes, he owes his existence to one Dr. Peter de Vries, a Dutch geneticist who added human genes to the fertilized egg of a horse and implanted the egg in the womb of a mare.[1] Mannie is thus an edited body; more specifically, an eclectic postmodern body. All at once, Mannie's eclecticism embraces technoscience's desire for control—to produce, on demand, an immaculate conception that is also an immaculate irony: a perfectly imperfect body. It is precisely Mannie's imperfection that makes him so appealing. Everything that is wrong about him is everything that is right. Like the patented mouse with a cancer gene known as OncoMouse™, Mannie's presence is a triumph of agency. He is neither high culture nor low culture, but a force that subsumes conventionalized categories—a figure whose exhibition on the

Figure 1. *Weekly World News,* 27 July 1993.

cover of a tabloid was in turn exhibited in the most accessible of exhibition sites America knows: the supermarket checkout lane.

A detour now. There will be many detours in this essay, and the first is circumlocutionary. I want to address the theoretical premises that underlie or otherwise inflect the seemingly disparate fields of thought discussed throughout this essay. My primary subject is bodies in a very general sense, and how, in the process of reproduction, they change and are changed.[2] As a subfield of body criticism, my secondary subject involves textual criticism, a field of practice that studies the dissemination of literary texts and how they too change and are changed in the process of being reproduced.[3] There are times when textual criticism and body criticism have mutual concerns—as with Mannie, who is both a text and a body, both a signifier for technoculture's triumph and a very real body. He is real not as a colt is real, but real as a textual body is real, appearing, as he does, on the cover of *Weekly World News*. Mannie is a threshold creature: his actualization as a textual body puts into a concrete form some of the most pressing issues facing body critics and textual critics today. If I had it my way, little plastic replicas of Mannie would be on the desks of textual critics and body critics alike—Jerome McGann would get one; so would G. Thomas Tanselle, and Donna Haraway, and Ira Livingston. Mannie reminds us in a very graphic way that every signifier is a body, and every body is a signifier. As much as bodies are biological entities, they are also social constructs: they include images and discourse, the tangible and the ephemeral, the literal and the figurative. We have come to think of body criticism as a specialized field of study that emphasizes the history of science and the history of criticism (both Haraway and Livingston figure in my thinking here), and textual criticism as an even more specialized field that emphasizes the continuity and transfer of information from one textual body to another (McGann and Tanselle, for different reasons, both figure here); yet, somehow, body criticism and textual criticism are mutually interpenetrating fields of thought. If we acknowledge here that editing applies to microbiological sciences as much as it applies to literature—to Mannie as much as to T. S. Eliot—how can we bring body criticism and textual criticism together in a way that says something about their mutual concerns?

My approach to this question involves the peregrinations of moving among a series of vignettes that constitute a virtual exhibition. There are visual displays interwoven with a fairly discursive assemblage of commentaries and detours in what amounts to a heuretic essay (the phrase belongs to Gregory Ulmer[4]) in its intermixing of art and theory. The art, however, is not quite the art I had originally intended—or even the form I had intended. The University of Wisconsin Press—financially constrained as most university presses are—insisted that the color images be printed in black and white. The small page size dictated a layout more linear than discursive. Some images that were originally part of this essay in its format as a lecture are not printed here because I was unable to obtain permission to reproduce them.

This essay is not really an "essay" as much as it is a "project." My sources vary considerably in relation to their supposed or hypothetical scholarly value: I believe that postcards and tabloids have as much to teach us about textual change as Keats and Shakespeare do, and so I have tried to focus, for the most part, on examples that have more or less fallen into the path of my life. As theory and as rhetoric, my essay makes its claims primarily by posing questions that derive from the various propositions, stories, and images that I have gleaned—an eclectic narrative that exemplifies itself as an edited body.

Another detour now. The year is 1906. A hot afternoon in July. Imagine it this way: you are sitting on your porch in Hadley, Massachusetts, when a postcard arrives from your sister, who is abroad for the summer (fig. 2). It's a nice card, almost a little funny: the interior of a greenhouse with shelves of pots filled with sprouting—babies. It is an unlikely coupling: Luther Burbank and Francis Galton. Agriculture and viriculture. A few weeks later, a second postcard from your sister arrives (fig. 3). It too is a nice card: kids growing in a cabbage patch that is actually a cauliflower patch. Cauliflower kids. Except that the cauliflower plants are really tobacco plants. It doesn't all come together quite right, yet it somehow comes together by not coming together. It is, as you first noticed, a nice card.

The turn from Romantic idealism to Modern realism might be described in terms of how we perceive the notion of difference. In the nineteenth century, biology was a relatively nascent subject. Mendel, Darwin, and Galton showed us that the biological body was a transitory body that changed, and could be changed, according to certain precepts that were slowly being understood as having something to do with the flow of information between bodies. Galton actually used the word "viriculture" to describe the selective breeding of humans as a means of "improving"—his word again—the human race. He later changed his terminology and chose the word "eugenics" to reflect this same editorial ideal. According to its Greek root, eugenics means "well bred." In the early twentieth century, the Anglo-American eugenics movement gained momentum through a variety of legislative maneuvers (such as enforced sterilization of "deviants" in the United States) and made eugenics a reality, not just a theory. It took the extremes of the Third Reich to force a reassessment of this activity. Nonetheless, some Americans actually lamented that the eugenics movement did not go far enough: Dr. Joseph DeJarnette, a proponent of sterilization in Virginia in the 1920s and 1930s, publicly remarked in 1934: "The Germans are beating us at our own game."[5]

At roughly the same time—a fact significant in the way it reflects a concurrency of scientific and cultural thought—textual critics were embracing a similar form of Romantic idealism. Like Galton, literary editors have always been concerned about the genes of the texts they edit. An assumption widely shared by textual critics is that, in the transmission of literary texts, both intended and unintended changes occur. In various ways, changes that depart from an author's affirmed or assumed intentions are typically char-

Figure 2. Unattributed postcard, ca. 1906–1908.

Figure 3. Unattributed postcard sent on 28 September 1906 from an undisclosed location in England. The postmark is only partly legible.

acterized as being abject; in the discourse of eugenics, departures from the ideal are sometimes given more precisely defined character as "deviant," "deformed," or "incurable." Editors typically see their job as one that involves the emendation of bodies in order to eliminate their supposed or purported imperfections through a variety of editorial procedures. Both biology and textual criticism thus face a similar situation: the transmission of bodies creates new bodies that are inevitably inflected by the vicissitudes of life, and by life's inherent potential for chaos.

But chaos has always been a troubling aspect of Western culture's desire for harmony and order. Tolerance of difference—let alone appreciation of it—has not been a particularly compelling feature of twentieth-century American thought. Instead, it was goodness—in body, life, and mind— that defined an early conception of Romantic modernism. In the 1920s and 1930s, during the heyday of the American eugenics movement, state fairs held competitions known as "fitter families contests" in which people were judged like chickens and cabbages. The question such contests posed was a dialectic between natural selection and artificial selection: how might the process of nature be hurried and controlled in such as way as to produce more immediate and precise betterment for the general good of humankind? It wasn't a new question though; it had already been implicitly posed and explicitly answered by Diderot in the *Encyclopédie,* in his definition for horticultural grafting:

> The graft is the triumph of art over nature. By its means, nature is forced to take on different arrangements, to follow other paths, to change its forms, and to substitute the good, beautiful, great in place of the abject; finally by means of the graft one can transmute the sex, species, and even types of trees.[6]

What Diderot does not say is how one might qualify the abject as being abject, or the good as being good. Cultural values, like the people to whom we attribute these values, are always in flux, and they are never quite so stable as we would like them to be. But what is clear is that for Diderot—as for most textual critics—the abject is a point of departure, the point at which one feels compelled to react with an ameliorative force, and thereby to act in a way considered both socially and morally benevolent. The entire eugenics movement was based on the supposition that the "burden" and subsequent "elimination" of those arbitrarily considered "less fit" was necessary in order to promote the moral and physical progress of humankind.[7]

Another detour, this time to a couple of exhibitions—Paris in 1829, New York in 1995. Ritta and Christina Sassari (fig. 4) were born on March 23, 1829. As the story goes, their parents were poor but managed to obtain enough money to bring them to Paris, where they intended to exhibit the sisters as a way of earning a living. The public exhibition of the sisters was prohibited by authorities who, however, did permit—or ignore—their private display. The sisters died less than a year after arriving in Paris; it is not recorded what fate befell their parents.[8]

Dinos and Jake Chapman were born in England in the 1960s. They are post-Generation-X artists. For the past few years they've been pretty hot. In a press statement accompanying a 1995 exhibition in New York, the Chapmans explained "We are sore-eyed scopophiliac oxymorons." Irony is rarely so blunt as the Chapmans make it. The single sculpture that they exhibited in New York at Gavin Brown's Enterprise—at that time a low-key storefront gallery on the lower West Side—is entitled *The Siamese Twat.* It presents what the Chapmans call "a scatological aesthetics for the tired of seeing."[9] This is one of the artworks for which I could not obtain reproduction rights. It's probably better that way.

The notion of the ideal is a purely subjective construction of desire, and in the space between Ritta & Christina and Dinos & Jake lies a long history of this desire's abetting itself. This desire to alter reality is a transcendent one whose operations involve the risk of irrevocability. Yet this is a risk many have taken, and a risk every editor necessarily takes: to ascribe a set of values to a textual body while knowing at the same time that those values are

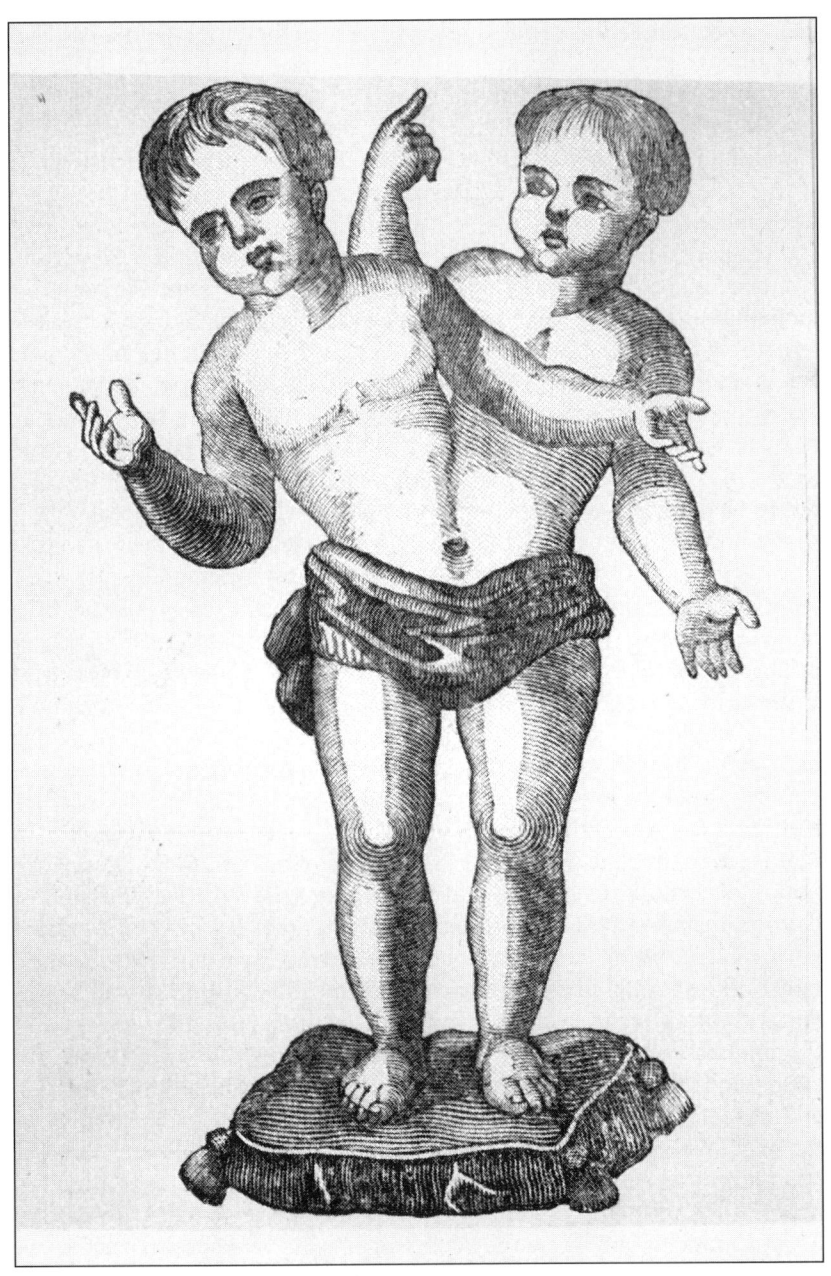

Figure 4. Ritta and Christina Sassari. (From C. J. S. Thompson, *The Mystery and Lore of Monsters* [London: Williams & Norgate, 1930], 85)

likely to be supplanted. That is precisely why no body can be perfect, and why no text can be ideal: because ideas of perfection and the ideal will always be supplanted by a new perfection and a new ideal. Take scars, for example—in a very simple and literal sense, the traces of trauma to the skin. Normally, scarring is seen as having a stigmatizing effect, particularly the scars of burns or unintended facial scarring. As Erving Goffman wrote, the word "stigma" itself refers to a bodily sign that exposes something unusual or bad about the moral status of the person bearing the stigma.[10] Slaves and criminals in ancient Greece were branded to mark their respective status. In modern Western culture, the scar is typically a sign of an undesired event—something that does not connote beauty as much as it connotes misfortune. But in a recent photo spread in the British hyper-pop magazine, *The Face,* scars were elevated to the status of being both fashionable and chic. "Tissue: A Portfolio of Scars" presented six individuals and their variously scarred torsos and faces in such a way as to turn stigma inside out: not to be scarred, not to be different, is to be unmarked.[11] This is the subversive real, and it shows how our ideas about the ideal are consistent only in their inconsistency. Ritta and Christina Sassari were, in their day, legitimized by their freakness. But similarly conjoined seven-year-old twins, Abigail and Brittany Hansel, were presented in precisely the opposite light in a 1996 spread in *Life* magazine: their freakness was legitimized. *Life* showed Abigail and Brittany living a perfectly normal life, doing all the things little kids do—swimming, riding a bike, dreaming about their future careers.[12] The people of "Tissue," like Abigail and Brittany, represent a new social turn that emphasizes the democracy of the body, and they demonstrate how those once perceived as bearers of stigma constitute a new social ideal of the real.

If there is a parallel to this turn in the realm of textual studies, it is in our notion of textual democracy: that what is normal in the transmission of cultural texts involves the production of texts that defy our illusions of normalcy, including condensed books, colorized films, bootlegged music tapes, appropriated images, relocated site-specific sculptures, and so on. Not merely different, such texts exist in conjunction with the people and the circumstances that brought them into being in the first place. Why do people condense books, colorize films, bootleg music, appropriate images, and relocate site-specific sculptures? Our contemporary understanding of the relationship between bodies and politics, between nature and technology, and between art and science has become an understanding of what lies *between* these domains rather than what lies within them. Ours is a culture of hyphenation. And where the hyphen occurs, it is the hyphen itself, as an agent of force, that makes impossible unions precisely what they seem to be: impossible. Mannie. *The Siamese Twat.* Kids growing out of cabbage plants. It seems to me that the mark of our age at the turn of the millennium is to *undo* the previous millennium's effort to taxonomize the world and its inhabitants into neat categories and divisions—to emphasize not the ontological "purity" of the categories themselves but rather their nature as indivisible and sometimes undefinable conflations; the perfect synecdoche is the Siamese twins, the product of a single egg that will not divide into two distinct bodies. By acknowledging our monstropomorphism and its various manifestations in both bodies and cultural practices, we come closer to acknowledging the impossible realities of our everyday lives—come closer, as it were, to our own ineluctability.

Alexis Rockman. Rockman paints these pretty normal scenes of our abnormal world. Barnyard scenes, for example, of raccoons mating with chickens. His source, however, seems to have been not a raccoon but a rabbit. Does this matter? Perhaps. In Rockman's more compelling works, he paints still-life portraits of our unstill lives. Take, for example, a work from 1991 entitled *Still Life* (fig. 5). It doesn't take a zoologist to notice that Rockman's bunny looks rather unbunnylike. Those who have traveled the highways of North Dakota and Montana—particularly the rest stops along the way—will recognize here something similar to the western jackalope. If you look closely, though, you will observe that Rockman's creature is not a jackalope (fig. 6). It's a wolpertinger. Wolpertingers have wings, jackalopes do not. And wolpertingers have asymmetrical paws, as well as teeth and an appetite that remind us of a certain now-extinct mammal.

The issue of mutations is significant here—not in a biological sense, but in an etymological sense that emphasizes changed and changing states. Siamese twins, jackalopes, wolpertingers, professors of interdisciplinary studies. Technoscience. Postmodernism and the posthumanities. As Barbara Stafford said of Enlightenment monsters, these creations resist the collapse into simplicity.[13] Facing, as we do, the conflations of history, etiology, and etymology, and seeking, as we also do, to filiate bodies into some kind of visual and hence tangible tree of life, we have the complex task of trying to see the ostensibly unseeable.

It is time to revisit our friend Mannie, the horse with a human face. It was not really a coincidence that I discovered Mannie on the day that the barcode reader broke down at Waldbaum's—it would have happened anyway. For about a year, I had been buying *Weekly World News* every couple of weeks or so. I like the photos. Especially the photos of Satan in clouds of smoke. *Weekly World News* also provides reporting—not really the right word, but I'll use it anyway—it provides reporting on the extremes of morphogenesis and morphodeviance: Batboy. Frogboy. The woman with three breasts. The marshmal-

Figure 5. Alexis Rockman, "Still Life," 1991, oil on canvas. (Courtesy of Gorney Bravin + Lee, New York City)

low tree (fig. 7).[14] The marshmallow tree is reputedly a conflation of several fruit trees, sugar cane, and a rare species of the rubber plant—a conflation involving hundreds of grafts over a period of seventeen years. Like Mannie the horse, the marshmallow tree is an eclectic body—the culmination and success of a certain human desire.

The portrait of Percy Shelley on the cover of the Norton edition of Shelley's poetry is also an eclectic body (fig. 8). It, too, is the culmination and success of a certain desire. The Norton Shelley was produced under the direction of the volume's editor, Donald Reiman, with the creative assistance of the artist Tim Gaydos. The portrait is derived from features of Shelley present in several contemporary works: the Amelia Curran oil portrait (and George Clint's redaction of it); the two 1821 pencil drawings by Edward E. Williams; the supposed Williams watercolor portrait; and the self-portrait of Antonio Leisman, which Thomas Love Peacock said was the closest likeness to Shelley as he remembered him.[15] From all of these bodies Professor Reiman made a new one, having offered specific suggestions to Gaydos on how to proceed.

Eclecticism is like a fatal attraction: it promises so much and delivers so little. Mary Shelley's *Frankenstein,* which was first published in 1818, is

Figure 6. Western jackalope (contemporary postcard).

about an eclectic body. It wasn't pretty and it didn't work quite right, but it was very much a distinct body, a body that in its individuality reflected the circumstances of its creation. The word "eclectic" is from Greek *eklektikos*, which means "selective." To choose, to select—and ultimately, to recombine. The eclectic body is, more than any other body, a body marked by authorship. Other bodies happen, but eclectic bodies happen because someone wants them to happen, and to happen in a certain way. The eclectic body draws attention not to itself but to the very desire that instigated its conception and brought it to existence. Dr. Frankenstein, Dr. De Vries, and Donald Reiman all created eclectic bodies—and all three, in their role as editors, cast themselves as creators of reconstituted bodies. A dominant editorial paradigm until recently, eclectic tendencies remain ubiquitous as an organizing principle in our everyday life: they offer us the possibility of mounting distinct and individual conceptions of a body or bodies and organizing them in a way that presents a particular vision of them.[16]

By its very nature, editing is a transgressive practice. Each time a text is emended or reprinted, it is altered in such a way as to construct a new textual body. What is ironic about this is that art cannot exist by any other means. That Shakespeare has come down to us in widely differing editions and formats—Johnson's Shakespeare, Bowdler's Shakespeare, Lamb's Shakespeare, Knight's Illustrated Shakespeare, Gary Taylor's Shakespeare—reminds us that editing is to a large extent about attitudes. The act

Figure 7. *Weekly World News,* 9 November 1993.

of transgression can thus be a benevolent act and not merely a manifestation of violence. It is somewhat disconcerting, however, given the record of unending change physically altering artworks, that many people continue to believe that art is immutable, that the artist's intentions are paramount, and that original works should be "preserved" from various agents of change. Perhaps this is simply a reflection of our desire for stability and order, our wish to think of art as something that will endure—unlike life itself. Art does endure, of course, and one reason it endures is because it is able to

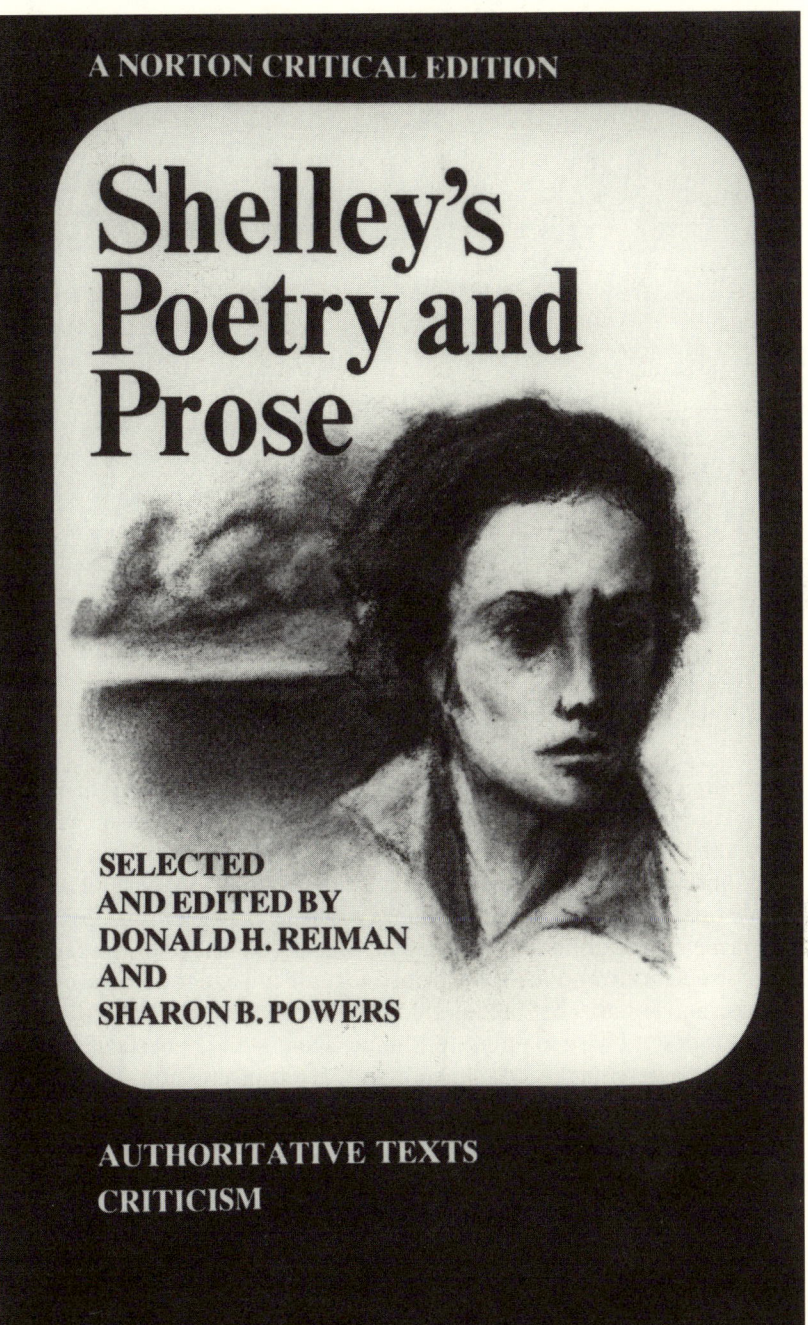

Figure 8. *Shelley's Poetry and Prose,* ed. Donald H. Reiman and Sharon B. Powers (New York: Norton, 1977), cover. ("Cover" by Tim Gaydos; copyright © 1997 by W. W. Norton & Company; used by permission of W. W. Norton & Company)

1. Figure of a colt with a man's face

Figure 9. Ambroise Paré, *On Monsters and Marvels,* trans. Janis L. Pallister (Chicago: University of Chicago Press, 1982), 6.

absorb and incorporate change of various kinds. The history of iconoclasm—a form of physical violence directed at artworks—is rich with examples that tell us not just about the people engaging in such acts of violence, but also about public and social attitudes in a more general sense.[17] People are typically shocked by change because of the ways it upsets our preconceived notions about how something should be. In this respect, the transformed body and the transformed text are alike, not because of their transformative status but because of the response they provoke.

At this point, I wish to return to Mannie again—and in particular, to the sort of transgression that Mannie presents. His transgression—like that of most mutants—is to subvert the natural order of the natural world. Historically, Mannie's antecedents are many. In the sixteenth century, the French doctor Ambroise Paré published *On Monsters and Marvels* (*Des monstres et prodiges*), a book that provides narrative and illustrated documentation on a vast number of mutant and conjoined bodies (fig. 9). Many of these bodies combine features of animals and humans and are attributed to transspecies couplings—what Paré described as "sodomists and atheists who 'join together.'"[18] In 1254, in Verona, a mare is said to have foaled a colt that had the well-formed head of a man.[19] In 1564, in Brussels, a pig is said to have given birth to a monster that had a man's face and arms and hands. Examples of monstropomorphic beings like these have always inspired speculation about their origins, and the very first sentence of Paré's book takes up this subject: "Monsters are things that appear outside the course of Nature."[20] But nature is today no longer merely "Nature"; and Mannie, being a conflation of nature and technology, a conflation of the biological gene and the digital image, is both nature and not. Mannie's contribution to body criticism is to remove us from our notions of complacency about the body and to define for us a set of possibilities in which the pose of life—like the pose of a mounted animal—might be unlike anything we know or knew. This is why new editions of canonical authors are sometimes received with disparagement or even disdain (think of John Kidd's reaction to Hans Walter Gabler's synoptic edition of *Ulysses*): it is the pose of the text that seems unnatural and detached from our expectations of what constitutes a *natural* text. And all this brings us, in a roundabout way, to the subject of taxidermy.

Taxidermy is known as the art of mounting animals for public display. This aspect of having an audience—of mounting animals for the public—is important. The *American Heritage Dictionary* defines taxidermy as "the art or operation of preparing, stuffing, and mounting the skins of dead animals for exhibition in a lifelike state." One of the chief aims of taxidermy involves the illusion of similitude: to convey a pose of life, and to reinforce, or supplement, this pose with a synecdoche appropriate to the ecosystem of the animal being mounted—a log, a rock, perhaps even prey, such as a mouse in the jaws of a weasel. At one point in the history of taxidermy, animals were literally stuffed: the skin was prepared using salt, alum, and arsenical soap, and then stuffed with dried organic matter such as straw. The result was generally quite unlifelike. If a stuffed deer came out looking like a stuffed couch, it was not an irony: upholsterers in fact did much early taxidermy.

The *Amateur Taxidermist*, a beginner's guide to taxidermy, was published in 1972. For mounting a squirrel (fig. 10), the author, Jean Labrie, imparts the following instructions:

To place the squirrel on a temporary base, pierce four holes in the base, of the same size as the stems of the legs. Insert the stems in the holes. Do not place the legs too far apart. The animal should look as much as possible as if it were alive, perhaps with the tail in the arc of a circle, the back slightly arched, a nut in the mouth or between the paws. Use your imagination, memories, photographs, books, and so on.[21]

Like Labrie, early taxidermists such as Oliver Davie (who wrote in the late nineteenth century) and Carl Akeley (who wrote in the early twentieth century) emphasized the importance of creating natural surroundings that were punctuated by the use of appropriate "accessories" such as branches and logs.[22] In a postmodern world, where nature embraces the urban as comfortably as it embraces the rural, accessorized dioramas of mounted animals can be found in our

THE AMATEUR TAXIDERMIST

Preparation for Drying

The modeling clay in the skull is not yet dry. Take advantage of this to correct, if necessary, the position of the eyes. With the large end of a needle, go around the periphery of the eyes. If the animal is to have the mouth closed, push a pin in below the jaws (you will remove this after the specimen is dry). If you are going to use a nut, place it between the teeth before you put in the pin. You can also prepare an artificial tongue of papier-mâché

The teeth of a squirrel are generally yellowed. If you wish to whiten them, rub them with a swab of

Fig. 77. The temporary base.

Figure 10. Jean Labrie, *The Amateur Taxidermist* (New York: Hart Publishing, 1972), 93.

Figure 11. Chipmunk and Teva sandals, L.L.Bean store, Freeport, Maine, summer 1996.

everyday life—whether at the L. L. Bean store in Freeport, Maine, or at Van Cleef & Arpels at the corner of Fifth Avenue and 57th Street in New York City where mounted black ravens can be seen wearing strings of black pearls (fig. 11).

A question now. What laws govern the way the pose of an animal—say, a deer is said to be "natural"? Our natural world is not just a world of fields and streams, but a world of interstate highways and Mack dumptrucks. Do deer know this too? The opossum that eats my cat's food from a yellow plastic bowl on my porch seems to know that the porch and the bowl and the cat food are part of its natural world. What does the deer know about blinding flashes of light that whisk by in the dark and leave behind a sudden breeze? How might all of this be posed as a diorama? Although taxidermists do not normally mount animals to make them look dead, they could perhaps validate their own theoretical practices by doing so. And so the diorama I have in mind involves a mounted deer perched, as it were, at the edge of a road, half in the breakdown lane, half on the verge—legs askew, and the body slightly bloated: the natural world.

Naturally unnatural. From the turnpike in Pennsylvania in 1997, I want to make a big detour to London in the early nineteenth century, and to Thomas Bowdler: one of my heroes, the editor to whom we are indebted for the word "bowdlerize."

Figure 12. Thomas Bowdler, ed., *The Family Shakspeare* (London: Longman, Hurst, Rees, Orme, and Brown, 1818).

Bowdler's Family Edition of Shakespeare's plays was first published in 1807. Over the next forty-three years, at least nine additional editions were published: 1818, 1820, 1823, 1825, 1827, 1831, 1839, 1849, and 1850. Bowdler prefaced the 1818 edition by saying that "Nothing is added to the original text; but those words and expressions are omitted which cannot with propriety be read aloud in a family" (fig. 12). Ostensibly a man of high moral probity, Bowdler saw himself performing a public service. Most editors do. Even censors do. Maybe that's why I admire Bowdler so much: he had the audacity to do what he believed, and the forthrightness to tell people why he was doing it. Like Mannie, everything that is wrong about Bowdler's Shakespeare is, for me, everything that is right about it.

Back to the twentieth century now. It is February 1995. I am house-sitting for a colleague in Ann Arbor, and part of my job involves sorting through her mail—the catalogues and junk mail go in one pile, and the first class mail goes in another pile, to be forwarded to her in England. My colleague, who is not just computer-literate but computer-astute, receives a regular supply of computer magazines and catalogues issued by suppliers of both hardware and soft-

Figure 13. Advertisement from the MacWarehouse catalogue, February 1995.

ware. In a catalogue for MacWarehouse was advertised a software program that enables people to create their own *Sports Illustrated* swimsuit calendars (fig. 13). It provides you with the bodies and you morph them yourself.

One of the characteristics of postmodern bodies is that their filiation is nonlinear. Their genealogies do not have straight lines. The collapse of nature into technology and the collapse of nature into itself have redrawn the ways we look at bodies. Two genders no longer define who we are. Fucking is no longer the only way to make a baby. As Donna Haraway wrote in her "Cyborg Manifesto," we're all creatures in a postgender world, being not just bodies but theories, fabrications, and chimeras.[23] Our natural world is a world we once called artificial. It is the word 'natural' that now wears scare quotes: 'natural,' with its Edenlike mystique and untainted purity, represents a perpetual nostalgia for something that is and is not present. Only we can't tell for sure what exactly is present and what is not. As in the Breck hair-dye commercials from the 1960s, it is the very uncertainty of the situation that attracts our attention: Does she or doesn't she? Ultimately, we do not just make bodies—we unmake them, remake them, and make them over. A real body today is an unstable body whose markedness is in being unmarked: in being everything and nothing, man and woman, white and black; and which, in cultivating markedness, is marked by others in other ways. As with texts in the hands of textual critics, the issue is one of competing authority. Who owns identity?

We are close to a point of implosion—of having so much information about bodies that we feel that in their movement as free radicals, there is only one response remaining: to construct something definite. There is a massive irony here in the compulsion to exercise control just at the moment when we feel we have lost control. As in the case of the so-called definitive edition, the desire here is that of authorship: to construct a text, to construct a body, and to sign our constructions, to label them, to assert a specific plan.

Madame J. W. Marshall was, at one time, a manufacturing artist in wax figures. As she says on the verso of her trade card issued in the late nineteenth century (fig. 14), her figures were used primarily for advertising purposes. Her clients included Jordan, Marsh & Co., A. Shuman & Co., and Chandler & Co. Madame Marshall took pleasure in stating that her figures were "as well executed as those made in London or Paris, at much less prices." Madame Marshall's figures included both stock figures and figures modeled to order.

For $35.67 you can buy your own E-Z Gene Splicer DNA Recombination and Transformation Kit from Carolina Biological Supply Company in Burlington, North Carolina (fig. 15). I did. It comes packed in dry ice, and you need a refrigerator and a freezer in which to store the stuff before you begin your splicing experiments. The kit includes *E. coli* bacteria, so you also want to make sure that everything in your refrigerator and freezer is properly labeled. When you are done with your experiments, however, it might be a little harder to label things. There's no telling what you might make.

The letters "D.I.Y." once meant "Do it yourself." The letters "E.I.Y." now mean "Edit it yourself." The postmodern Prometheus does not work, like Madame J. W. Marshall, with clay and phenotypes, but rather with genes and genotypes. This is the difference between classical genetics and postmodern genetics. Microbiology is a high-end kind of editorial activity, yet somehow it has also become a kitchen-table activity. How ironic. Cutting and pasting words, cutting and pasting pixels, cutting and pasting genes—ours is a culture of cutting and pasting, of grafting, breeding, transplanting, recombining. These metaphors of biological processes, so successfully applied among plants and animals, have extended their range to include conflations between humans and animals, between plants and fish, between biology and technology.[24] What we have done with our postmodern cutting and pasting is create sutureless sutures. We do not even need a hyphen now to describe our new monstropomorphism. The posthumanities, like technoscience, are hyphenless constructions. The gap of the hyphen is too wide.

And yet, we hyphenate—producing, as it were, an unceasing succession of unceasing bodies, all of which, in their vicissitudes, exemplify the multiple viability of posthumanity.[25] At the end of the twentieth century we are,

Figure 14. Undated trade card.

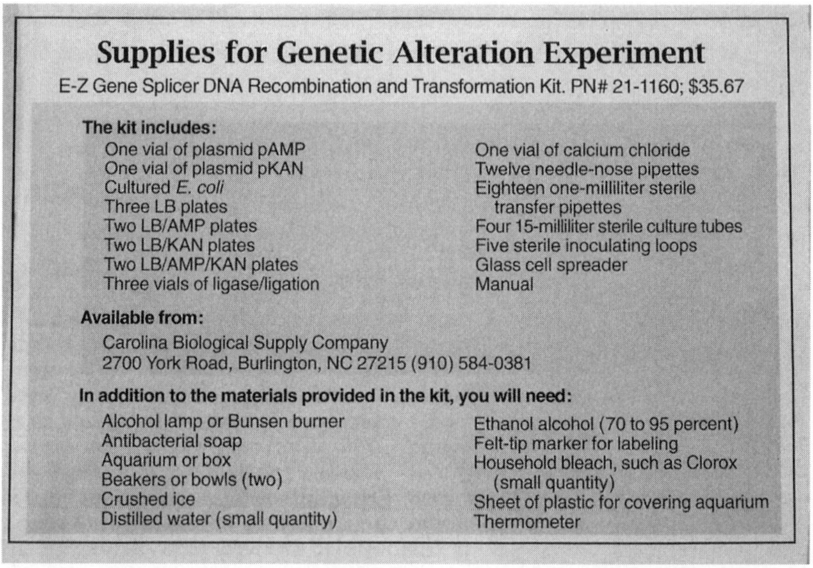

> **Supplies for Genetic Alteration Experiment**
> E-Z Gene Splicer DNA Recombination and Transformation Kit. PN# 21-1160; $35.67
>
> **The kit includes:**
> One vial of plasmid pAMP
> One vial of plasmid pKAN
> Cultured *E. coli*
> Three LB plates
> Two LB/AMP plates
> Two LB/KAN plates
> Two LB/AMP/KAN plates
> Three vials of ligase/ligation
> One vial of calcium chloride
> Twelve needle-nose pipettes
> Eighteen one-milliliter sterile transfer pipettes
> Four 15-milliliter sterile culture tubes
> Five sterile inoculating loops
> Glass cell spreader
> Manual
>
> **Available from:**
> Carolina Biological Supply Company
> 2700 York Road, Burlington, NC 27215 (910) 584-0381
>
> **In addition to the materials provided in the kit, you will need:**
> Alcohol lamp or Bunsen burner
> Antibacterial soap
> Aquarium or box
> Beakers or bowls (two)
> Crushed ice
> Distilled water (small quantity)
> Ethanol alcohol (70 to 95 percent)
> Felt-tip marker for labeling
> Household bleach, such as Clorox (small quantity)
> Sheet of plastic for covering aquarium
> Thermometer

Figure 15. Advertisement from *Science* (January 1993).

it seems, facing both an explosion and implosion of interest in the very idea of the body, and in how it represents, all at once, everything we are and everything we want to be. Textual critics should not expect from this discourse a directive on how to edit texts; rather, they might glean from this experience insight on how they might find value in texts they had once discredited, and see how the vicissitudes of human nature have had a corresponding influence on the textual bodies they have produced. Texts, as bodies, are extensions of the bodies that create them, and therein lies the mystery. Our natural world is no longer just a natural world, but a world that lives and breathes in the space between *The Origin of Species* and the *Weekly World News*.

Notes

1. *Weekly World News*, 23 July 1993.
2. Among the principal recent sources on body criticism that have influenced my work, and which are representative of efforts to distinguish between human and posthuman bodies, I would cite Barbara Maria Stafford, *Body Criticism* (Cambridge, Mass.: MIT Press, 1991); Donna Haraway, *Primate Visions* (New York: Routledge, 1989), *Simians, Cyborgs, and Women* (New York: Routledge, 1991), and *Modest_Witness@Second_Millennium.FemaleMan©_Meets_OncoMouse*™ (New

York: Routledge, 1997); Nicholas Mirzoeff's *Bodyscape* (London: Routledge, 1995); and two anthologies of essays, *Posthuman Bodies,* ed. Judith Halberstam and Ira Livingston (Bloomington: Indiana University Press, 1995), and *Deviant Bodies,* ed. Jennifer Terry and Jacqueline Urla (Bloomington: Indiana University Press, 1995).

3. My principal exponents in the field of textual criticism include Jerome McGann (on the notion of textual democracy) and Paul Eggert (on the relationship between art and textual criticism), as well as a number of New Textual critics whose work looks closely at the social peregrinations of texts, and the critical value of these peregrinations. Many of my thoughts and ideas about this subject have been explored in my *Textualterity: Art, Theory, and Textual Criticism* (Ann Arbor: University of Michigan Press, 1995). In this essay, my intention is to look at some of the more general implications of the notion of textual eugenics, and the underlying importance of human agency.

4. Gregory Ulmer, "The Heuretics of Deconstruction," in *Deconstruction and the Visual Arts,* ed. Peter Brunette and David Wills (Cambridge: Cambridge University Press, 1994), 80–95.

5. Daniel Kevles, *In the Name of Eugenics* (Berkeley: University of California Press, 1985), 116.

6. Stafford, *Body Criticism,* 254.

7. See, for example, Leonard Darwin's *The Need for Eugenic Reform* (London: John Murray, 1926).

8. C. J. S. Thompson, *The Mystery and Lore of Monsters* (London: Williams and Norgate, 1930), 84–85.

9. Exhibition announcement, Gavin Brown's Enterprise, New York, autumn 1994. See also *Chapmanworld* (London: ICA, 1996), n.p.

10. Erving Goffman, *Stigma: Notes on the Management of Spoiled Identity* (Englewood Cliffs, N.J.: Prentice-Hall, 1963), 1–2.

11. Sean Ellis, "Tissue: A Portfolio of Scars," *The Face* 4 (May 1997): 168–73.

12. "Together Forever," *Life,* April 1996, 44–56.

13. Stafford, *Body Criticism,* 259.

14. R. Neale Lind, "Scientist Grows Marshmallow Tree!" *Weekly World News,* 9 November 1993, 39.

15. *Shelley's Poetry and Prose,* ed. Donald H. Reiman and Sharon B. Powers (New York: Norton, 1977), front and back covers.

16. In textual criticism, the extreme opposite of an eclectic text is an unreconstructed text—a text whose interventions, whether intended or not, are read in relation to their historical circumstances and their reasons for existing. An extreme example of such a text might be the *Reader's Digest* condensed version of *Tom Sawyer* (1989), in which references to Jim's negritude have been altered and omitted. The effort to undo problematic race relations in the nineteenth century in turn reflects on the newer problematic of race relations in the late twentieth century, thereby unmasking our contemporary social and cultural hypersensitivity. In textual criticism, editors can erase words but cannot easily erase evidence of their erasures. For a discussion of issues related to the *Reader's Digest* condensed *Tom Sawyer,* see my *Textualterity,* 39–46.

17. See David Freedberg, "Iconoclasts and Their Motives," *Public* 8 (1993): 8–47.

18. Ambroise Paré, *On Monsters and Marvels,* trans. Janis L. Pallister (Chicago: University of Chicago Press, 1982), 67.

19. 1254 is the date cited on p. 6; 1224 is cited on p. 71.

20. Paré, *On Monsters and Marvels,* 3.

21. Jean Labrie, *The Amateur Taxidermist: A Step-by-Step Illustrated Handbook on How to Stuff and Preserve Birds, Fish and Furred Animals,* trans. Florence Wall (New York: Hart, 1972), 91.

22. Oliver Davie, *Methods in the Art of Taxidermy* (Philadelphia: David McKay, 1900), 130; Carl Akeley, *In Brightest Africa* (Garden City, N.Y.: Garden City, 1923), 9.

23. Haraway, *Simians, Cyborgs, and Women,* 149–81. See also Susan M. Squier, "Reproducing the Posthuman Body," in *Posthuman Bodies,* ed. Judith Halberstam and Ira Livingston, 113–32, esp. 119.

24. For an expansive discussion of trans-species couplings, see Haraway's *Modest_Witness@Second_Millennium.FemaleMan©_Meets_OncoMouse™,* 49–118.

25. Judith Halberstam and Ira Livingston, "Introduction: Posthuman Bodies," in their edited volume *Posthuman Bodies,* 1–19.

Rachel Blau DuPlessis

Response
Shoptalk—Working Conditions and
Marginal Gains

Who could disagree? The essays in this volume by Daniel Ferrer, Joseph Grigely, and David Greetham offer a sense of living among cultural vectors whose dimensions and implications—for authorship, reading, pedagogy, publishing, scholarship, and aesthetics—are witty and challenging. They continue the materialist reading of the social, institutional, and hermeneutic practices around texts that we also associate with the theoretical and editorial accomplishments of Jerome McGann. Texts themselves—their creation and their subsequent publication—are part of social processes and bear the marks of those processes: as they are disseminated, in Grigely's words, they are "changed in the process of being reproduced."

Thus, in all instances, time—a difficult and unspoken dimension filled with the potential for loss and erosion, meddling and tampering, knowing better than and making good on—has entered to inflect authorial production, reception, dissemination, and the further critical/scholarly/editorial (re)production of texts. We do not always want to see time at work: we still have a structure of feeling that is partly formed by the "not marble" topos; we somehow think that the intellectual property of a poem (closer to an ideal state of timelessness) will outlast physical manifestations of personhood, beauty, and "builded monuments." But as Lawrence Lipking notes, "Poets may try to design their own memorials, but all they can be sure of is the body of their work; the monument, the way the work will be remembered, must be left to other hands."[1] We can still think of Art, perhaps with a shameful (shamed) nostalgia; it is, as Greetham shows, part of our (Renaissance-Enlightenment-modernist) heritage. But Grigely is properly confrontational: "Given the record of unending change physically altering artworks, [how can] many people continue to believe that art is immutable, that the artist's intentions are paramount, and that original works should be 'preserved' from various agents of change[?]"

Ferrer, Grigely, and Greetham all discuss a new textuality that proceeds beyond the idealized fixing of text in authoritative or definitive editions, the former activity of textual scholarship. Instead, they propose that the scholarship named "textual" document and analyze the layered composites of textual, visual, and artifactual materials and the social processes that surround and inflect the production and reproduction of texts. Textuality is rich with the situational, the accidental, the contingent, the relational. This culturalist "psychoanalysis" of the text is called "genetic criticism." It is a materialist practice. Is it materialist enough?

In this new and expanded field of endeavor, the three critics have different attitudes to what used to be called "the text"—the thing someone might hand one when one asks, "Got anything good to read?" Ferrer says that the "final object [constructed by genetic criticism] is not a printable text but a movement, the process of writing, that can be only approximately reconstituted from existing documents and only imperfectly represented, be it by a narrative, a 'genetic' edition, or a hypertextual presentation." This is a worthy form of scholarship, rich in detail, but it may presuppose that, once upon a time, displaced from genetic documentation or diplomatic editions, something was published, *bon à tirer*. Grigely suggests that any imperfect, bad, deformed, chopped, or cut text can be scrutinized by criticism (no quarrel there), and that other "cultural texts" may "defy our illusions of normalcy: condensed books, colorized films, bootlegged music tapes" (etc.). Although Grigely may be closer to a model that is disinterested in aesthetic hierarchies of value, he is still wide-eyed at amusement itself, and he certainly shows Art in the way his essay is compounded. As for what to read, he accepts implicitly that texts as such are "emended or reprinted," noting what is now incontrovertible: they become, in each new manifestation, "a new textual body." The new textuality takes the iconic term "text," and makes it become Heraclitean, heteroclite.

Greetham contextualizes our nostalgia for fixed and permanent texts in the broadest sweep of philosophic traditions. Counterposing Plato (modern idealists) and Aristotle (medieval and postmodern pragmatists), he suggests that the premodern and the postmodern could productively encircle modernist idealizing, universalizing textual ideologies. His witty use of the medieval (not least in the lush, eloquent, and scholastic footnotes that complement his essay) suggests that modernism is an aberration, and yet again that there is little or nothing new under the sun ("we have indeed become medievalists again"). In the name of history and temporality, he offers a strange assertion of atemporality, as if the pressures and technologies of the "postmodern" present were truly analogous to the medieval. But Greetham draws back after flirting with the atemporality that he otherwise denies, and he also reengages with the modern. Textuality is now constructed in a "battle of the books" between these two paradigms and their different analyses of "textual authority, variance, resolution, and teleology"; his final position seems to be that the two paradigms would interact to correct and modify each other. So we will have something to read, after all.

What, then, *are* we going to read? It is not a more conservative concern that makes me want simply to examine how and where the text—say, editions of Djuna Barnes's *Nightwood* or H.D.'s *The Gift*—emerges in new textuality. My examples are motivated: both women writers, and both stellar, original, magisterial modernists who have had major works cut, trimmed, bowdlerized, and partially presented for the best possible reason, the temptation of publication.[2] The situation in regard to both works had been rectified by the late 1990s, but to achieve rectification, the editors of the new editions presumably worked as if putative finality were a goal, no matter how theoretically retrograde that claim. Perhaps it is not so much finality as closure within the humilities of informed judgment: the satisfaction of the maximum of claims, of loose ends, so that the edition, too, is *bon à tirer*. It was probably clear to both the editors of these women writers' works that texts are artifacts in time, made, unmade, and remade by a variety of hands, including prior editorial interventions. An editor (whatever the ideology of his or her production) is not making an iconic or static thing when an edition is created, but entering into and engaging in a process of transmission that is (in principle) ceaseless, though it has certainly tended to cease abruptly in the cases of nonhegemonic, less studied work. Transmission, like translation, involves acts of intervention, agenda'd and rife with the contingent special pleading and interpretation. Every choice is motivated and belongs in certain ways to its own time, technology, and regimes. There is no neutrality. We are in the arena of partisanship and appropriation.

Texts, then, become something like a musical score performed at a certain time under a certain interpretive paradigm and changed at another, although the notes are the same (though never incontestably all there): Bach on the piano, Bach on the harpsichord—different ideas about the sound, different historical understandings lead to different performances. The text is a snapshot caught in an album, possibly at an awkward angle in unfashionable clothes—what made the text smile like *that*? She looks dreadful that way! Do we not want to offer her a makeover? Thus, sometimes texts are "restored" to look like what people assumed and (maybe) hoped they could have been or ought to have been—perfected to the taste of the time. These notions of restoration and improvement are, in these essays, presented as inadequate editorial interventions but fascinating topics for study. We have learned a great deal about these matters from the case of Emily Dickinson, and from the uncovering of her unique and original use of textual, disseminating, and bibliographic institutions of production by Susan Howe, Martha Nell Smith, Sharon Cameron, and others.[3] And still, can one not fantasize about being the person finding the fascicles and not taking up the scissors to snip the threads that bound them?

But if one talks eloquently about social processes surrounding texts, one must also talk of social needs, calling attention to the uses to which texts are to be put. The expansion of the canon has necessitated a pragmatic look around; to read Charlotte Smith, one must first know of her existence (news to some) and then have some reasonable, decent text of her work (thank you, Stuart Curran).[4] One would like "original works" of literature not to be lost totally, not to be destroyed; one wants them available, accessible, maybe annotated, within reach of people literate enough to care or excited enough to learn to care. A lot of that Pollyanna-ish list depends on the politics of institutions of reception and dissemination. None of the new textual recoveries with their expanded reading lists precludes genetic textuality; indeed, all such recoveries might benefit from such criticism (e.g., the history of the differences between editions of *The Gift* in 1982 and 1998 is an important topic). It is possible, however, that the energies of and resources for one kind of textual scholarship—getting a decent edition of some work published—might conflict with the energies and resources necessary to engage in a full genetic documentation.

It would be paradoxical and unproductive if what emerged from these essays were a new textuality that did not account for texts—the production of editions. Let me talk for a while about texts: the kind of thing a person might have on a syllabus, or in hand, or on a bookshelf. Here I am departing a little from the subject matter of this volume, but I am trying to examine a blind spot in the analyses.

My simple experiences with my own manuscript files as a poet make me agree with Daniel Ferrer that any reconstruction of textual order or sequence of composition (even done by the author herself) is fairly fictional. It is, in his term, a narrative, made by a critic "to reconstruct, from all the evidence it can muster, a historically attested chain of events." (The "it" is "genetic criticism" acting as a critical agent.) Or, to cite the related work of Pierre-Marc de Biasi, "The *avant-texte* does not therefore designate the material manuscripts . . . but rather the critical discourse by which the geneticist [a kind of textual critic], having established the objective results of their analysis (transcriptions, relative dating, classification, etc.), reads them as successive moments of a process."[5] So the story gets told with some end in view. It is a critic's game, and a critic's marginal gain. It is the critic who has the privilege of sequencing and telling an effective story, one with a *telos* or end of the making of just this (art)work.

The oddest thing, from the perspective of the author, is that in all instances of reception, dissemination, and textual editing, it is the critic and not the putative author who benefits. In the modernist case, to follow Greetham, the critic solves, heals, binds, and perfects the situation left by the contingencies and inadequacies of authors. It is as if materiality and staining existed only in the past, while in the present we have sanitary perfection, freeze-dried food, and the clarities of textual utopia after the contingencies of the past. But in the postmodern textual situation, the textual editor is working as an equal with the author in the textual workplace. The only difference between modern and postmodern textual critics seems to be their attitude toward the future, toward poesis, toward ongoingness. The modern textual critics hold time off with their monuments; the postmoderns jump into that sea and understand that their work is just one part of a "signifying chain" of critics, textual events, publication events, and material practices.

Nonetheless, buried in the new textuality there is still some model of Singular Authorship. In Pierre-Marc de Biasi's suggestive chart titled "Typology of Genetic Documentation," a perceptive and intelligent summary of the making of any work, the missing factor is *others,* the work of others— any other hands, eyes, corrections, other stream of creative pressure on the author at the points of making the work (de Biasi, 34–35). No other agent is named; the input of others is not an explicitly excluded possibility, but it is underplayed. No other person besides the implied agent "Author" seems to be implicated at any stage (before the textual critic, that is). Yet there are many textual situations one could postulate in which single authorship is blurry. Some works do take shape via helper figures at the point of production—a production that is pluralized, even if ultimate authorship can still be assigned (Toklas typing, reviewing, adding to Stein; Mrs. Moore commenting on Marianne Moore's drafts, pencil in hand). And this is not to speak of the many point pressures of coterie work: he'll write a poem for this reading to answer someone else's poem at the prior reading; she'll write this kind of poem because that particular magazine has a deadline. The sociality of artists making works in a nexus of relations as part of the genealogy of work is downplayed by the new textuality when it focuses on transmission and not on the multiple origins of production. When plural authorship is obfuscated, plural helpers resisted, and group inspiration rendered invisible, we are still near the realm of "genius."

I have seen H.D.'s *Helen in Egypt* manuscript: to the best of my knowledge, H.D. simply wrote the poem into one of her small blue notebooks, in pencil, page after page, with no textual changes. However, after the poem was written, she added a layer of prose gloss (published in italics). She decided to add this material in a scintillating atmosphere created by the presence of two men helpers, Erich Heydt and Norman Holmes Pearson, and in the aftermath of a 1955 recording session in which she audio-taped part of the poem.[6] Text *does* emerge in the workshop of confluent forces.

Perhaps the new textuality leads us to a biography of the works, rather than to the biography of the author. This is a suggestive result. For example, Ilse Grumbrich-Simitis writes: "Such biographical material as is included in this book almost exclusively presents the reader with Freud at work—Freud observing, listening, feeling surprised and stimulated, reading, learning, associating and fantasizing, concluding and conceiving, noting, drafting, rejecting, making fair copies, busying himself with his manuscripts, correcting proofs, editing, and publishing."[7] The point of the present essays by Greetham, Grigely, and Ferrer is that any text contains and is the result of a *work*shop.

Text versus work is, then, a false binary. Any document is a site of labor, an apparatus of production, the work of several hands on deck. It has a material configuration and material limits. Thus, some general economic and materialist remarks might be illuminating. There are issues of the workplace or the class-and-reward system of the workers (authors, helpers, editors, scholars) at the point of production or at the point of dissemination and textual reproduction. These particular issues are among the most silent as social issues impinging on textuality.

I sometimes wonder whether anyone could fully describe a workplace, even our own white-collar but proletarianized "shops" with all their forces: assignment, competence, resentment, jealousy, policy, fiefdoms, cost accounting, bottom line, anger, cynicism, "government in exile," alternative sources of information, paper flow, scheduling, decoding messages, invitation to meetings, reading between the lines, personnel problems, personal problems, power, misuse of power, bullying and passivity, how people get chewed up, who is in *sauve qui peut* mode, arrangements, deals on the side, the politics (I suppose this is a novel) of any institution—the sociality of work and the way that affects the work that gets done. I think it is almost indescribable. Then there are the class, ethnic, and gender cultures of each person's origins; there are the matters of luck and chance (birth order, illness or health, timing, and social supports) that filter the workplace variously and perform in it accordingly. I think we have a high degree of deeply embedded knowledge of these forces and that we make intuitive, informed, and sometimes risky choices within a worksite based on changing mixes of these elements. But they are so rich as to be almost unspeakable. Almost inarticulate; like planing on a wave, enduring an avalanche of conflict, deciding between alternatives along a narrowing margin of possibility. Working conditions.

Now think of all these workplace forces, all these working conditions and more, as involved with the work of texts. One has, first of all, authorship, and all we know of struggles to set up a workshop, given the pressures against it. Feminist criticism has been eloquent about the ways the production of the person precedes and intersects with the production of the artwork by that person. Then there exist such institutions as cohorts, groups of artists, publication, viewing, storage, and performance prospects in cities, theaters, and reading sites. There exist gender streams, class streams, racialized streams of access and cohort bonding, exclusion, downplaying, discouraging, enhancing, benefiting—struggles around authorship inflected with one's social subjectivity and position. Barrett Watten has discussed these "micropolitics of literary culture," and two younger critics—Libbie Rifkin and Ann Vickery—have published significant analyses of the poetic career and of a literary cohort.[8] There are responses to events in the social world. There are libraries, special collections, departments of humanities, committees of oversight, press boards with their publication policies, and editorial decisions. All have institutional cultures rife with the forces of "shops." There are anthologies and their weird politics—intellectual, emotional, and poetic—of inclusion and exclusion, representativeness and symbolic belongings, pleasant relations with the right persons, betrayals and ignorances that get solidified, even temporarily, into what we peculiarly call "canon." Generally, posthumous worksites and institutional conglomerates may involve the intersection of the following forces: executorships, curatorships, presses, family ownership of a poet's manuscripts, libraries of full access and those of less, assignment of editorship of texts, who benefits, editorial rivalries in the reconstruction of the same textual situation (or condition), courtier–queen relations in the suit for editorial privilege, stealing, hiding, concealing of material by those to whom it is entrusted, slow routes of access, loss inside the library by misshelving, mislabeling, or misdating, claims of priority, proprietorship, "rights" of use that bar the use by others, permission to cite—denied. Biographical speculation barred. Biographical speculation embraced. Engineering of authorial scarcity drives the value up. I allude to just a few of the workplace situations that I know of or have heard of that create the "author" and the "worked text" or the "edition" we know.

Texts and social class, texts and power, texts and careers, textual economics, texts and rewards. The issue of textuality itself as a "working condition." Can the new textuality bluntly, fairly, willingly evaluate these forces—some relegated to the level of gossip and private knowledge, but all at work in the making and documenting of texts?

So far, I have asked where the book or reading matter emerges, and how one is to make reading editions within the new textuality, and I have suggested that its practitioners should more fully explore the working conditions and workplace conditions that might illuminate social subjects and textual productions (including their own). Now, just three more questions.

The first concerns declassé texts. Would anyone "do" any of this genetic textuality ("the study of textual invention," according to Ferrer) with formula work such as romances, gothics, "girl books" (and "boy books"), the genre-snows of yesteryear that no one cares about right now? Well, maybe, for those few that accumulate some kind of historical status; and maybe a different kind of study—across many such texts—is plausible. But for the most part, it is an achievement just to preserve these books from the shredder or from rotting in wet garages so they can become texts for studies on, say, Edwardian girlhood or the construction of boyhood. It is clear, however, that genetic textuality would be more effective when applied to certain kinds of cultural products and not to others. And, since it is the critic who can certainly benefit, it is likely that textual critics will want to exercise their postmodern skills on large authors, big authors, authors worth considering, authors with an oeuvre that has received several generations of critical attention—that is, authors of established value.

One reading of this evaluation of texts from a critical perspective will note that often, under this regime, "to those that have, it shall be given": Shakespeare, Joyce, Yeats, James. In *Yale French Studies* 89, *Drafts,* the authors spoken of are Hugo, Flaubert, Valéry, Joyce, and Auden. That is, the critical warrant to look at sheer majority and agreed-on authorial power and the temptation for a genetic textual critic to work on big, serious authors may result in a reading list with striking demographic limits. To those limits, three decades of intense critiques—feminist and otherwise—have already been addressed. Whose work matters enough to be submitted to the regime of a new genetic textuality? The answer to this question is always contingent, but it depends on extra-textual debates about value, canon, audience, and even sometimes market that cannot be ignored.

The second question is, what texts can be imagined as benefiting from these strategies? Temptations to the scholar include messy textual situations, many drafts, richly articulate *avant-textes,* a panoply of materials, and complicated publication histories; even no publication, just workshop and a concerted career of thinking, as with George Oppen's working papers, posthumously published in various forms, or the work of private writers of aphorisms and keepers of journals. This is all to the good. But in a regime of *avant-texte* and genetic readings, an author could fall by the wayside just by doing the writing in his or her head. That is, an author who leaves no traces, producing no or few manuscript drafts, and then writes out a text in a clean copy will frustrate some (though not necessarily all) of the acts of genetic textual discussion. One would not want a new textuality to put a premium on writers who alter, who have messy textual situations for which thick narrative is possible, ripe for the labor of a critic, and thereby to neglect those who produce clean copy.

Third, adherents of the genetic textual ideal of studying versions want something closer to diplomatic editions. However, one may encounter material, economic limits to this desire. Versioning, instability, suggestive plethora, or hypertext models may not be available choices when material has to be produced in a given form or not at all. The pure choice of an editorial free agent, an agent who can act fully on these convictions about textual versions, may not be possible. There may be limit terms—terms that are part of the working conditions under which we do what we can, not always what we desire. One can study the signifying practices of texts only if one has once had that initial text—something to read. And there are, at least in book form, striking material limits to the investment a publisher (or any parallel institution) would want to make in nonstandard textual conditions. Hypertext may be an answer, but it is still a material resource, and choices to deploy it may have economic limits. When I edited the letters of George Oppen, I was faced with this situation.

Oppen is a still underknown writer of high quality, high density, and high interest. Even to date, his value is not known to many; he is not yet a "must-read" of the modern/contemporary period, as, say, Frank O'Hara and Charles Olson are. (Their credibility, one might add, has to do with the devotion of early editorial interventions that established something close to copy-text, even if it was semi-fictional.) Where Oppen is concerned, there could certainly still be a struggle for his place in a syllabus. Indeed, by the triage of representativeness that can beleaguer groups or cohorts, Oppen might have to struggle with his peers Louis Zukofsky, Charles Reznikoff, and Lorine Niedecker for shelf space as the representative "objectivist." His letters have a sculptural and exciting textual surface, with many "irregularities" deviating from norms of space, punctuation, and use of the page; however, no publisher could possibly want, at this point, to devote material resources to that fact at a time when most anthologies of the twentieth century do not even enter or index Oppen's work. All these decisions are material and economic choices made in time, and one of the temporal factors is the degree of "ripeness" or "readiness" of an author's "reputation."

Here textual editing is precisely the making of something to read: a translation and a creation of certain illusions or gestures, a working in the sphere of "as if" to create a literary object. One needs to create illusions that lead the reader to acknowledge some part of variant, creative textual situations that authors seem to want. So in a printed text: make some gesture toward spatial irregularity. Follow and do not normalize certain gestures (such as exfoliating open parentheses); don't follow, and do normalize, certain others (irregular indenting and white gaps which are arguably intellectually expressive and visually appealing). But there were material limits; to have strained the (generous) capacity of Duke University Press, and particularly its editor Joanne Ferguson, to a commitment to this author (by insisting, say, on a visual text close to that of some of his letters in page space use), I would have lost the marginal gains I saw in making available the work of this writer.

So, simply put, the two textual paradigms—modern/copy-text and postmodern/versioning—occur in a space (could we call it a Platonic space?) in which material, pragmatic considerations about the establishment of a textual paradigm are not brought into high relief. The analyses in the three essays of this section do not discourage the point I am making about material conditions; nonetheless, this set of material, economic considerations can push an editor of a text into a modernist attitude toward the task of editing as a judgment about the workplace, the workshop, and the marginal gains. Is postmodern textuality a material luxury?

Notes

1. Lawrence Lipking, *The Life of the Poet: Beginning and Ending Poetic Careers* (Chicago: University of Chicago Press, 1981), 139.

2. In the case of H.D., it was not her temptation but the temptation of her estate, a decision made to bring her work to the attention of a general public. The publisher, New Directions, sped up the text by removing a whole chapter, significant parts of others including motifs that linked chapters, and, *passim,* any meditative moments of lyric reflection with a spiritual cast. The situation in regard to *The Gift* (w. 1941–44) has been rectified in an edition published by the University Press of Florida and edited by Jane Augustine that "makes available for the first time the text as H.D. wrote and intended it to be read, including H.D.'s coda to the book, her Notes, never before published in its entirety." (This summary is from the card catalog description of the work.) H.D., *The Gift: The Complete Text,* edited and annotated, with an introduction by Jane Augustine (Gainsville: University Press of Florida, 1998). The situation of *Nightwood* (1936) is summarized as follows on the dustjacket of the 1995 edition: "The version of *Nightwood* published in 1936 and revered ever since both as a classic modernist work and a groundbreaking lesbian novel differs in many respects from the book Djuna Barnes actually wrote. Unable to find a publisher for her earlier, more explicit versions, Barnes allowed her friend Emily Coleman and her editor T. S. Eliot to cut much material—ranging from a word to passages 3 pages long—to create a book 'suitable' for publication" (Djuna Barnes, *Nightwood: The*

Original Version and Related Drafts, ed. with introduction by Cheryl J. Plumb [Normal, Ill.: Dalkey Archive Press, 1995]).

3. See Susan Howe, *My Emily Dickinson* (Berkeley, Calif.: North Atlantic Books, 1985); *The Birth-mark: Unsettling the Wilderness in American Literary History* (Hanover, N.H.: Wesleyan University Press, 1993); "Women and Their Effect in the Distance," *Ironwood* 28, vol. 14, no. 2 (fall 1986): 58–91; "Postscripts to Emily Dickinson," in *Dwelling in Possibility: Women Poets and Critics on Poetry,* ed. Yopie Prins and Maeera Shreiber (Ithaca: Cornell University Press, 1997), 80–84. See also Martha Nell Smith, *Rowing in Eden: Rereading Emily Dickinson* (Austin: University of Texas Press, 1992), and two essays in *The Emily Dickinson Handbook,* ed. Gudrun Grabher, Roland Hagenbüchle, and Cristanne Miller (Amherst: University of Massachusetts Press, 1998): Martha Nell Smith, "Dickinson's Manuscripts," 113–37; and Sharon Cameron, "Dickinson's Fascicles," 138–60.

4. Charlotte Turner Smith, *The Poems of Charlotte Smith,* ed. Stuart Curran (New York: Oxford University Press, 1993).

5. Pierre-Marc de Biasi, "What Is a Literary Draft: Toward a Functional Typology of Genetic Documentation," *Yale French Studies* 89, *Drafts* (1996): 38.

6. H.D.'s comments in *Between History and Poetry: The Letters of H.D. and Norman Holmes Pearson,* ed. Donna Krolik Hollenberg (Iowa City: Iowa University Press, 1997), 176–77, 180.

7. Ilse Grumbrich-Simitis, *Back to Freud's Texts: Making Silent Documents Speak* (New Haven: Yale University Press, 1996), 11.

8. Barrett Watten, "What I See in 'How I Became Hettie Jones,'" *Poetics Journal* 10 (June 1998): 98–121, 107; Libbie Rifkin, *Career Moves: Olson, Creeley, Zukofsky, Berrigan, and the American Avant-Garde* (Madison: University of Wisconsin Press, 2000); Ann Vickery, *Leaving Lines of Gender: A Feminist Genealogy of Language Writing* (Hanover, N.H.: Wesleyan University Press, 2000).

TEXTUALITY AND THE VISUAL

Morris Eaves

Graphicality
Multimedia Fables for "Textual" Critics

"Textuality," as textual critics have understood it, involves them in problems of "authority" and "transmission," and of course "representation," interwoven central concerns of the discipline. My simple aim is to point out, as provocatively as I can, some telling ways in which the textual has coexisted with the graphical or, more plainly, ways in which texts have lived with pictures, and to suggest that graphicality is as relevant to authority, transmission, and representation as is textuality, and that, for all but the most abstract philosophical purposes, graphicality is inextricable from textuality. In these circumstances, I realize, "picture" and "graphic" beg to be defined. Since that is too tall an order for the present occasion, much less the present writer, I will dodge the problem by substituting a thumbnail account of the special fate of pictures in the history of technologies of reproduction over the past three centuries or so, on the assumption that pictures can be defined, in some measure, by what people have had to do to make them. Then I will introduce a specific historical example with intriguing implications for textual criticism: the peculiar posthumous fate of the illuminated books of William Blake. That will provide a useful if indirect look at graphicality from the oblique angle of two other associated issues, canon formation and arts mixing.

The Life of Pictures

Let us start with the attractive commercial proposition that the Western demand for pictures has always outstripped the supply. This is unadulterated speculation, but I suspect that picture hunger, bordering on starvation, has been a chronic affliction of Western audiences for centuries. For most of that time, severe technological limits left picture-makers lagging far behind word-makers in their ability to multiply the optical excitements they concocted. Even as late as the eighteenth century, when printing presses were efficiently churning out seditious and repressive words almost as fast as writers could provide them, the output of engravers—the chief image-reproducers of the day—was pathetically small by comparison, and painters were still hiring assistants to copy their paintings brushstroke by brushstroke. In the next century, photography, the steam engine of imaging, revolutionized the technology, put the power of making images into the hands of anyone who could master the camera machine and film chemistry, and then combined forces with lithography to create a powerful hybrid printing medium that swept engraving right down the back steps of history.

In the twentieth century, new technologies—film, X-ray, television, xerography, ultrasound, video—have added so much picture-making power to the previous sum that a tradition of cultural criticism has grown up around a standard lament over the "flooding of imagery"[1] that conveys the perils of a contemporary life menaced by nuclear weapons and cheap pictures. Indeed, because of longstanding cultural attitudes toward pictures, this sea of imagery, as a threat to civilization, has come to stand more effectively for the dangers of "mass media" than a sea of words ever could have. The wailing and gnashing of teeth over the proliferation of images may, however, give the entirely false impression that the technical problems of producing pictures have been solved and that graphicality has replaced textuality as the condition of contemporary existence. As many images as there are, we would have many, many more if the economic and technical conditions were more favorable, and if the antipictorial prejudice that has dogged images everywhere in every medium were less virulent.

In eighteenth-century printing, texts and pictures were reproduced by different technologies—on different platforms, as we now say. They were created by different skills practiced by artisans working with different tools and materials in different shops, printed on different presses, and, in many instances, sold in different marketplaces. Except for woodcuts, which were typically crude and much less durable than metal type, all engraved illustrations were printed separately from the texts they illustrated and were assembled into one unit only at the end of the process. That separation of graphical and textual modes of production ensured deep inefficiencies, slowed production, increased costs, and doubtless resulted in far fewer pictures in books and magazines than audiences would have desired. John Boydell's Shakespeare Gallery project of the late eighteenth century, the most ambitious of several London "galleries" of the period, is a striking case in point. Boydell sensed a commercial opportunity in the unslaked thirst of his customers for pictures in illustration of texts. For texts he chose the most notable British poet, hoping to use the logic of association to increase the value of a far less notable group of British painters (other "gallery" projects imitated Boydell's associative logic by substituting for Shakespeare such texts as the Bible, Milton, and Hume's popular narrative of English history). Boydell's second principle was additive and multiplicative: to add the advantages and the appeal of separate media by packaging them in various combinations at various price points, including printed plays with or without engraved illustrations, illustrations with or without plays, prints one by one or grouped in portfolios, and prints in large versions or small. Boydell's marketing logic was ingenious but fundamentally flawed. The death, in bankruptcy and a lottery sell-off, of his bold and innovative attempt to integrate the production and marketing of paintings, prints, and texts points straight to the catastrophic problems that pictures created in his system. Even as they added value in certain respects, they subtracted it in others, and the subtractions were ultimately decisive in bringing the downfall of the Shakespeare Gallery (as well as others).[2]

In the post-Boydell era, the successive inventions of lithography and photography and their amalgamation in photolithography, the medium that gradually came to dominate twentieth-century printing, made it possible to reproduce pictures and texts from the same plates of the same press at the same time. But, as anyone knows who has tried to get even a few monochrome "halftones" published in an article or book (such as the one you are reading), pictures remain an inconvenience in printing, and for pictures "in color," as we say, the obstacles remain formidable. "We don't do books of photographs much any more," the director of a university press with a reputation for such books told me recently, "because they have become too expensive to print, even when we ship the printing abroad, which used to help."

Pictures are special cases. Pictures are problems.

Dead Man

In the light of this history of media realignments, consider Jim Jarmusch's film *Dead Man* (1995), set in a vague and mythical western United States in the nineteenth century, well stocked with sociopaths and psychopaths, religious fanatics, and lost souls around campfires and in trading posts and lawless frontier towns.[3] Almost everyone is armed and easily provoked.

Bodies pile up. The violent death of a young woman named Thel, shot by her former lover when discovered in the arms of a character named William Blake, sets up a running joke anchored in the film's two lead characters—Blake, a wide-eyed, plaid-suited accountant from Cleveland, and Nobody, an itinerant, overweight Native American who rescues and protects the wounded Blake after Thel's death. The Indian has returned to the West after spending his youth in England, where he landed after being kidnapped for exhibition, only to end up as a student who learned much, it seems, about the other William Blake.

For our purposes, Jarmusch's Blake joke inspires a silly but useful question: If, as he tells the other Blake, the Indian studied Blake after his stint as a traveling exhibit, what Blake did he study? The Indian is shown in flashback as a boy in proper English clothes, sitting at his desk with a book. This, of course, leads directly to a second question about the filmmaker and scriptwriter, the boy's inventor. Who is Jim Jarmusch's Blake? These questions take us to the heart of the editorial matter.

Posterity to the Rescue

The years from about 1805 to 1811 were the most difficult and painful of Blake's life, after the souring of his relationship with his patron William Hayley during three years in Felpham, and capped by the nightmare of a provincial trial on charges of assault and sedition (a capital crime). Depressed by the subsequent failure of his new projects back in London, humiliated by mockery and questions about his sanity, he tried for the first time to formulate in prose some of his ideas about art, including the historical situation of British art and of his own art in particular. Infected by personal disappointment, the writings often take a bitter turn, and at key points they resort to conspiracy theories to explain how a major original artist could have won so little public recognition in a quarter-century of ceaseless striving that had produced a large body of work in several media. "I am hid," he wrote in the margins of his Joshua Reynolds.[4]

Blake's conspiracy theories helped save him from despair by explaining, in terms favorable to him, his failure to find an audience; this relieved him to some extent of the blame that was regularly laid at his feet by friends who found his stubborn refusals to comply with contemporary tastes maddening and by observers who found him simply mad.[5] But his very negative analysis of past causes and present effects did not stand by itself. It had a positive counterpart in a vision of a just future when originality would be recognized as sanity, and insanity, the label with which original artists have often been branded, would be put back where it belongs, on the foreheads of imitators and their commercial allies: "It is very true what you have said for these thirty two Years I am Mad or Else you are so both of us cannot be in our right senses Posterity will judge by our Works" ("Public Address," *E* 573).

This "posterity" is the idealized future form of Blake's audience, which will finally awaken from "the fatal Slumber into which Booksellers & Trading Dealers have thrown you" ("Public Address," *E* 576) to faith in its own judgment, fulfilling Blake's wish that "every Englishman ought to be a judge of painting."[6] In compensation, one supposes, for his disappointments with contemporary audiences, Blake creates a future audience that is immensely powerful, even millennial. Its coming he associates with the Last Judgment: "For the Son of man shall come in the glory of his Father with his angels; and then he shall reward every man according to his works" (Matt. 16:27). "It is the same in Art," Blake declares, "by their Works ye shall know them" ("Vision of the Last Judgment," *E* 564). The future audience will be able to expose the imitators: "theirs is the Contempt of Posterity" ("Public Address," *E* 580). Once posterity sets things straight for artists, the first shall be last and the last shall be first. Lo and behold, at the millennium we stand in posterity's shoes, apparently in fulfillment of Blake's prophecy that the audience would at last wake up and recognize his worth. As I have argued elsewhere, this posthumous space is where textual critics do most of their work, typically by observing the golden rule of posterity: do for others what they can no longer do for themselves.[7]

Cecil Lang, the editor of Swinburne's letters, declares that "Swinburne's criticism has rendered several distinct services to literature. . . . He rescued Blake. The work on Blake is on the whole dated, but its historical importance can scarcely be overestimated."[8] This claim cannot take us by surprise, because William Blake is always eligible for rescue, and among his rescuers Swinburne is neither first nor last. Rescue has always been one of the coordinates by which we fix Blake's position, and it has become, oddly, part of his cultural value. His "tardy fame" (*Blake Records* 1) enrolls him in that small company of cultural exemplars of the principle that the audience is not always right the first time around, which is also the principle that makes business for posterity's rescue squads. To put it another way, Blake, like Melville, has come to stand for error and misunderstanding in arts history. The stories of such dead European white males remind us that even the old, unextended hegemonic canons are founded on amnesiac histories. Blake's misfortunes have made him one of the heroes of those cautionary tales designed to scare us into eternal vigilance and unremitting reassessment.

What, precisely, did Swinburne rescue Blake from? One strong answer is certainly "From oblivion." By Swinburne's time in the latter half of the nineteenth century, Blake was, as his Victorian biographer Alexander Gilchrist called him, "Pictor Ignotus."⁹ A second answer, at least as compelling, might be "From himself." The very need for rescue puts Blake in a compromised—and one might say feminized—position that to some extent empowers his rescuers at his own expense. A hero who needs to be rescued is a vulnerable hero who can double as a victim; he may even be, as is often suggested, his own worst enemy, whose bad decisions posterity must reverse. This, in turn, points to a third answer hinted at in Cecil Lang's formulation: one of Swinburne's "distinct services to literature" was to rescue Blake from his chosen profession, painting and engraving, for, of all things, literature.

We shall consider such complications of fate in the course of this discussion, which moves the issue of Blake's artistic originality into the posthumous public realm in which he claimed to invest hope for ultimate recognition, but where he no longer has any authoritative voice with which to protest misunderstandings, and no way of revising his originality (an arresting oxymoron) as one might revise the terms of a human relationship or the strategies of a political campaign. It is too late. A new game begins, with a new constitution and new politics and, most important, with a shift of the burdens of responsibility off the shoulders of the artist onto the shoulders of the audience. Here representation, in the broadest sense, becomes the name of the game, even when what is being represented is the dead artist's originality. When the artist was alive, we might have been excused for believing that he was representing himself. Now that he is dead, it becomes clear that there is no excuse for thinking that.

Within this framework I want to introduce the role of the sponsor, who is closely related to the middleman in the economic argument but, in art, closest to the patron. The sponsor is the historically extended form of the patron whose sponsorship may not occur during the artist's lifetime or require money and whose own tastes may not be primary motives. Think of the canon—of major legitimate artists and masterpieces—as a club, of the sponsor as the one who accompanies a candidate for entry, and of the sponsor's task as finding a way of gaining admission for the candidate. Canonization is like a series of diplomatic negotiations. It requires a lot of selective editing, some willed blindness to obvious facts, some plastering over, a narrow focus on priorities, self-induced temporary amnesia, and so on. But if the sponsor is successful, the candidate appreciates in value.

Swinburne and Blake are an auspicious example of the sponsor–artist pair. Swinburne is historically removed from Blake by several decades, and Blake is present to Swinburne less as an artist—as Michelangelo was present to his Medici patrons, Handel to George I, or Blake to Hayley—than as a transmitted body of work recalling an artist. To support Blake's work, Swinburne spends intellectual effort rather than money; we can say that his effort is repaid in metaphors that register the altered lot of Blake in posterity.

Blake's Miscalculation and Victorian Attitudes

We can understand Swinburne's historical position more clearly if we start from the premise that Blake's decision to make illuminated printing the vehicle of significant work was a grave political mistake that cost him recognition and serious regard in his lifetime and for decades afterward.[10] Illuminated printing, which Blake used to produce such works as the *Songs of Innocence and of Experience, The Marriage of Heaven and Hell,* and *Jerusalem,* employs a form of watercolored relief etching that he believed he had invented. The process was appealingly domestic and autographic, as well as reasonably fast, flexible, and inexpensive, at least by comparison with the standard methods of reproductive engraving. Both the form and its range of aesthetic effects seemed new enough to warrant a new name. Blake christened his works in the medium "Illuminated Books" (prospectus of 1793, *E* 693). Most important, Blake's medium is intercanonical. It straddles two strongly defined conventional canons whose borders are institutionally guarded. Knowledge and the artistic status that depends on knowledge are traded in a cultural economy that his medium does not fit. Consequently, there is a weak institutional base for knowing illuminated printing; Blake's continuous medium, which in our time has often been celebrated, highlights institutional discontinuities and challenges institutional memory. By cultivating a single medium that joins two arts, Blake put tremendous stress on the ability of ordinary legitimizing processes to function, and that stress had an unfortunate effect on the course of his reputation. I shall argue that Swinburne divulges, almost despite himself, the line of thought that reestablishes the necessary continuity and fit, but at the cost of contradiction and misunderstanding that have taxed later readers.

The profound problem of definition created by illuminated printing emerged during Blake's lifetime. In a letter to his steady customer Thomas Butts, Blake wrote from Felpham that his patron William Hayley was pressuring him to abandon his talent for poetry to concentrate on art: "But I do not wish to irritate by seeming too obstinate in Poetic pursuits. . . . I know myself both Poet & Painter" (6 July 1803, *E* 730–31). If we understand Hayley's attempts at coercion as a reflection of socio-intellectual resistance rather than personal animosity, then we can see that the pressure of enforcement he applies to Blake is part of a more general pattern. An important variation later appears in Dawson Turner's offer to buy a set of designs separated from the text of the illuminated books, and Blake's offer to sell: "tho to the Loss of some of the best things," he protests, "For they when Printed perfect accompany Poetical Personifications & Acts without which Poems they never could have been Executed" (9 June 1818, *E* 771). It would be a mistake to lose the significance of Turner's action by too hastily siding with Blake. His customer Turner is applying economic pressure to edit the illuminated books under well-established cultural guidelines that separate poetry and poets from paintings and painters. We would grant Turner an editorial role more readily if he were making similar strong demands as Blake's representative (his agent, we would say today) or as a publisher's editor (as Blake's Maxwell Perkins, perhaps).[11] Most of Blake's associates were similarly predisposed to define him as a visual artist. His friend Frederick Tatham represented *Jerusalem* as a collection of sublime designs with verbal alloy (*Blake Records* 520). Allan Cunningham, one of the first to give Blake a significant place in the canon of English painters, described *The Book of Urizen* as "twenty-seven scenes" interspersed with "wild verses, scattered here and there" (*Blake Records* 487).

We should understand these not (merely) as manifestations of blindness to the facts but as unsuccessful attempts to re-present Blake's medium, and hence Blake, for maximum historical and economic impact. I would call these attempts editorial: however wobbly and haphazard, they seek an edition through which Blake's work can be known and remembered. Since Blake's memory during the early decades was preserved largely by people interested in pictures, the pressures of definition often made him out to be a visual artist, but there were always other, relatively weaker, pressures making him out to be a poet, especially through verbal extracts from the *Songs of Innocence and of Experience.*[12] But Blake's multiple pursuits, especially as they violated conventional expectations, had made it most difficult for an audience to convene. An investor might say that Blake had halved his chances by trying to double them. He had taken away the rallying points: he had refused to attempt major paintings in oil, refused to attempt major poetry in print, put major effort into minor media like graphics and watercolor, buried epic poems in etched and watercolored imagery, and trapped sublime designs in webs of words. The works in illuminated printing, based on an artistic technology that fits many categories and none, symbolize the near impasse in which he had left himself.

As one would expect, this cultural confusion—a bundle of aesthetic, technological, and economic confusions—is forcefully registered in a critical tradition that defines him as an outsider through metaphors that place him and his work beyond the circle of normal adult life. That is, positive and negative judgments of Blake's work are tied to metaphors that refuse to recognize him as a bona fide member of the group that he addresses. He is not allowed to aspire to the egalitarian status of Wordsworth's poet, "a man speaking to men," but instead is forced to communicate from a position of social irresponsibility or aresponsibility, usually in one of two forms, the child or the lunatic. Echoes of both can be caught in Cunningham's reference to Blake's "wild" verses, "scattered here and there" as one would expect of an untidy mind, childish or mad.

Alexander Gilchrist, the first and still the most significant in the line of literary Blake biographers, had to confront these nagging problems. Among his handy Victorian solutions was his skillful management of the image of Blake as an outsider. He wisely spent his corrective energies on the most destructive image, Blake the madman, which he effectively defused by turning it into a biographical problem that would succumb to biographical techniques. With the aid of eyewitness testimony, he assembled freefloating anecdotes into a coherent picture of a sane man whose apparent insanity was mainly a misunderstanding. But he achieved his victory over one image of Blake, the lunatic, by replacing it at key points with the other, the child, the misunderstood innocent, the man without a mask trying to thrive in a world of hypocritical adult disguises.

Gilchrist shapes this image through such unlikely tales as the one that finds Blake and his wife in their garden playing Adam and Eve, complete with recitations from *Paradise Lost*. Gilchrist turns the story to his purpose by blocking the three major intersections where the argument could turn against Blake as a libertine (in the connection of nudity with sexuality), a religious fanatic who might have millennial political aims (returning to Paradise by building the Kingdom of God in our midst), or a madman (doing in his backyard what his counterparts are doing in Bedlam). Gilchrist prefers the explanation from innocence: the Blakes were caught playing a game of pretend that adults might misunderstand. "For my reader here frankly to enter into the full simplicity and naïveté, of Blake's character, calls for the exercise of a little imagination on his part" (1:112).[13]

Gilchrist strengthens the image of a childlike Blake by preferring *pictor ignotus* to *poeta ignotus*; the result is a storyline that climaxes in the production of two visual masterpieces, the Job copperplate engravings and the Virgil wood engravings—illustrating works of apparent religious and intellectual piety fit for the Sunday-school room and classroom, respectively, and, equally important, illustrating works whose canonical status was undeniable. No bizarre apocalypse here; no "Urizen," no "Elynittria." The venerable association of the visual arts with pleasure, in contrast to the hard adult intellectual labors of literacy, silently reinforces Gilchrist's biographical argument to produce a drawing and coloring and engraving Blake whose work is pious play. He acted out "in his own person" the phase of art history characterized by "immaturity of expression." "And Blake in some aspects of his art never emerged from infancy" (1:1). By contrast, his poetic career is treated as a phase of unfulfilled promise which peaked early with the *Songs* before taking a wrong turn into the obscure verbiage of the other illuminated works. Blake may threaten as a literate but insane, fanatically religious adult male; but, composing poems from his heart and decorating them with pictures he becomes the creative child in all of us.

Reviewers were alert to these aspects of Gilchrist. The Christian poet James Thomson, reviewing the *Life* in 1866, found in Blake a child-saint who "did not act the infantine, for he was infantine, by a regeneration as real while as mysterious as ever purest saint experienced in the religious life."[14] Likewise, the appearance of a "boyish" Blake of "unmistakeable innocence" and "pure pleasure" in Swinburne's *William Blake, a Critical Study* (1868) reminds us that his book began as an essay to accompany Gilchrist's *Life*.[15] But as Blake's sponsor, Swinburne intends to use the familiar image of Blake the child in a significant new way which we can best approach through a transition from biographical images to editorial ones.

Bringing Up Blake

The images of a candidate communicated through a critical tradition are not simple reflections of the candidate but active agents—sponsored images. What they are sponsoring, however, is not quite a person nor quite a product, but a person in some relation to a product, as life in some relation to works. If literary canons tend to rest on three documentary pillars—the biography, the critical study, and the edition—the edition is the central support, without which nothing, and the most important material object in the process of canon formation.[16] In editions, sponsorship takes physical form. Since editorial consequences are practical consequences that embody changes of interpretation in changed evidence, it can be revealing to cast biographical and critical questions in their editorial form. In the 1860s, when Gilchrist gave Blake his first biography (paired with a second volume of selections from his work), and Swinburne gave Blake his first critical study, biographical and critical traditions were indeed editorial traditions in the making.

All editorial policies make lists of priorities. Policies that regard texts primarily as the creations of individual authors identify essential aspects of the text with essential aspects of its author. We acknowledge this autobiographical connection whenever we identify texts with persons ("I am reading William Blake"). As part of an editorial policy, this identification encourages us to refer the text to the person who created it, as Swinburne does here: "Where both text and design are wholly his [Blake's] own, and the two forms or sides of his art so coalesce or overlap as to become inextricably interfused, we have the best chance of seeing and judging what the workman essentially was" (108).

It seems appropriate, then, that a few pages later Swinburne laments the loss of some of these essential characteristics of inextricable interfusion from a print-only edition of Blake's *Songs of Innocence and of Experience:* "These [songs] at a first naming recall only that incomparable charm of form in which they first came out clothed [as illuminated books], and hence vex the souls of men with regretful comparison [to the merely printed text]. For here by hard necessity we miss the lovely and luminous setting of designs, which makes the *Songs* precious and pleasurable to those who know or care for little else of the master's doing" (112–13). But we soon discover that, in fact, Swinburne's lament is just a sentimental detour on the way to approving a printed edition, as he soon reveals: "Nevertheless this decorative work is after all the mere husk and shell of the *Songs*" (113–14).

Actually, the contradiction is only apparent. Swinburne begins with an *ubi sunt* lament that remembers the illuminated *Songs* as a debutante as she "first came out clothed" in an "incomparable charm of form." The *Songs* in this original form are like Burke's Marie Antoinette, a nostalgic vision of lost youth that was once "lovely and luminous . . . precious and pleasurable." The peculiar result is less a personalized than a socialized work caught in the image of its coming-out in society, which we, the audience, observe from the outside as sponsoring adults. The logic of this primary metaphor suggests that, no matter how much the memory of a beautiful young girl may "vex the souls of men," only a misguided guardian would want her to go through life dressed as a debutante. Young girls are charming but immature, after all—Gilchrist had said that Blake's art was "immature"—and the real person is obviously to be found in the mature woman, just as the real plant anticipated in the blossom is to be found in the fruit. It is the unexpressed ratio, clothes:person::husk:fruit, that authorizes a division of the *Songs* into a dispensable graphic shell and an indispensable textual core.

The further associations that make the husk pictorial and the authentic core textual are silently but strongly supported by what I have called "picture prejudice," a prejudice against the sensual luxuries of pictorial media—against paintings, but also against such varied manifestations as stage spectacle, shaped poems, film, comic books, and television, and most recently against the addicting influence of computers—and in favor of the monochromatic intellectual severities of print.[17] In one of its deeply rooted forms, this antivisual tradition identifies reality with ideas in language and associates pictures with excess and the ornamentation or distortion of reality, and thus with entertainment, fantasy, and luxury. Often the distinction is gendered—male language, female images. By tying his apology for a printed edition of Blake's *Songs* to the opposition between words and pictures, Swinburne makes surrendering the admittedly lovely, luminous, precious, and pleasurable designs a way of surrendering childish (perhaps more specifically, girlish) illusions.

Having conceded the existence of an immature Blake, Swinburne then associates him with the illuminated book, as the artistic product of innocence and pure pleasure. That move allows Swinburne to restore Blake, the book, and the audience itself to the adult world in three steps. He uses metaphors of natural growth to divide design from text, uses a cultural prejudice to make design superficial and text essential, and then reintroduces the growth metaphor to support a program of instruction that moves the student from the superficially beautiful to the essentially true. What had seemed to be "inextricably interfused" text and design finally turns out to be only the holistic illusions of an elementary stage of understanding appropriate to "those who know or care for little else of the master's doing."

Swinburne's radical reconception of the illuminated books as only the early stage of an organism that must undergo a transformation if it is to grow into maturity and yield its fruit to an attending public is supported by the familiar notion of the passage from childhood to adulthood as a process of giving up surpluses and excesses and getting down to business. Though he does not say so, his reconception assumes the presence of supervising parental figures—editors—who know best. In conventional terms, unornamented texts are for adult male sensibilities while illustrations—like Blake's Virgil illustrations for a Latin schoolbook—are optical bait for women and children intolerant of verbal instruction. Maturity is achieved by learning to knock out the visual props or, in Swinburne's terms, peeling away the pictorial husk to get to the verbal core. Utterly reversing the visual predisposition of those early spectators who perceived the illuminated books as pictures with indecipherable captions, Swinburne discovers a fundamentally verbal structure: "We are to recollect . . . that these books [the *Songs*] are not each a set of designs with a text made by order to match, but are each a poem composed for its own sake and with its own aim, having illustrations arranged by way of frame or appended by way of ornament" (186). He adds that the commentary on the illuminated-book illustrations that appeared in Gilchrist's *Life* was, though "final and faultless" as far as it went, nonetheless a distraction from the proper object of interpretation. The "illustrative parts merely" had received excessive attention: "So much otherwise has it fared with the books themselves, that . . . the clothes are all right and the body is all wrong" (186). Here the body-garment metaphor reappears in support of the notion that the words are "the books themselves."

"For here by hard necessity we miss the lovely and luminous setting of designs": Swinburne finds support for his view of the illuminated books not only in the antivisual tradition that supplies his metaphors but also in a stern yet benevolent determinism. By "hard necessity" we know he means the technological and economic constraints that make an accurate reproduction of an illuminated book impractical by making it unusually complicated and expensive. He makes a virtue of this necessity by showing that it automatically—mechanically—strips off the visual husk to reveal the verbal core of the illuminated books. Thus, to rationalize the printed edition, Swinburne underwrites the institutions of printing and publishing that support it. What at first may seem only a practical (technical and economic) editorial obstacle to pictures is legitimized as an angel of commercial providence that remodels the *Songs* for the best, after all.

The editorial implication is powerful. Blake may have created the "original" illuminated books, but a public technology has improved them through the very processes of reproduction that Blake had complained about in his public announcement of illuminated printing in 1793:

The Labours of the Artist, the Poet, the Musician, have been proverbially attended by poverty and obscurity; this was never the fault of the Public, but was owing to a neglect of means to propagate such works as have wholly absorbed the Man of Genius. Even Milton and Shakespeare could not publish their own works.

This difficulty has been obviated by the Author of the following productions now presented to the Public; who has invented a method of Printing both Letter-press and Engraving in a style more ornamental, uniform, and grand, than any before discovered, while it produces works at less than one fourth of the expense.

If a method of Printing which combines the Painter and the Poet is a phenomenon worthy of public attention, provided that it exceeds in elegance all former methods, the Author is sure of his reward. (1793 prospectus, *E* 692)

Blake casts his explanation in the form of a new technical solution to an old problem. His rationale is aggregative: the old "difficulty" was caused, he claims, by a lack that has been supplied by a "both . . . and" method of printing that allows a "style more ornamental, uniform, and grand" as it "combines" painter with poet and "exceeds" all the old methods in elegance.

Indeed, as Blake promised, the medium of illuminated printing delivered the "strange and beautiful integrity"[18] that Swinburne cites as evidence of "the master's doing." If the aim of an edition is to give "the best chance of seeing and judging what the workman essentially was,"[19] then the challenge of editing Blake will be greatest "where both text and design are wholly his own"—in the illuminated books, or what Swinburne commemorates as "the singular amalgam" (287–88). But it began to dawn on Swinburne's generation that this appealing logic and the expensive facsimile editions it justified had been mistaken, at least as an entrance strategy. The continuous integrality of the illuminated books, which embed the textual and the pictorial in one physical medium, is a solution that creates a whole new set of problems for individual consumers and the institutions that serve and are served by them. Swinburne saw that the obviation of these problems demanded not the aggregation but the separation of poet and painter. The terms of Blake's legibility would have to be renegotiated.

In Swinburne's apology for the editorial restorations that would at last make Blake available to a broad literate audience, the technology of reproduction that matures illuminated originals into plain print is made out to be as natural as the technology of reproduction that matures children into adults. The operation of this technology is restorative in the sense that it strips away the visual accretions in which Blake's medium had hidden his texts from his posterity, which would be found first among the readers of poetry. Now we know what Swinburne was hinting at when he said that the coalescence of text and design reveals "what the workman essentially was." The hard necessities of technology and economics, as they edit the materials of art, reveal in time that Blake "essentially was" not what he thought he was, a workman crafting a "singular amalgam," but a poet whose work belongs by rights to the canon recorded in literary history.

Dead Man, Walking

The argument, then, is this: Swinburne's sponsorship turns on a point of profound accommodation. Sensing the difficulties presented by Blake's originality in its most assertive physical form, the illuminated books, he realizes that Blake's immediate future in the canon depends on a conversion to something less original. The most important form of the conversion, the editorial form, is as aggressively physical as the originality itself. As such, the edited and adapted reprint acquires the power to displace the original in cultural memory. The ultimately successful representation of Blake in printed editions utilizes, in his favor, the separation between "conception" and "execution" that he had identified as the chief weapon of his enemies.[20] Blake's motivation for keeping content and form together in theory was perfectly consistent with the medium of illuminated printing that the theory helps to explain. It is equally true that such private theories had to be shelved, as sentimental obstacles, if Blake was going to be successfully revived.

Swinburne cleverly exploits the metaphor of the child-artist, from the center of the nineteenth-century critical tradition, in two ways. He takes advantage of the incomplete action it implies, and especially of the room it leaves for guidance by others through a process of editorial socialization. He also pictures maturation as a subtractive process that loses the excessive and reveals the essential, rather than as an additive process that moves from the partial to the full. He associates the child with the illuminated book and maturity with the print-component extracted from Blake's medium. In these terms, the process of maturation is not a matter of individual development and growing self-respect in the direction of ultimate self-fulfillment— what in shorthand we might call the Romantic ideal—but of socialization, compromise, self-sacrifice, and the respect of others. Swinburne's canonical politics doubles as an editorial manifesto. The modern myth of editing that primarily values the authority of original sources and the author's intentions echoes in Swinburne's respect for "the master's doing," especially the "singular amalgam" of Blake's illuminated medium. To counter it, the metaphor of socialization underwrites a process of accommodation forceful enough to alter the physical character of the illuminated books.

Swinburne's primary aim, however, is to rationalize the editorial separation of print-component from design-component. To do so, he depends on the myth of canon formation that primarily values social and historical processes, especially the purifying effects of transmission.[21] He brings three plots into parallel alignment: maturation (child to adult), editing (corrupt to purified text), and canon formation (unselected to selected body of work). Drawing implicitly on the mutually reinforcing strength of all three, he unseats the myth of authorial origins by associating it with childhood and replaces it with a myth of social authority associated with adulthood. Applying this myth, Swinburne finds the remedy his generation needs: a rhetoric and a medium of representation strong enough to bring Blake in from the cold intercanonical darkness, where his shade had wandered for decades, over the threshold of the House of Art. The decision to sponsor him as a candidate for the poetry salon puts Swinburne into the avant-garde of poets, literary critics, and editors—rather than artists, curators, and collectors—under whose control Blake's twentieth-century reputation would begin to flourish.

Artists sentenced to lives of cultural misalignment become posterity's exciting opportunities. Blake and his kind signal above all the ever renewable adventure of arts history, demonstrating by their example that histories are not just flat maps of known lands with masterpieces for capitals, but deformed four-dimensional structures with wilds and outbacks, folds and crevices where treasures hide to reward the discoverer. Artists such as Blake turn their audiences into a hardy if sometimes self-congratulatory breed of explorers and speculators, thrilled by anticipations of belated revelation. In that vein Swinburne plays John the Baptist to Blake's Christ: ". . . I, their first commentator—the voice of one crying in the wilderness, Prepare ye the way of the Blake (though I could not in conscience add, Make his paths straight— . . .)."[22] In that final parenthetical remark about what might be conscionable preparation of "the way of the Blake," Swinburne must be thinking of two passages in *The Marriage of Heaven and Hell,* one a Proverb of Hell—"Improvement makes strait roads, but the crooked roads without Improvement, are roads of Genius" (*Marriage* 10, *E* 38)—and "The Argument," which tells how the Just Man, who "Once . . . kept his course along / The vale of death," was driven off the path by "the villain" of goodness, who took over the best road and forced the Just Man into "the wilds / Where lions roam" (*Marriage* 2, *E* 33), turning the world upside down and leaving the unimproved crooked roads to the evil genius, and the straight and narrow roads to the virtuous "villain." But the dilemma that Swinburne touches on is this: If "the Blake" is to be brought into town from the wilderness, how is he to stay off the straight and narrow way? As it turned out, Swinburne, whatever his qualms of "conscience," saw clearly the straight road Blake had not taken and steered him right onto it. It was a printed edition, streamlined for efficient reading. Those who are won over to the illuminated books by their designs are those who "know or care for little else of the master's doing," counterparts in the audience of "the Blake" to those who were attracted to the Messiah only for his magic.

Swinburne's remedy was never unanimously endorsed, as a glance at the hundreds of lithographs in the Ellis–Yeats edition of 1893 will show.[23] He was erratic in his own editorial preferences, and his Blake book was not successful. As an individual commentator, he was neither particularly consistent nor particularly influential.[24] Credit belongs, of course, not to Swinburne himself but to the kind of thinking he brought to the Blake problem. Hard necessity favored a literary Blake; a printed edition went to the top of the post-Gilchrist agenda. The dawning of this realization may have been partly responsible for taking some of the steam out of ambitious but premature projects to publish the illuminated books in facsimile, along the lines of the Pearson proposal in the 1880s (*Blake Books* 487–88). The legible Blake was the wave of the future. As W. M. Rossetti wrote in reaction to the Pearson facsimile of *Jerusalem* (1877), "We cannot omit the present opportunity of saying that the publication in ordinary book-form, without designs, and without any attempt at facsimile of text, of the *Jerusalem* and the other Prophetic Books, is highly to be desired. Difficult under any circumstances, it would be a good deal *less* difficult to read these works in an edition of that kind, with clear print, reasonable division of lines, and the like aids to business-like perusal."[25] Here is the straight road of literacy and legibility. A succession of editors, including W. M. Rossetti (1874), Sampson (1905), Keynes (1925), and Plowman (1927), opened the way for the next (and perhaps the last) generation of Blake's literary editors, notably David V. Erdman and G. E. Bentley, Jr.[26] Wherever their own editorial loyalties have lain, the influence of their printed editions has been powerfully reinforced and extended by the institutions of literacy that give dignity to the reprint and credibility to the argument from technological and economic hard necessity.[27]

The Imagination Which Liveth Forever

The latest biography of Blake, by Peter Ackroyd, inherits the results of seventeen decades of strenuous posthumous efforts to fix his position by telling his story.[28] The Blake whom Ackroyd buries is worth adding to our brief survey of dead men. Ackroyd shapes the final paragraph of his final chapter, "The Imagination Which Liveth for Ever," around the "numerous rumours about Blake's 'lost' works," including, most notoriously, "reports . . . that Frederick Tatham," the painter who became Blake's executor, "destroyed many manuscripts which he had inherited from Catherine":

> But this is conjecture. What remains is enough, and more than enough, to demonstrate the true genius of William Blake, who lived in a world which distrusted and despised him. After his death George Richmond kissed him, and then closed his eyes "to keep the vision in." Yet there was really no need to do so. That vision had not faded in his pilgrimage of seventy years, and it has not faded yet. (368–69)

The quietly stirring finale that Ackroyd offers at Blake's grave may seem distant from partial editorial constructions. But in what is said and not said, and especially in its generalized diction, lie clues to the tangled web Blake wove and to our attempts, as his late-arriving caretakers, to remodel it along more productive lines.

Ackroyd takes up a position on the borderline between Blake's death, in "a world which distrusted and despised him," and a future that has by now recovered and preserved a "vision" that "has not faded." "Vision" is not just an honorific choice. It makes the leap between then—when Blake's eyes were closed by a painter, George Richmond, to store their "vision" away for later use—and now, when Blake's "vision" has been transformed from the ocular faculty on which painters and engravers depend into the nonspecialized mental faculty of which the Blake of the third millennium has become the veritable prototype: an artist's vision, but also a poet's and a prophet's "vision" that can join "genius" and "imagination" as the favorite trio of universal descriptors of this revalued Blake's multimedia artistic authority. The vision that "has not faded yet" is not the same vision that George Richmond wanted to keep in. The space for Blake to die a painter-engraver and rise a writer-poet can be sensed right across the roomy, noncommittal lexicon of Ackroyd's last paragraph. The phrase "'lost' works" is as neutral in respect to medium as "vision," and the association of those conjectural disappearances both with reports that Tatham destroyed "manuscripts," and with Blake's statement about epic poems as long as Homer's and tragedies as long as Shakespeare's, reinforces the slippage toward the literary.

In Ackroyd's story, Blake's wife Catherine was joined at the gravesite by Richmond, Frederick Tatham, and John Linnell, all artists. The earliest accounts of Blake were written almost exclusively by picture-makers and the picture-minded, and the commercial traces left by Blake during the same period consisted of sales by artists and art collectors. But since the first full-dress biography by Gilchrist, Blake's biographers have been literary people.

That includes Ackroyd's predecessors, Ackroyd himself (a novelist and biographer by trade), and his successors G. E. Bentley, Jr., and Aileen Ward, professors of English.[29]

To make Blake consumable, his sponsors had first to make him legible. This radically edited, textual Blake is presumably the dead man whose living words were the centerpiece of the Victorian education of Jim Jarmusch's Native American. Jarmusch has Nobody tell the perplexed accountant Blake that William Blake was "a poet and a painter." And the youthful Nobody is shown at a desk in his proper English clothes, thumbing a copy of Blair's poem *The Grave* with Blake's engraved illustrations. But *The Grave* seems to be there chiefly for its title, which resonates with the film's title and all its other death obsessions. "You were a poet and painter. But now you are a killer of white men," Nobody tells Blake. "That weapon will replace your tongue . . . and your poetry will be written with blood." For Nobody, as apparently for Jarmusch, Blake is a poet, and Thel and Scholfield are primarily names from his poems rather than figures visualized in his pictures. The weight of representing Blake in Jarmusch's pictorial medium is carried almost entirely by Blake's words. Or, more cautiously, if there are visual manifestations I did not see them, whereas the literary Blake is present at every turn in direct quotation. Of course, no one expects Jarmusch's Blake scholar to carry prints and paintings around in his saddlebags. But that is precisely the point: Blake's pictures are not needed to represent "Blake" adequately; Nobody's oral renderings can do the job.

Graphical Fables for "Textual" Critics

I opened this discussion with the claim that, because pictures and texts are joined at the hip and yet enmeshed in histories of separation, and because the digital revolution promises new vantage points from which graphicality and textuality might be seen more clearly and fully for what they have been if not for what they "are," we should drive on toward a thorough review of such key terms as "picture." In the ranks of textual critics, what exploration there has been of the graphical in some relation to the textual has generally taken one of two contrasting forms. One well-rehearsed line of thought constructs a near-opposition between texts and pictures that is anchored in strong distinctions between their very modes of existence. The verbal-readable, in this view, is delivered by arbitrary linguistic and typographic codes whose physical existence in a "medium" is only an approximate instance of its (shall we say) real existence in a nonphysical mental realm. In contrast, the pictorial-seeable is delivered as what-it-is, a physical object such as a painting or sculpture that makes it possible to speak sensibly of "the original" versus "copies" and "reproductions"; texts, however, are never productions, always only reproductions of a ineluctable, hypothetical mental original that Thomas Tanselle, among contemporary textual critics, has insisted we call the "work" as opposed to its "texts."[30] Tanselle has enlisted in the cause of textual-critical argument a venerable opposition with its basis in the notion, classically articulated by G. E. Lessing, that readings are temporal codes and seeings spatial codes, calling for different kinds of comprehension. In the words of one art critic, "Reading is one thing and seeing another."[31] If the art critic protests too much—at the very least, we know that we must see to read in the usual sense of the term—we must acknowledge that the single most influential way of seeing the graphical and textual has been through the lens of this opposition.

If Tanselle has founded a "rationale of textual criticism" in part on an opposition between pictures and texts, Jerome McGann has founded a "critique of modern textual criticism"—Tanselle's being an instance of the modern sort—in part on the continuities between pictures and texts. In exploring the aesthetic and editorial implications of what he calls "bibliographical codes" and "linguistic codes," McGann has undertaken to open up textual originality to graphical elements previously sequestered in a separate realm of the bibliographical.[32] As it happens, bibliographical codes are mostly graphical elements (font design and page layout, for instance) which, along with a few textural elements (the feel of paper, the heft of a book that is elegantly slim or imposingly fat) have typically played little part in editorial decisions. More precisely, editors have usually read bibliographical codes as evidence for altering linguistic codes, graphical means to a linguistic end. Thus, changes in page layout or paper may have "bibliographical" implications for a conclusion about the authority of a text, but when it comes time to represent that conclusion on the pages of an edition, the text is the thing.

In view of his arguments for the visual presentation of textual elements, it makes sense that McGann should recently have been pioneering the theory and practice of electronic editing in connection with his Rossetti Archive (1993– ; http://jefferson.village.virginia.edu/rossetti). The latest alteration in the cultural fate of pictures has come, of course, with the digital revolution, which has also brought us a Blake Archive (1994– ; http://www.blakearchive.org). Much of the speculation that swirls around electronic media and the prospect of "media convergence" involves graphical elements. Perhaps the most influential vision, backed by Nicholas Negroponte, director of MIT's Media Lab, regards every analog medium as now potentially translatable into a single composite digital one—a stream of digital bits that can be back-translated into the medium or media of choice on demand.[33] The same bitstream, we are told, will carry picture, text, and sound if not (at first) touch and smell: print it out as a "book," if you like, watch it as a "film," or listen to it as a "CD" (new media under their old names). Before these pigs fly, let us stop a moment to ponder the implications of this convergence for pictures. At last they would be right there in the bitstream of the Many-in-One Universal Medium, along with everything else that anyone might want copied and sent.

Perhaps the most unexpected and intriguing overlap between the textual theorist Tanselle and the media theorist Negroponte is their common investment in the opposition of the material and the immaterial. Tanselle has found it important to regard the mental realm where "works" reside as immaterial, and Negroponte to regard the digital realm as immaterial. Neither, so far as I am aware, has questioned this key opposition in his arguments, though the immateriality of human brains, computers, and electrical signals seems eminently open to inquiry.

But those who have used desktop computers know that, compared to texts, pictures remain a thorn in the side even in cyberspace. Going back a few years, we can recall that a basic difference between the IBM desktop platform and the Apple was manifest in the ability of Apple machines to handle graphical with textual elements. (I once asked a bookish colleague for his reaction to the first Microsoft Windows graphical interface on display at the university computer store, where he had gone to pick out a new IBM machine for himself: "Beneath contempt" was his whispered response to all those vulgar "icons.") Even the Macintosh used its integrative interface to segregate word and image processing into separate applications. Today, though the movement toward convergence continues apace, images resist easy technological assimilation. They devour money, memory, and expertise. They take more memory, more processing speed, more network bandwidth, more expensive equipment—not just cheap and simple keyboards but scanners, along with bigger and better monitors and better and faster color printers. As the Microsoft juggernaut speeds ahead, it exterminates the relatively uniform standards that have made the Macintosh the overwhelming favorite of graphics professionals. Video and audio on the (relatively) amazing multimedia scene of the World Wide Web remain grotesquely primitive, complicated, and elusive beside the reassuringly streamlined and stable letters and lines of standard, searchable, intermeasurable ASCII text. Pictures remain formidable problems, and the relation of the graphical to the textual remains an unsolved foundational issue.

Notes

1. The phrase is Robert Jay Lifton's from *Boundaries: Psychological Man in Revolution* (New York: Random House, 1969), 44, echoing what by then had already become a potent tradition constructed by at least two generations of intellectuals

troubled by contemporary culture, including Walter Benjamin, Lewis Mumford, Dwight Macdonald, and a host of others. The tradition is, of course, still very much with us.

2. For discussion of the commercial design of Boydell's gallery and its significance in the history of British art, see Morris Eaves, *The Counter-Arts Conspiracy: Art and Industry in the Age of Blake* (Ithaca: Cornell University Press, 1992).

3. Jim Jarmusch, writer and director, *Dead Man* (12-Gauge Productions, 1995).

4. Unless otherwise stated, quotations of Blake are taken from *The Complete Poetry and Prose of William Blake*, ed. David V. Erdman, newly rev. ed. (Berkeley and Los Angeles: University of California Press, 1988), and indicated by the abbreviation *E*. This quotation is from the annotations, p. 636.

5. The coherence of Blake's conspiratorial theories is discussed in historical context by Eaves, *Counter-Arts Conspiracy*.

6. G. E. Bentley, Jr., *Blake Records Supplement* (Oxford: Clarendon Press, 1988), 44. Subsequent references to Bentley's books, including *Blake Books* (Oxford: Clarendon Press, 1977), *Blake Records* (Oxford: Clarendon Press, 1969), *Blake's Writings*, 2 vols. (Oxford: Clarendon Press, 1978), and *William Blake: The Critical Heritage* (London and Boston: Routledge and Kegan Paul, 1975), are cited parenthetically by short titles.

7. Morris Eaves, "'Why Don't They Leave It Alone?': Speculations on the Authority of the Audience in Editorial Theory," in *Cultural Artifacts and the Production of Meaning: The Page, the Image, and the Body,* ed. Margaret Ezell and Katherine O'Brien O'Keeffe (Ann Arbor: University of Michigan Press, 1994), 85–99.

8. Algernon Charles Swinburne, *The Swinburne Letters*, ed. Cecil Y. Lang, 6 vols. (New Haven: Yale University Press, 1959–62), 1:xviii. Cited hereafter as Lang.

9. Alexander Gilchrist, *Life of William Blake, "Pictor Ignotus,"* 2 vols. (London and Cambridge: Macmillan, 1863). *"Pictor Ignotus"* was dropped from the title for the 2d edition in 1880.

10. Jerome McGann describes some of the results of the conflict between the "institutions of publishing" and Blake's illuminated-book project in his *A Critique of Modern Textual Criticism* (Chicago: University of Chicago Press, 1983), 43–47, 53–54.

11. Though the outcome of the negotiations between Turner and Blake is unclear, we have traditionally acknowledged the editorial role of other buyers by honoring their purchases with names invented for the purpose, such as the Large and Small Books of Designs that Blake assembled from the illuminated books and other sources. The initial impetus may have come from Ozias Humphry in the mid-1790s. Dawson Turner must have asked for something like the selection Blake had made for Humphry, since Blake begins his letter to Turner with a reference to "Those I Printed for Mr Humphry" (*E* 771). In *Nollekens and His Times* (1828), J. T. Smith described what we now call the Small Book of Designs as "another publication by Mr. Blake" that "consisted only of a small quarto volume of twenty-three engravings of various shapes and sizes" (*Blake Records* 472). See also David Bindman, *Blake as an Artist* (Oxford: Phaidon, 1977), 96–98; and Martin Butlin, *The Paintings and Drawings of William Blake,* 2 vols. (New Haven and London: Yale University Press, 1981), 1:131–32, 141–42.

12. For examples, see the "Table of Blake's Poetry Reprinted in Conventional Typography before 1863" (*Blake Books* 74–75). The *Songs* began to appear in anthologies during Blake's lifetime, and a print-only edition of the *Songs* appeared in 1839, twelve years after his death.

13. Compare the skeptical treatment of the same episode in *Blake Records,* 53–54.

14. Quoted in Deborah Dorfman, *Blake in the Nineteenth Century: His Reputation as a Poet from Gilchrist to Yeats* (New Haven and London: Yale University Press, 1969), 177. The image of Blake as a child became so ingrained that later writers seem to have felt compelled to cast even their disagreements in its terms. Francis Thompson characterized Blake as an adult opportunist only disguised as a child, not the "pet lamb" some adults suppose him to be but "a very ill-behaved ram assuming the airs and privileges of his infancy." Coventry Patmore heard in Blake's poems a crazy child speaking "mere drivel" and "delirious rubbish." Paul Elmer More admitted that, while the childlike Blake may have been "the sincerest of poets," sincere adults will have to admit that they listen to him as they listen to the sincerest children, with condescension: "A little investigation will detect a slight note of insincerity in our enjoyment and, having enjoyed this, we fall back on the poets who accept fully the experience of the human heart" (all quoted in Dorfman, 184, 186, 189). Dorfman's review of the documents that record the growth of Blake's nineteenth-century reputation is essential. See also Bentley, *Critical Heritage*; and Joseph Anthony Wittreich, Jr., ed., *Nineteenth-Century Accounts of William Blake* (Gainesville, Fla.: Scholars' Facsimiles and Reprints, 1970).

15. Algernon Charles Swinburne, *William Blake: A Critical Essay* (1868), reprint ed. Hugh J. Luke (Lincoln: University of Nebraska Press, 1970), 139–40.

16. We can acknowledge the general truth of this proposition without ignoring complications. Each of the three, for instance, may do double or triple duty, as illustrated in different ways by Pope's translation of Homer, Boswell's *Life,* Wordsworth's *Prelude,* and T. S. Eliot's essays in criticism.

17. In *The Printing Press as an Agent of Change: Communications and Cultural Transformations in Early-Modern Europe,* 2 vols. (Cambridge: Cambridge University Press, 1979), Elizabeth Eisenstein notes, in relation to printing, "the persistence of a venerable philosophical tradition of proud ignorance concerning material and mechanical phenomena" (1:24). Visual artists, as workers who cannot avoid the messiness of materials, have often had their status lowered beneath the poet's and thinker's by this prejudice, which combines readily with the other.

18. Swinburne to W. M. Rossetti, 17 July 1874, in Lang, 2:311–12.

19. Fredson Bowers's notion is that manuscript accidentals deliver "the real flavor of Hawthorne" (quoted in McGann, *Critique,* 20) better than the accidentals in printed editions. By implication, the substantives in the manuscript perhaps deliver the food, Hawthorne himself.

20. Blake's stake in the integrity of conception and execution is discussed by Eaves, *William Blake's Theory of Art* (Princeton: Princeton University Press, 1982).

21. On what it means to value transmission and reproducibility in an editorial policy, see Eaves, "'Why Don't They Leave It Alone?'"

22. Swinburne to W. M. Rossetti, 17 July 1874, in Lang, 2:311–12.

23. Edwin J. Ellis and William Butler Yeats, eds., *The Works of William Blake, Poetic, Symbolic, and Critical,* 3 vols. (London: Bernard Quaritch, 1893).

24. As for inconsistency, Swinburne wrote W. M. Rossetti about Rossetti's forthcoming (print-only) Aldine edition: "Of course my serious opinion . . . is that an issue of such books as Milton, Jerusalem, etc., without their setting of illustrations, or in any form but what is barbarically called 'facsimile,' would be simply absurd. . . ." But in the same passage he recommends that "the greatest of all the Prophetic Books and of all Blake's writings," *The Marriage of Heaven and Hell,* "is not a poem at all, but ought to head a fellow volume of his . . . Prose Works. . . . But I should like to see the 'Marriage' simply in type without commentary. . . ." (5 Mar. 1874, in Lang, 2:285). Later the same year, he repeats even more strongly his objection to "the separate critical publication of the letter-press," again because of "the unity and indivisibility . . . of the two forms . . . the text is an integral part of the design and the design an integral part of the text" (17 July 1874, in Lang, 2:311). Swinburne also showed himself to be a scrupulous modern editor in preferring "Blake's worst bad grammar" to W. M. Rossetti's mendings (30 Oct. 1874, in Lang, 4:349). As for the influence of his views on Blake, Swinburne later said that his book "was received— with reviling and ridicule and such general contempt that almost all copies were sold as 'remainders'—so W. D. [Watts Dunton] says, correcting my own impression that they were sold as waste paper" (2 July 1903, in Lang, 6:170; see also 4:284). But we must not confuse failure to gain a popular following with failure to influence. The influence of Swinburne's *Critical Study* appeared in many forms, as he later realized: "'And thus the whirligig of time brings in his revenges': if a man has the good sense to live long enough" (2 July 1903, in Lang, 4:170; see also 4:208). Eric Robert Dalrymple MacLagan and Archibald George Blomefield Russell dedicated to Swinburne their printed edition, *The Prophetic Books of William Blake: Jerusalem* (London: A. H. Bullen, 1904).

25. William Blake, *Jerusalem: The Emanation of the Giant Albion,* 1804, copy D, the Pearson facsimile (London, 1877). W. M. Rossetti quoted in R. W. Peattie, "William Michael Rossetti's Aldine Edition of Blake," *Blake/An Illustrated Quarterly* 12 (1978): 7. On the late-nineteenth-century facsimiles, see Robert N. Essick, review of the Manchester Etching Workshop facsimile of *Songs of Innocence and of Experience, Blake/An Illustrated Quarterly* 19 (1985): 39–51; and Morton D. Paley, "John Camden Hotten, A. C. Swinburne, and the Blake Facsimiles of 1868," *Bulletin of the New York Public Library* 79 (spring 1976): 273.

26. W. M. Rossetti, *The Poetical Works of William Blake: Lyrical and Miscellaneous* (Aldine Edition of the British Poets; London: G. Bell, 1874); John Sampson, ed., *The Poetical Works of William Blake* (London: Oxford University Press, 1905, 1913, and later printings); Geoffrey Keynes, ed., *The [Complete] Writings of William Blake,* 3 vols. (London: Nonesuch Press, 1925; 1 vol. Nonesuch, 1957; Oxford Standard Authors, 1966 and later printings); and Max Plowman, *An Introduction to the Study of Blake* (London and Toronto: J. M. Dent, Everyman's Library, 1927).

27. The Santa Cruz Blake Study Group's review of Erdman's edition, in *Blake/An Illustrated Quarterly* 18 (1984): 4–31, considers some of the editorial issues raised by a printed edition of an illuminated book.

28. Peter Ackroyd, *Blake* (New York: Knopf, 1996).

29. Bentley's biography is slated for publication by Yale University Press in 2001 under the title *The Stranger from Paradise* (Blake again the unrecognized outsider). Ward's biography has been long underway.

30. See G. Thomas Tanselle, *A Rationale of Textual Criticism* (Philadelphia: University of Pennsylvania Press, 1989), 16–18, 26–33.

31. G. E. Lessing, *Laocoon: An Essay on the Limits of Painting and Poetry,* trans. Edward Allen McCormick (Baltimore: Johns Hopkins University Press, 1984); John Russell, "Italy Reclaims Its Treasures from the Past," *New York Times,* 26 June 1988, section 2, page 1.

32. See, for example, the introduction to McGann's *The Textual Condition* (Princeton: Princeton University Press, 1991), 13–16.

33. Nicholas Negroponte, *Being Digital* (New York: Knopf, 1995).

Mary Ann Caws

Taking Textual Time

> I have seen many fair pictures not in vain.
> —Emerson, "Experience"

To the discussions in this volume of textualities and technologies, computer graphics, and theories about literacy and electro-literacy, I feel that I need to add my particular concern of the moment. It has to do with the greatly diverse speeds at which people see and read and listen, and the difficulties those differences provoke: in short, with the *problematics of pacing.* It has not yet been sufficiently addressed, in my view. Many textual critics worry a great deal about the notions of place and of space; it is time to worry about pace—about the rhythm of the mind as well as of the eye, step, or hearing.[1]

We can consider the issue of rhythm from the point of view of the reader, of the viewer, or of the listening audience—or of all three. Clearly, in each case the problems are different; the urgency of considering their combination is no less clear, given that we do not live in a simple age. We have to listen as well as look, and we have to manage our and others' texts. Some of us tend to think of ourselves as unitary receivers and locate the complex and interesting issues in the text or image or sound outside ourselves. But I want to worry about us, for a moment, and how we do or do not follow instructions for reading, seeing, and listening. My example will invoke the particulars of an architectural/philosophical construction and various reactions to its exhibition.

Given our way of being and our varying powers of direction, action, and reaction, we textualists, weaker or stronger (presumably, we are all a combination), can take to the lists, as it were.[2] "Up, old heart," we can shout with Emerson, and go to it: repacing ourselves.

Fine, but how? Let me first sketch out the issue in four scenes. Picture first an exhibition of textualists doing what they do best, or at least most often—reading.[3] The various attitudes depicted depend on what material object the reading/thinking process that precedes the writing takes as essential. I will call the reader "you."

Scene 1: You are ensconced in your favorite chair, reading a text at your own rhythm. Life is short. You read it quickly here, slowly there. What halts you at various points is some difficulty, like a knot in the otherwise smooth surface. You focus on that point, rereading the passage to smooth it out like the rest. The repetition of reading itself compounds the thickness of that very place. Your attention has been seized. You figure out the problem and then speed up again to your normal pace. Anyone watching you might see your brows furl slightly, then unfurl. You are doing some active reading.

Scene 2: You are at your computer, whose muffled noise of something working in there reassures you about continuance. From the Internet, you call up two images you want to work with, and you compare them with a text to which they seem to relate. You are at the controls and in control. But what method is available for this comparison? How do you find the right rhythm? In the back of your mind, a problem has arisen: Where is the Descartes who will write a discourse on this method?

Umberto Eco's discussion, a few years ago, on a much-consulted wire service of what he calls the "software schism" may be as close as we are likely to get to a Discourse; and then he doesn't write in Latin, although he probably could. For the sake of contrast and debate, he posits that the Macintosh operating system represents Catholicism, with sumptuous icons, offering everyone the chance to reach the kingdom of heaven, at least at the moment the document is printed. DOS, on the other hand, is Protestant, allowing free interpretation of Scripture, demanding difficult personal decisions, and presuming that not all will reach salvation. Windows, in presenting this schism, allows elaborate rituals in the cathedral but permits you to return to DOS to modify anything you choose.[4] At least you know what you have to wear in this cathedral, church, or temple of learning: the vestments of conviction, however "shabby."[5] But you may not know at what pace the ritual will be conducted. Will your choice of system make a difference? Will you be able to follow what is going on?

Scene 3: You are in the permanent gallery of a museum, wandering from picture to picture as you always do, perhaps thinking about something else. You recognize all the paintings and maintain an even stride. Suddenly, a new piece catches your eye, and you slow down to acquaint yourself with the unexpected, to put it—after giving it a name or a school or a subject—with the rest, to iron out its distinction. You see a painting labeled *Landscape* by an artist unfamiliar to you, with the date 1967. Across the painting, a phrase is written: "A LINE IS A CRACK." You read that slowly, thinking it over (what kind of crack, what does it open on to, does it give light?); you reread it, looking at the lines on the rest of the picture—no clue—and then pass on. You have spent more time on the statement than on the picture. The statement sticks.

The next time you walk through this room, you will not change your stride in this spot. Perhaps somewhere else; you might even be looking for a new difficulty, to let a different light through the crack, as Charles Bernstein puts it.[6]

Scene 4: You are at an exhibition. The paintings on the wall are strange to you; you want to read all the available information. But your intake of the verbal text is not correlated with your absorption in and of the picture itself; the reactions to the verbal and to the visual are differently temporalized, and the activities do not match. Something feels askew. At first preoccupied with the problem of absorption, you become obsessed, *post-occupied,* realizing the irony of the thing.[7] "You cannot do two things at once," someone is saying everywhere in the world at this moment, in some language or other. You are occupied with reading as doing   the pragmatic approach.

The same artist of the "line as crack" aphorism has constructed the series of conundrums on the wall here. Each poses a different problem, and each slows you down until you are standing still, trying to think about meaning. These are pictures of thinking; these are investigations of the meaning of meaning. This is creative, ongoing mapping in a most particular sense, making a model of the mind. There is no possible instant apprehension of these "paintings," no passive acceptance that viewers can agree to before passing on to something else. You have a feeling that there is nothing else, as you are forced into the multidiscourse of the work, into a dialogue or a conversation.

Now, which of these four ways of reading text and image teaches the most, and most effectively, about reading reimagined? We know what it is like to read in a chair, to work at a computer, or to stroll about in a museum among familiar and less familiar things; but in the fourth scenario—experiencing an exhibition of the totally unfamiliar, assailed by new expectations of text and image and object, as by an auditory imposition of someone else's voice—the competing textures and changes in rhythm force a remodeling of the mind, a rethinking of meaning, a readjustment of pace. Do we have time to worry about timing? Does a combined conceptuality, visuality, and aurality actually require all this effort? Who needs a model of mind, anyway?

There was a time when we chose our texts and read them at the speed we chose. There was no time budgeted for that one? No bother, we could just read something else in its place. We were not seized yet. Some of the texts that chose us then and choose us now to read them insist on placing our thoughts in their sites, to move at their pace. They make us read the way they want. They change our rhythm differentially, according to their own pace. We have to adjust.

One of the most exigent visual texts that has recently chosen some of us has stretched out over the years. It is the accumulated work of two architectural philosophers, one Japanese and one American, living in New York, constructing in Japan, in the Hamptons, and elsewhere, and in their minds: Shusaku Arakawa, a Japanese conceptual philosopher-artist and a friend of Marcel Duchamp in his first years in New York, and Madeline Gins, an American conceptual artist, writer, and thinker. They created the image-texts called *The Mechanism of Meaning* (hereafter *MM*), in which they referred to the philosophical/perceptual issue of the meaning of meaning, in order to investigate conceptual art style. In these image-texts, we knew we had to read just the way they directed us to. What *MM* presented, in its complex working out of the methods of meaning and of grasping and constructing and receiving meaning, was an advanced realization of the "Mapping of Meaning," the ur-subtitle or subdivision Arakawa had couched on his almost bare canvases of the early 1960s (fig. 1).[8] The exercises revolutionized, in slow or quick tempo depending on the receiver, in handwriting and in print, the conception of thought held by many textual critics, and the presentations of thinking—verbal, pictorial, architectural—originally called "models of mind." All those diverse exercises were impossible to render verbally, so they were exhausting to the nonvisual onlooker. *We learned to look. We thought about thinking.*

What looking at Arakawa/Gins's ways of thinking about thinking manages to teach is a free-ranging imagination based on anti-linearity—exactly what this present volume aims at doing for textuality. In this case, doing is meant to be being.

These models of thinking, these operations of textuality are still relevant, and they reappear in Arakawa/Gins's exhibition at the Soho Guggenheim in 1997 and its accompanying catalogue, *Reversible Destiny*. Here they

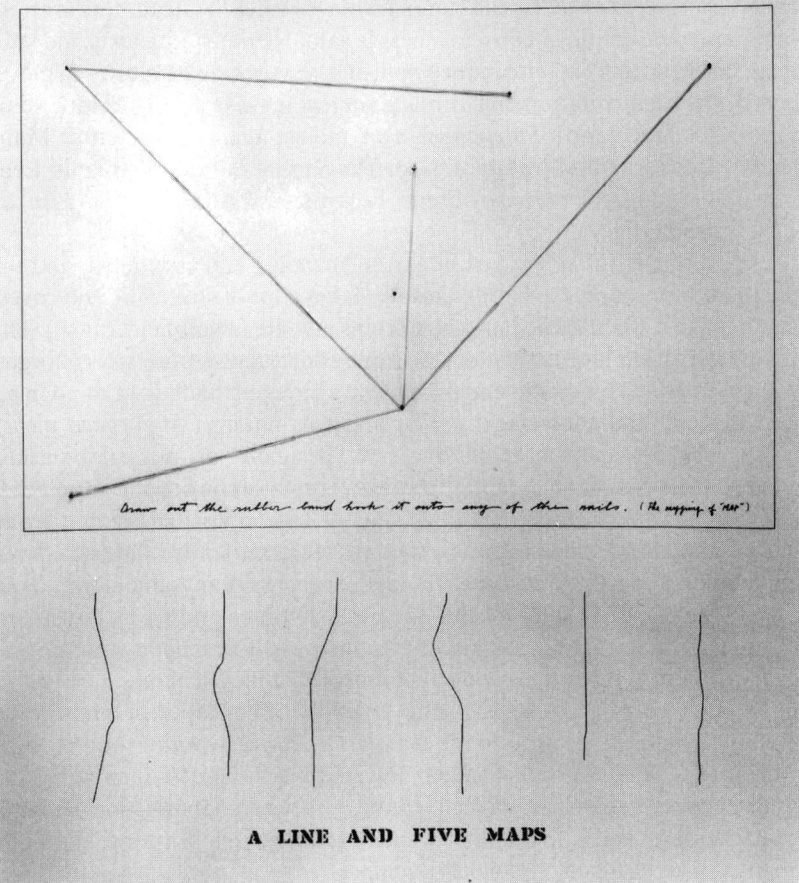

Figure 1. Shusaku Arakawa and Madeline Gins, *The Mechanism of Meaning*, 1963–1973, section 11, "Mapping of Meaning," panel 1. (Courtesy of Arakawa and Gins)

grouped their examples under subdivisions, titles that confronted directly viewers' too-straight ways of imagining. Look. In forcing the sighting and sitings of ambiguity and our reading of it as well as we could—a process best illustrated by the diverse (re)presentations of a lemon (figs. 2, 3) under the subdivision "Presentation of Ambiguous Zones" (fig. 4)—they were working against our textual habits of definition: being clear, inhabiting a clear textual decision, reading clearly.

It is around this zone, though under the subdivision "Splitting of Meaning," that the meditation on "A LINE IS A CRACK" appears; under it is "SAY one THINK two" (*MM,* 43; fig. 5) or "Perceive A as B" (50). Rather like the child's exercise of rubbing the tummy while patting the head, this exercise of potential doubling of consciousness is valuable in reading texts and subtexts.[9] Still another exercise in the "Splitting of Meaning" is a divided glove, posed above a meditation on twins and on rectangular pieces of cloth, reminiscent of Duchamp's *Stoppage-Etalon* and set against one-half of Mantegna's *Dead Christ* (*MM,* 45; fig. 6). The Virgin and Saint Anne in Leonardo's painting, celebrated by Freud, become the *Portrait of Mona Lisa,* by La Gioconda (fig. 7).

Logically, what is split apart in and by meaning is reassembled, and the pragmatic approach, the hands-on style, takes a lot of stretching and covering to make it work in the business of thinking "Reassembling" (fig. 8). The "Meaning of Intelligence" works the same effortful way: you have to forget, you have to find something nonexistent, you have to stretch your mind in regard to seeing and not seeing, thinking and not thinking ("If possible, please forget about any shape not marked shape," or again "any place not marked place"); the entire panel is labeled "ABOUT," as if pointing to the impossibility of doing what we are asked to do (fig. 9). The impossible exercise grows more complicated still in regard to rhythm: "Intermittently," they say, showing a landscape (two landscapes, in fact), "disregard any time not marked time" (89). Now, of course, nothing is marked "time," and we by now know enough not to look for it. We are thus trained—self-trained, if you like—to disregard instructions. This is, as in figure 8, what it is all about.

Yet it is also, already, about the reversibility of concepts, of our ways of thinking, well on the way to *Reversible Destiny,* a working out of anticyclical time. Take the panel called "Reversibility" (fig. 10). It stretches the concept of reversal; it has its own stretch marks and hanging *lines* as mnemonic devices; and it insists that we look at an object "for more than one minute." This is, again, about self-pacing.

But it was hard for the beholder of this work to hold onto any one thing, any one time. Across the mental exercise pages of Arakawa/Gins's thinking of meaning, already conceptually trying, arrows start off in all directions, until the forming of what they called "BLANK." Blank, like Spanish *blanco,*

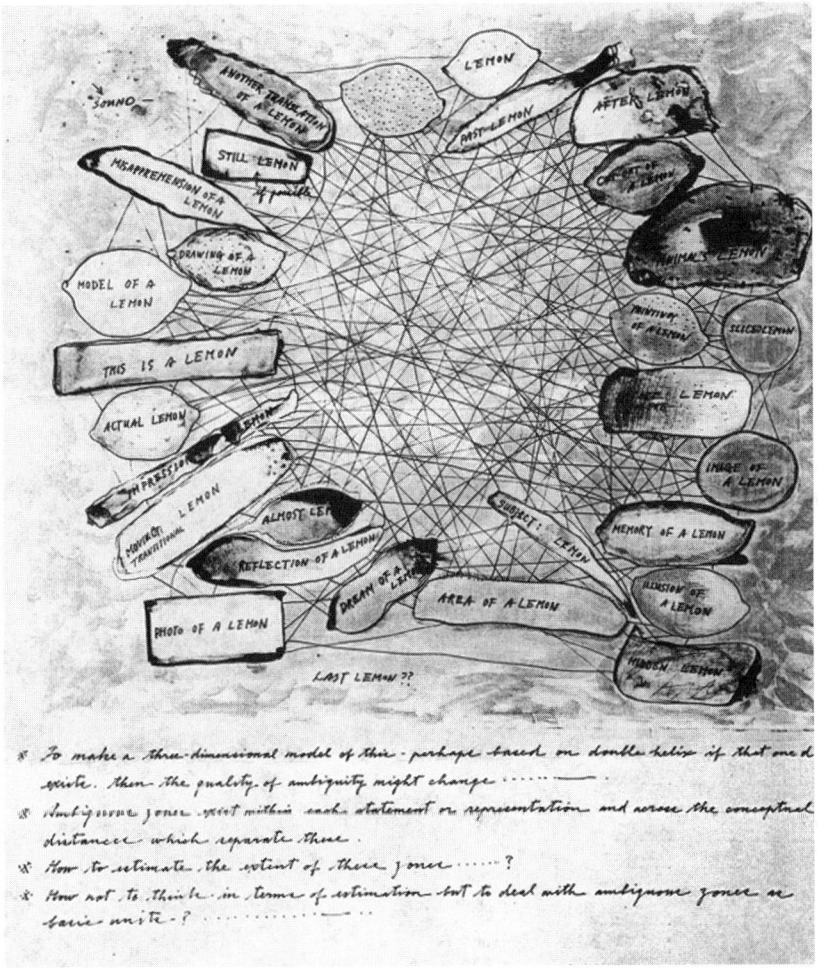

Figure 2. Shusaku Arakawa and Madeline Gins, *The Mechanism of Meaning*, 1963–1973, section 3, "Presentation of Ambiguous Zones," drawing. (Courtesy of Arakawa and Gins)

is target and whiteness and emptiness—oddly coinciding with those gaps in reception theory in which Iser, Jauss, and assorted others put so much stock. Are we to fill them in? Is completion turning out to be a good thing?

If "BLANK" represents "the inability to see the overall in the absence of a single organizing principle" (Bernstein, 192), like the vanishing point in single-point perspective or a blind spot in the optical field, it strangely corresponds also to the tenets of other works on blindness and anti-visioning.[10]

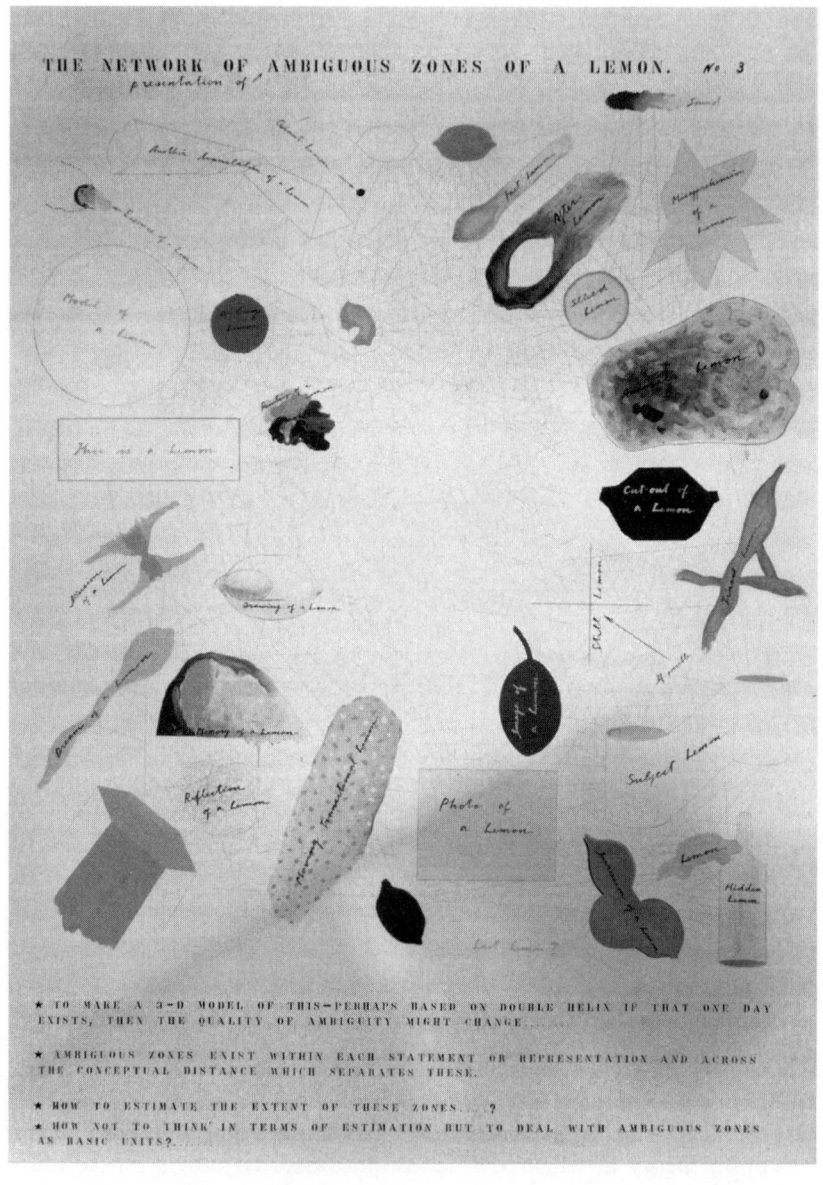

Figure 3. Shusaku Arakawa and Madeline Gins, *The Mechanism of Meaning*, 1963–1973, section 3, "Presentation of Ambiguous Zones," panel 6. (Courtesy of Arakawa and Gins)

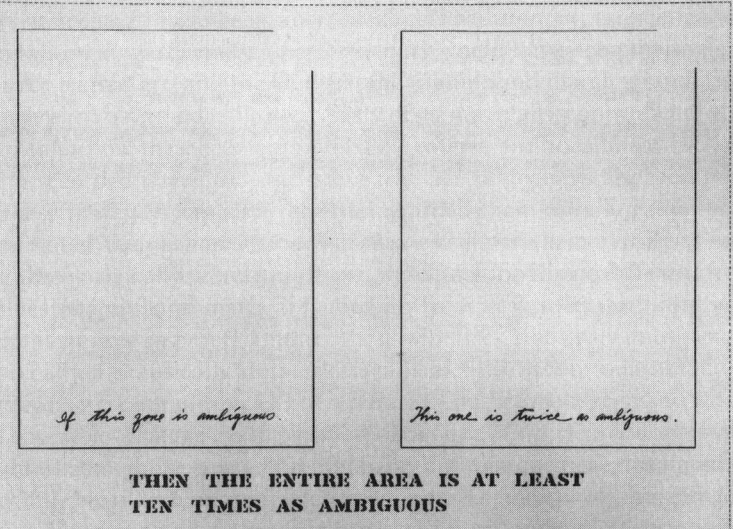

Figure 4. Shusaku Arakawa and Madeline Gins, *The Mechanism of Meaning,* 1963–1973, section 3, "Presentation of Ambiguous Zones," panel 1. (Courtesy of Arakawa and Gins)

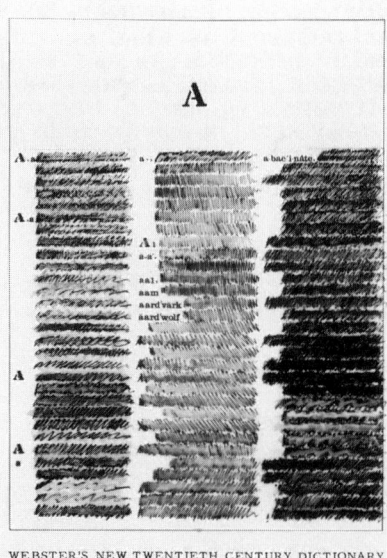

Figure 5. Shusaku Arakawa and Madeline Gins, *The Mechanism of Meaning*, 1963–1973, section 7, "Splitting of Meaning," panel 3. (Courtesy of Arakawa and Gins)

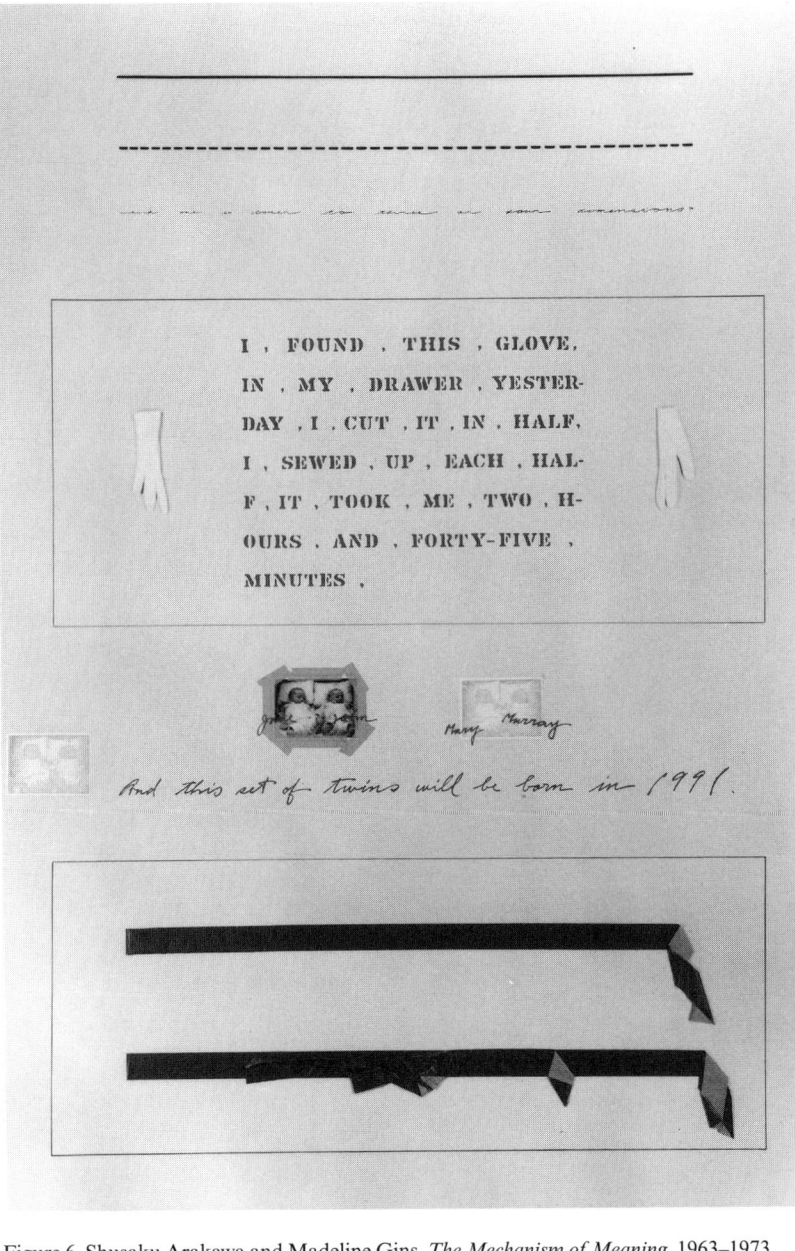

Figure 6. Shusaku Arakawa and Madeline Gins, *The Mechanism of Meaning*, 1963–1973, section 7, "Splitting of Meaning," panel 5. (Courtesy of Arakawa and Gins)

Figure 7. Shusaku Arakawa and Madeline Gins, *The Mechanism of Meaning,* 1963–1973, section 7, "Splitting of Meaning," panel 1. (Courtesy of Arakawa and Gins)

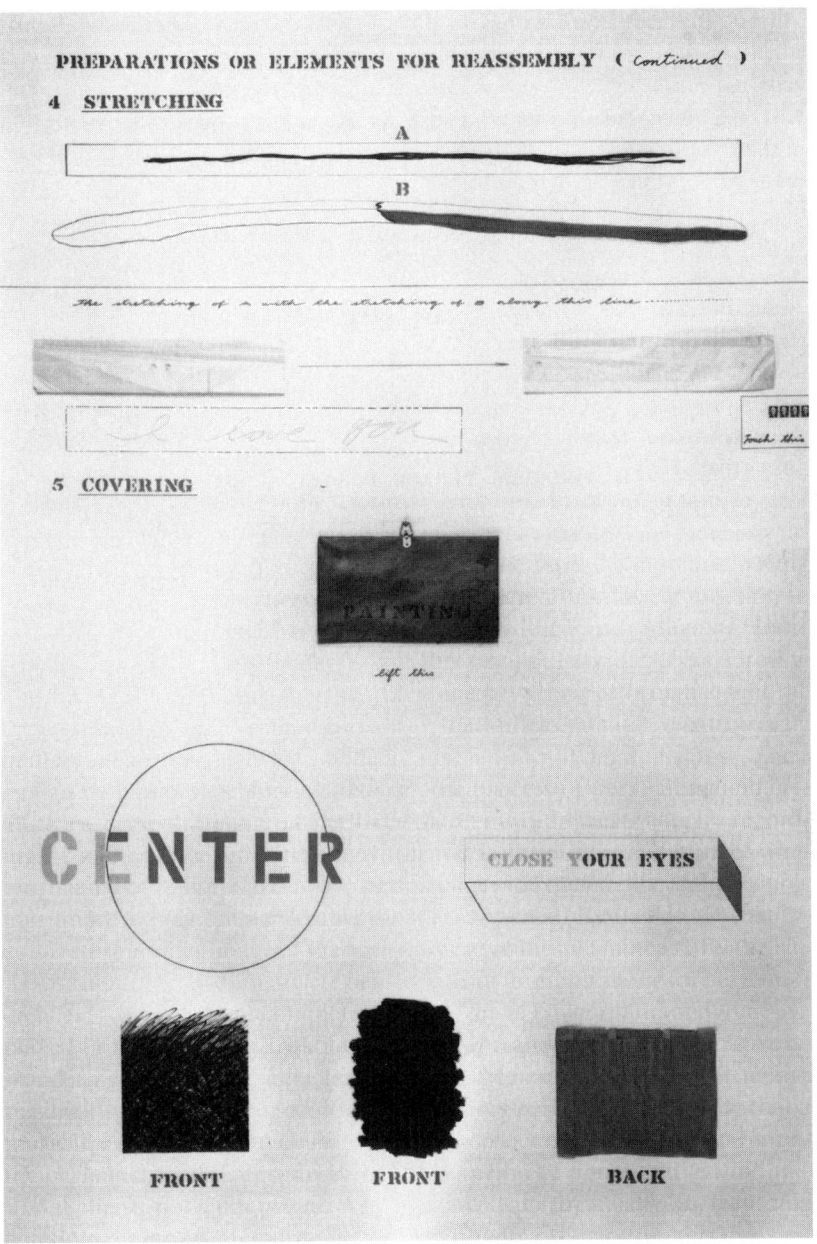

Figure 8. Shusaku Arakawa and Madeline Gins, *The Mechanism of Meaning,* 1963–1973, section 8, "Reassembling," panel 5. (Courtesy of Arakawa and Gins)

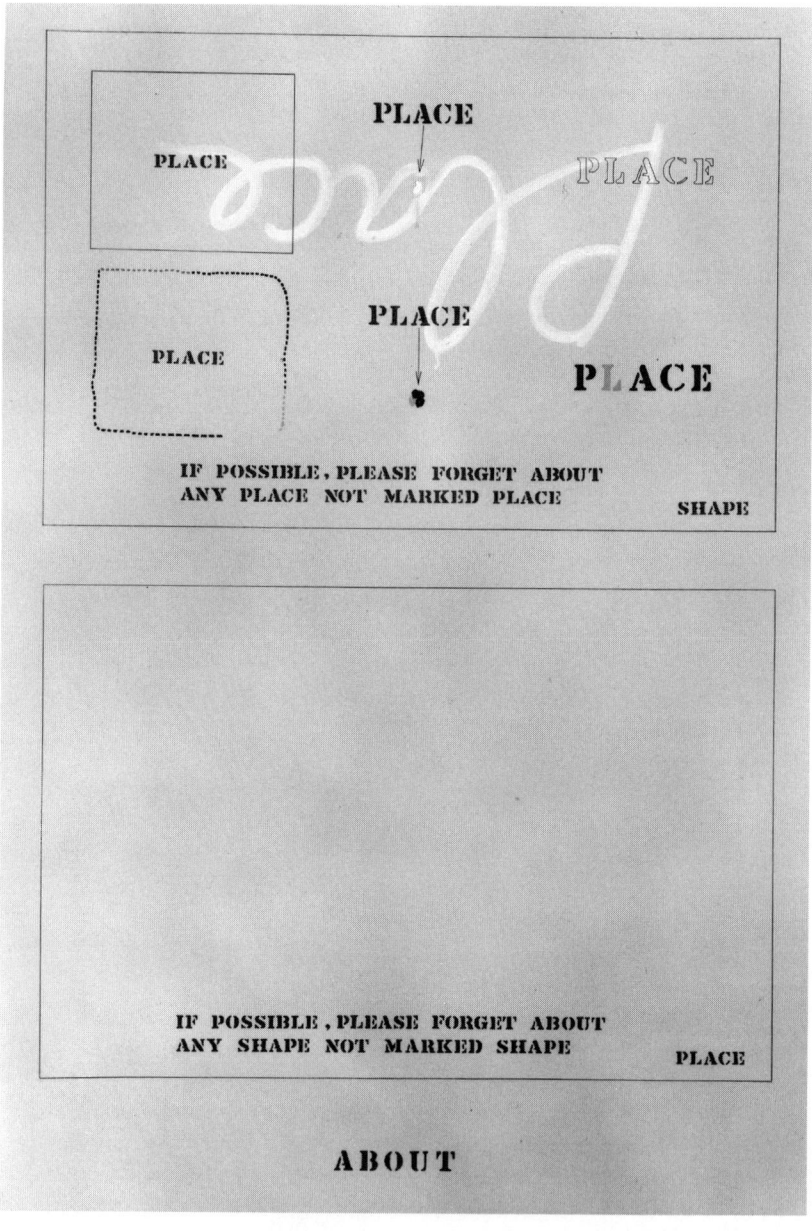

Figure 9. Shusaku Arakawa and Madeline Gins, *The Mechanism of Meaning,* 1963–1973, section 15, "Meaning of Intelligence," panel 3. (Courtesy of Arakawa and Gins)

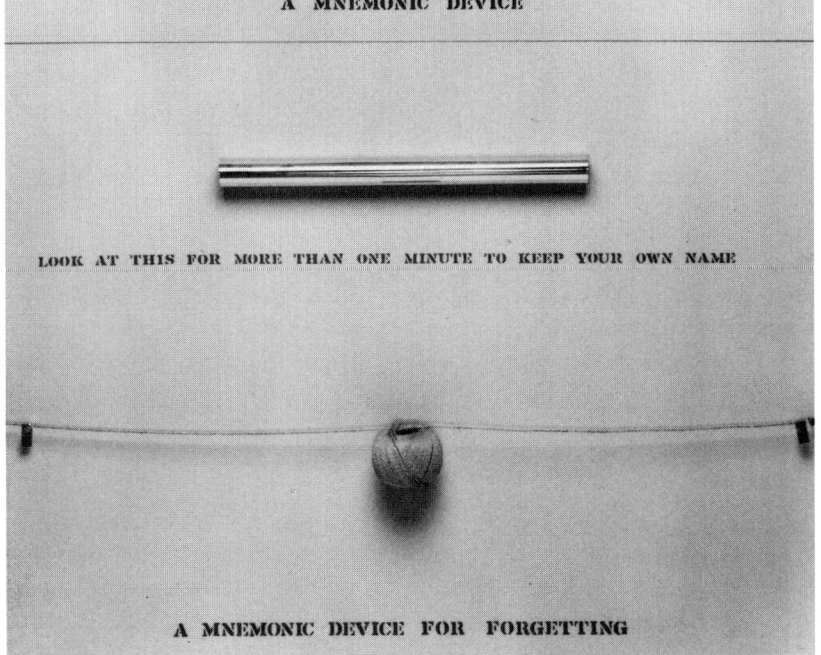

Figure 10. Shusaku Arakawa and Madeline Gins, *The Mechanism of Meaning*, 1963–1973, section 9, "Reversibility," panel 1. (Courtesy of Arakawa and Gins)

For those of us who had spent a good part of our then lives in admiration of contemporary sketchiness—of the paintings from Cézanne on that we were tempted to complete in our minds—the temptation was clear. We just wanted to fill in the BLANK and get on with it. We didn't know how to read it, and we didn't want to take the time.

Actually, beholders had to close their minds and eyes early. The first thing I remember from the first version of *MM*—a book that blew my mind, as they say—is being asked *not* to look at a black dot. I was riveted by one Dutch perspective: Vermeer's broom beside an opened door, leading into another room, alongside an Oriental scroll (65). These could be shown on the page as clearly as concrete poems. Thus, I could deal with them, and with the ways thoughts were pictured. I could turn the page at my own speed. But they took reading. They were about the texturization of textualization—what I like to think of as an "architexturization"[11] (fig. 11). Though it is supposed to lead to a meditation on the distance or nearness of the experience of textures, this image, like many others, may equally well lead to a diversion, also the point.

There was already a visible, tangible upbeatness about *MM*. We may have had our doubts, but there was room for those and optimism too. Under "Neutralization of Subjectivity" (that is, the unlimiting of humans' natural ego-centered reactions, as in Zen consciousness), we read, "Although it is uncertain how nonsensical any or all meaning is or may turn out to be, probably there will never be a reader of this book dispossessed entirely of the mechanism of meaning" (11). Exercises force us to construct, constrict, and delineate our own space (fig. 12). "Susanna and the Elders" comes under the same heading, so that Susanna confronting herself in the mirror models, paradoxically, the letting go of the excessive involvement the reader/observer has with herself (figs. 13 and 14).

In these panels and in these pages reproducing the panels, reading time is occasionally built in: "Look at any close objects as you open and close your eyes for several minutes" (12). Or, after a particularly intricate text concerning the imagination of the full and the empty, and elaborate instructions: "Stop Thinking about This" (13).

Inviting the impossible arrests the thinking process. Think of the panels that read "Do not think of this black dot," or directions as nonavailable for following as "Turn left/as/you turn right." Impossibilities arrest the mind, or at least slow it down to a point where normal reading rhythms, the pace of understanding that we might have thought we understood, are undone. We are reversed, on our way to being redestined.

Always, Arakawa/Gins have been interested in the reverse side of things: don't look, when you are looking. (How to represent not looking? So blind-

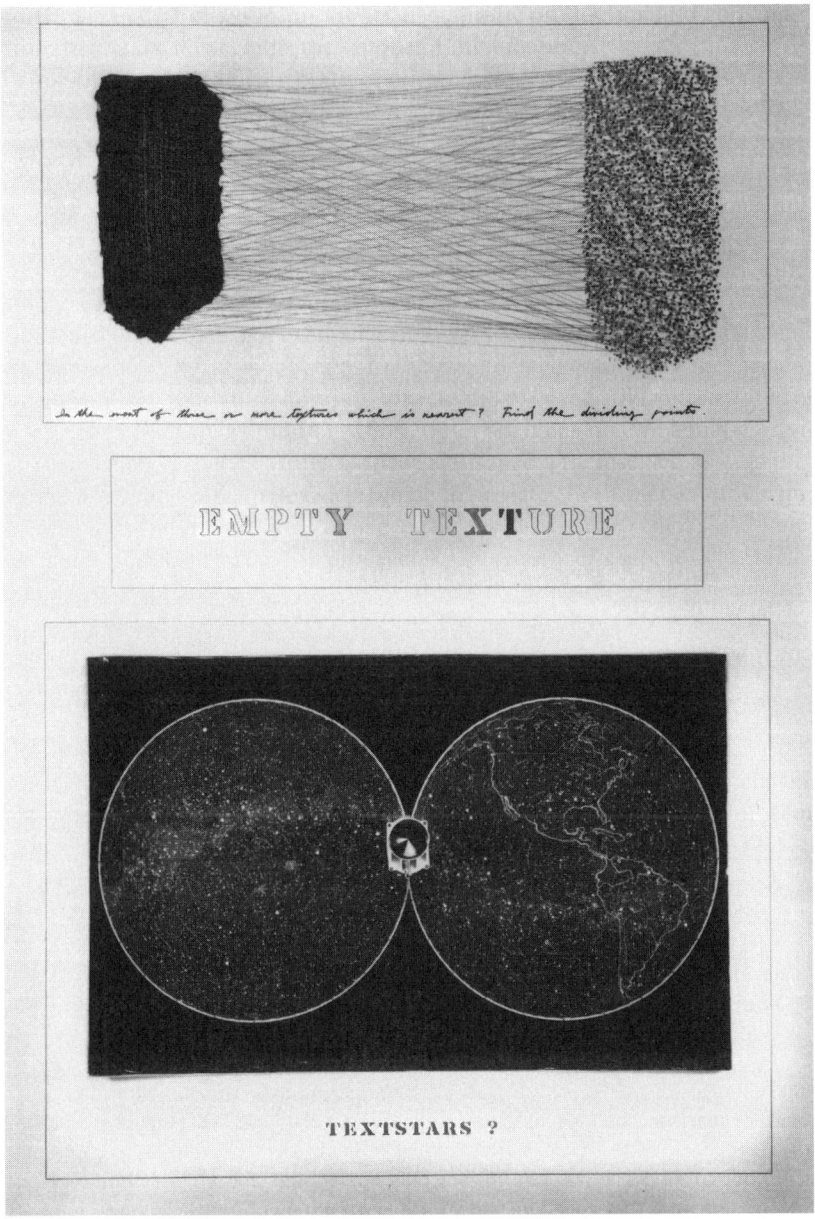

Figure 11. Shusaku Arakawa and Madeline Gins, *The Mechanism of Meaning,* 1963–1973, section 10, "Texture of Meaning," panel 5. (Courtesy of Arakawa and Gins)

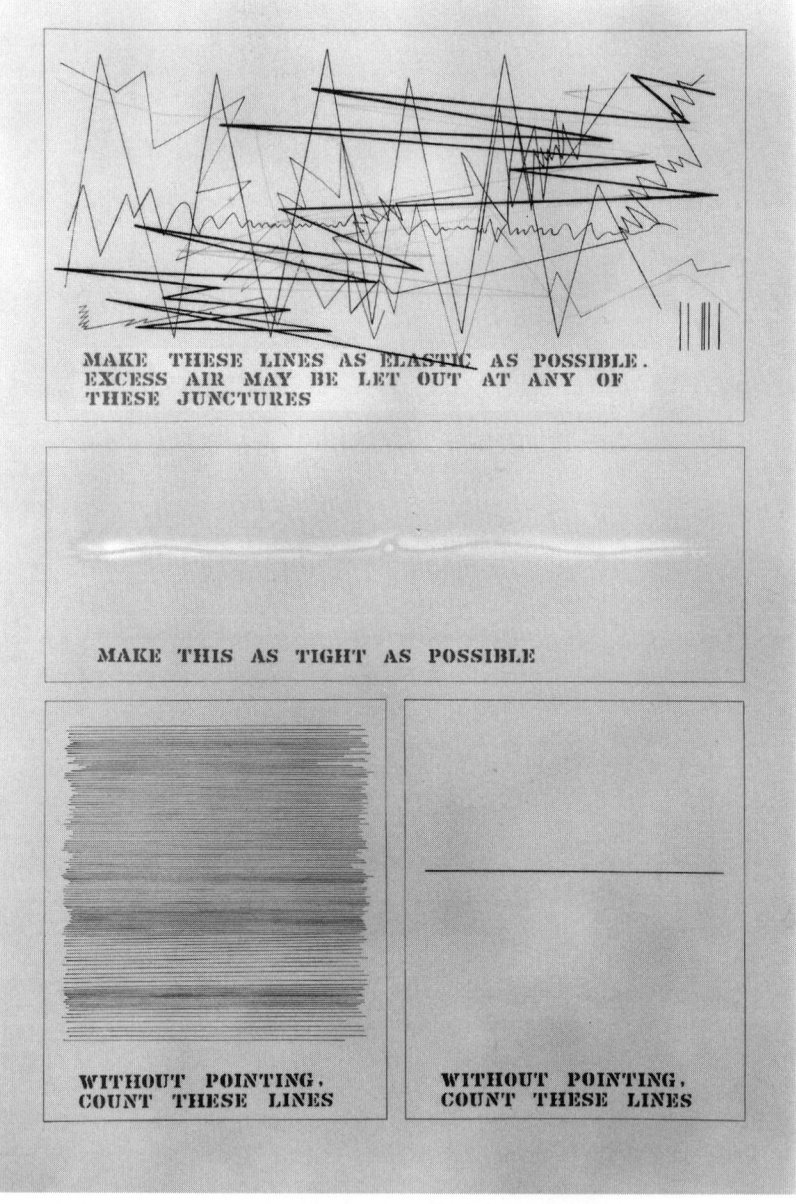

Figure 12. Shusaku Arakawa and Madeline Gins, *The Mechanism of Meaning*, 1963–1973, section 1, "Neutralization of Subjectivity," panel 2. (Courtesy of Arakawa and Gins)

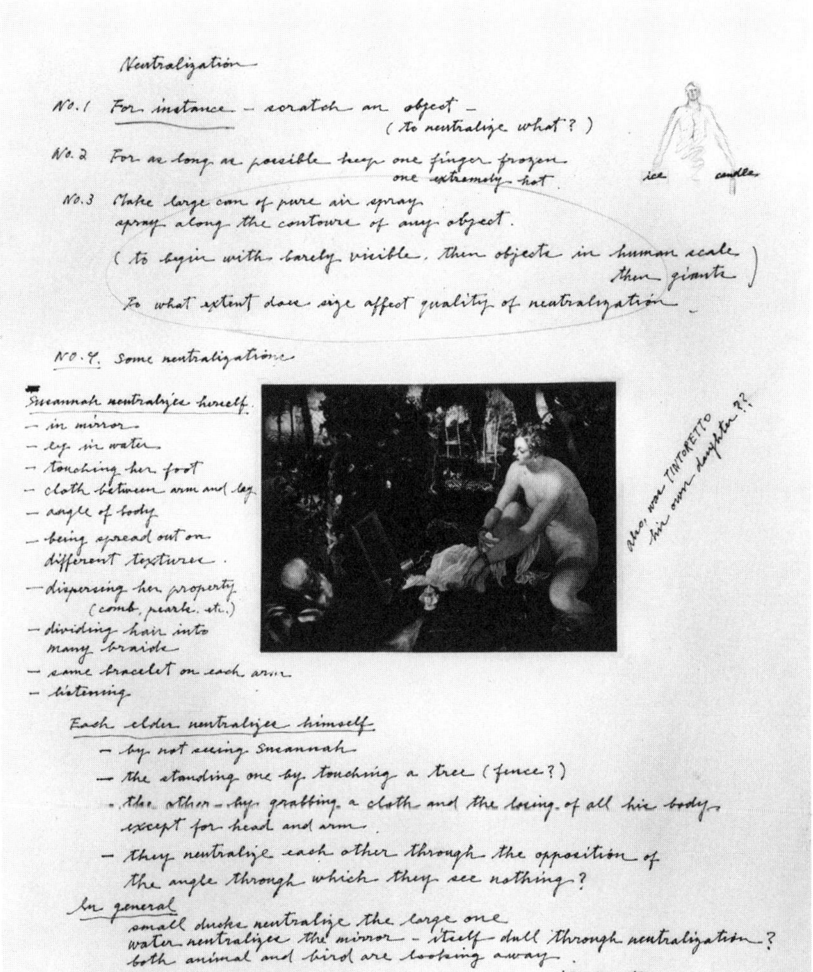

Figure 13. Shusaku Arakawa and Madeline Gins, *The Mechanism of Meaning,* 1963–1973, section 1, "Neutralization of Subjectivity," drawing. (Courtesy of Arakawa and Gins)

SUSANNAH NEUTRALIZES HERSELF
- IN MIRROR
- BY/IN WATER
- TOUCHING HER FOOT
- CLOTH BETWEEN ARMS AND LEG
- ANGLE OF BODY
- BEING SPREAD OUT ON DIFFERENT TEXTURES
- DISPERSING HER PROPERTY (COMB, PEARLS, ETC.)
- DIVIDING HAIR INTO MANY BRAIDS
- SAME BRACELET ON EACH ARM
- LISTENING

EACH ELDER NEUTRALIZES HIMSELF
- BY NOT SEEING SUSANNAH
- THE STANDING ONE BY TOUCHING A TREE (FENCE?)
- THE OTHER BY GRABBING A CLOTH AND THE LOSING OF ALL HIS BODY EXCEPT FOR HEAD AND ARM
- THEY NEUTRALIZE EACH OTHER THROUGH THE OPPOSITION OF THE ANGLE THROUGH WHICH THEY SEE NOTHING?

IN GENERAL
- SMALL DUCKS NEUTRALIZE THE LARGE ONE
- WATER NEUTRALIZES THE MIRROR—ITSELF DULL THROUGH NEUTRALIZATION?
- BOTH ANIMAL AND BIRD ARE LOOKING AWAY

BESIDES THIS LIST THERE MUST BY MANY MORE NEUTRALIZATIONS IN OPERATION IN THIS PAINTING.

Figure 14. Shusaku Arakawa and Madeline Gins, *The Mechanism of Meaning*, 1963–1973, section 1, "Neutralization of Subjectivity," panel 5. (Courtesy of Arakawa and Gins)

ness was to be next.) Their experiments and thinking have become progressively harder to read. Those of 1990 are active, interactive, conceptually upsetting to the domesticated mind. CLOSE YOUR EYES, said the sign over the exhibition. How could we possibly prepare, I wondered then and still now, for our own textual consumption, what is only to be seen *without* our eyes? How Can We Read This?

Don't Look Now

Let me read back my experience, confronting those paintings of Arakawa called "Paintings for Closed Eyes," which were at the Ronald Feldman Gallery in New York from 20 October to 10 November 1990. Perhaps, when our eyes are not looking, we can better adjust to someone else's thinking speed.

My eyes wide open, I stare at the front wall. In large black letters on the white, a statement:

If then it is by the spectator or posterity that the work of art is finally formed,
Who after all is the spectator or what are the essential properties of the witness?
Arakawa

The gravity strikes me. This goes beyond reception theory, to question the receiver. Witness is to be borne to something, and to the witness itself, involved in some essence, in seeing beyond form to what comes after. No empty words. No blank.

But now the point was the experience: I walked in, rubber bottoms to my shoes. I knew from previous Arakawa exhibits—like the *Building Sensoriums, 1973–1990* (15 Sept.–13 Oct., Ronald Feldman Gallery), by Arakawa with Madeline Gins and John Knesl, that I should be prepared for mind shifts, like one-way bridges: for walking over, along, up, inside. Entering the *Stuttering God* construction by the trinity of artists, I was warned to wear nothing with buttons exposed; indeed, I found myself imprisoned for a time in there, building up my sensorium, when my sleeve button, tiny but efficacious, caught in a mesh inside, in a web like an internet (*MM,* 121; fig. 15). This is an extreme example of what Arakawa sees as the viewer entering the depiction, the model of thinking.

You are not sitting at a computer. You are not allowed a static pose. You are confronted with a ramp, up which you have to move, to see the *Paintings for Closed Eyes* (fig. 16).

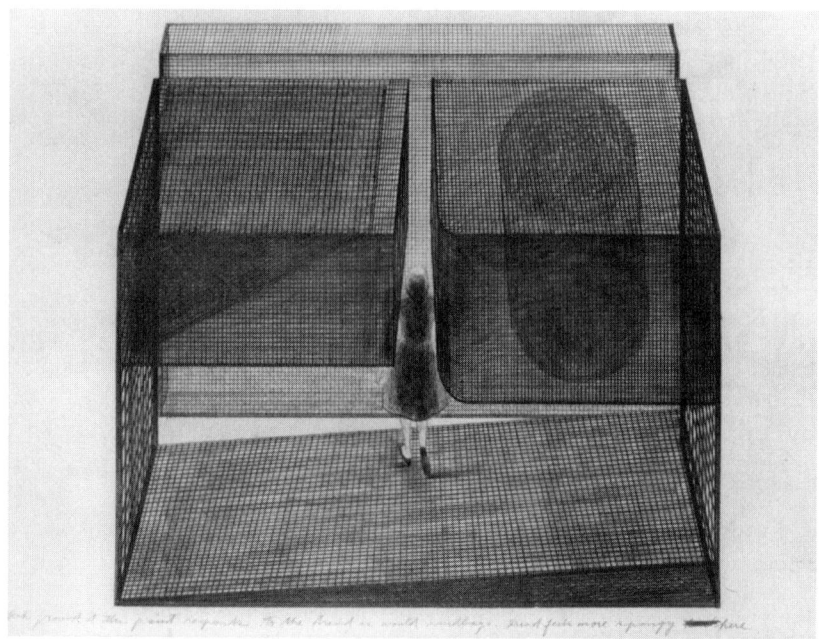

Figure 15. Shusaku Arakawa and Madeline Gins, *The Mechanism of Meaning*, 1984, section 16, "Review and Self-Criticism," sketch for *The Bridge of Reversible Destiny (The Where of Nowhere)*. (Courtesy of Arakawa and Gins)

Inside this one, bareness and high tension now. I have to walk up ramps at differing inclines, supplied, when the incline is steep, with climbing ropes. The first one I tried was a low slope, ropeless, but definitely a slope in the mind. WALK ON THIS, *it says, and I walk up, on anatomical drawings—of a hand, of a throat—and a whirling spiral, and the right side of a check for $15.25. In the center is a blank white space, above the throat, as if someone or something were crying up into blankness. A hand is outstretched, under a convergence of abyss and coastline merged. As indeed the images tend to merge for me, all of them whirling. I am dizzy.*

What I experience is that walk up a throat, with a hand, unattributed, held up in panic, exposed from inside, with that abyss to my right (Pascal's, I remember, was to his left). Then I stand still. I close my eyes, having already seen the black lines, like horizontal slashes, on the huge white canvases in front of me. CLOSE YOUR EYES, *it says at the bottom of the canvas, as it had said:* WALK ON THIS. *So it is an exhibit constantly in three-time step. Look, walk up, close your eyes.* ONE-TWO-THREE, *walk down, repeat.*

Was I still thinking? I didn't have time, I had to read without looking.

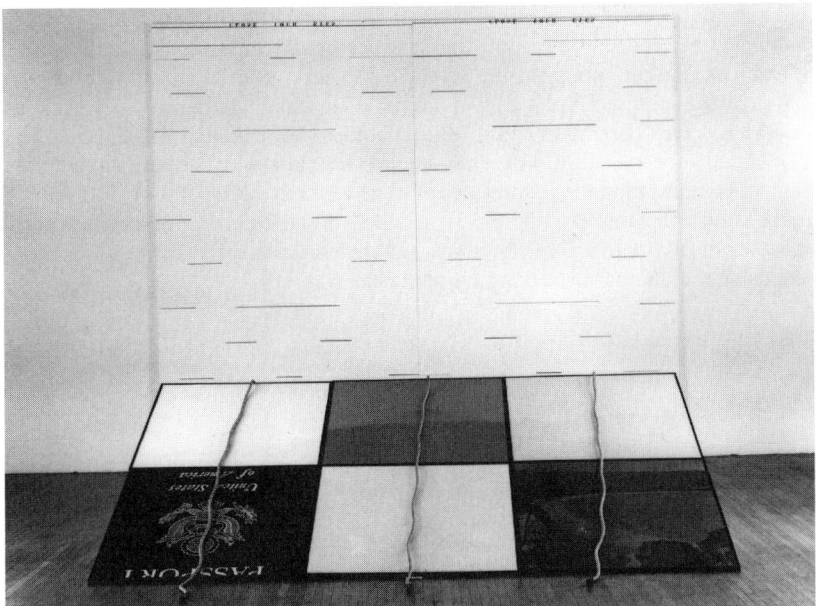

Figure 16. Shusaku Arakawa and Madeline Gins, *Paintings for Closed Eyes, Abrupt Resemblances,* 1989–1990, diptych: acrylic and pencil on canvas, 132 x 90 inches each panel; ramp: aluminum boards, photgraphs, plastic, plywood, and rope, six panels, 48 x 48 inches each. (Courtesy of Arakawa and Gins)

Now this first ramp is set at an angle to the canvas, which feels right. I am not yet ready to see it—or not see it—straight on. Next I try one with a rope, a friend and Madeline Gins climbing up behind me, holding on. For dear life, as they say.

Then we try one with three ropes, each up an incline of dark and light squares, but at the bottom left lies a passport reversed. Walking on the upside-down passport, I notice there is no sideways angling to this ramp; it is to be a straight passage. It feels like standing on shipboard, and the rope is a thick sailor's rope. We are sailing straight into the text ahead. Not angling for anything. CPO2E YOUR EYE2, *it seems to say, so I translate and do, meditating on what it is to travel with this particular part of a reversed passport. I slide back down reluctantly, knowing the world outside this gallery is less fun. No climbing ropes out there, different sorts of ropes to learn, and you can't close your eyes for a minute.*

How can I possibly represent the *experience* that exhibition forced on me? In his text for *Reversible Destiny,* "The Road to Critical Resemblances House: Report of a Mapping," Charles W. Haxthausen does it in words:

First, the ramp renders explicit the space of beholding by heightening the beholder's awareness of his or her own physical presence before the work. Second, the contrasting orientation of the images on the platforms—near and far, foreshortened, upside down, and so forth—creates a sense of tension between the viewer's body and what is seen, thereby reinforcing the beholder's sense of body as an agent of the perceptual process. Third, and most important, the steeply sloping angle to the ramps heightens the tactile experience of viewing; the creaking of the platforms also adds an aural dimension to the experience. One must exert energy in moving against the force of gravity to ascend the ramps and then maintain one's equilibrium as one stands on the sloping surface to gaze at the painting. (29)

"To have looked at this with closed eyes," *reads a wall text. I have. Like seeing inside.*
I have. But that was then.

But the philosophical/textual mind of this team of architects had something else in store, harder on the rhythm of reading and thinking and on their relation to the meaning and memory of meaning. For quite a few years now, Arakawa and Gins have been developing what they call and build as *Reversible Destiny*. We, their readers, viewers, and friends, are diversely mystified by the forcing of two kinds of seeing and thinking, and by the videos and audioguides for the exhibitions. Nothing moves at our pace, whatever that may once have been. The readerly mind—even the computer-ready mind in all its availability—finds itself strangely perturbed by the slowdown inflicted by those oral inflections on the audioguide, as a chosen direction we are offered. It is as if, knowing that neither the purely verbal nor the purely visual will make a sufficient response to our newly perceptual world, we now had to deal with the voice as well.

Look here, they say. Zen talk. Now you are standing here. Look in the right corner . . . listen to the lullaby, look at the child. Like a museum, but not. On the second floor of the Soho Guggenheim, there are large posters of Meaning on every wall, notebooks with which to agree or disagree, a call for interaction. The question is not about the catching of our attention but its holding; it is about *time.*

We may have learned to read surrealist texts rapidly, or poetic texts slowly; to scan grocery lists and class lists; to dramatize what needs it. Yet we have not learned—if I can take my own case, that of my adult son who accompanied me to the exhibition at the Guggenheim, and that of the others around us—to think these texts through on their own rhythm. Our lack of temporal reading adjustment becomes more aggravated with this serious life-concerning enterprise, in which we necessarily cooperate or leave.

Here is the issue: How do we learn, impelled by a project of someone else's thinking, to adjust our own speed of reading and reaction to these diverse inputs? Ponder all the divergent conceptions we can accommodate in our thinking; imagine how many different models we can consider for possible ways of seeing; consider how much sharper and wider will be our eventual vision and envisioning of textuality, formed through our multiple and various readings.

"Chardin Reading Proust" is a chapter title in a recent book on visualizing the world's favorite embedded author, who can change readers' lives from his reclining position.[12] The next chapter reverses it, like our destiny once we know how to think and read at the same time: "Proust Reading Chardin."[13] Textualizing visually is contagious; we are hooked. There is not a lot that textuality cannot teach our inner clocks, even when they run down.

Reversible Destiny

To Not to Die, Arakawa and Gins called an earlier project, that one in book form; it, too, was pointed against what most of us consider our inevitable fate. Yes, of course, we want to ensure our own mental passage, and we are open to it. But again, building is the problem. (How) is it at all possible to render, in any site *but* an art gallery, any of the experiments Arakawa and Gins have been constructing for years?

What they are building, here and there, and in their and our minds, is the most ambitious project of all, and the hardest to read: *Reversible Destiny.* If one reads the model of the city, one may be persuaded, eyes open, to do what the directions sometimes say: see and join up. On the other hand, the presentation of the project, with its various city parts and different dwellings, looks like a relief map with small sleek figures. It is hard to read. One has to see it slowly.

These *are* still the ways of meaning; these *are* still the models of mind that force a reconsideration of textual timing. The "perceptual landing sites" of *Reversible Destiny* demonstrate, as our thinking lands on them and takes off again, how those mental operations presented as models of thinking have evolved as "escape routes" from mortality and limited thinking; the textuality of meaning and being increases its complexity (and our potentiality) and demands a still wider range of reading rhythms.

The act of writing and thinking backward wants to install itself in our minds and build a house. Oddly, the reworked project with its apparent labyrinths consists primarily of entrances. I take this as grounds for hope. Some elements of textual thinking and building will linger longer than others, and among them are the possible ways of visualizing meaning's meanings—until we tire or rush past the slow truths.

Let me try a different way. In questioning: What is it to think backward? Is it just like writing backward, taken a step further? Does that mean reversing our seeing, our being, our living, our dying? All these reversals have to do not just with Arakawa's lifelong fascination with Leonardo da Vinci and his mirror writing, but also with another form of textualizing the mind—not just the page, not just the gallery experience. Virtual thinking, with a vengeance, against mortal thinking.

What Arakawa and Gins are naming and believing in as "reversible destiny" has this as its primary article of belief: what the mind conceives it can install, once it is prepared. Their relentless optimism undoes the tradition of the *vanitas,* of the *memento mori,* except that this is a memento *nonmori*—like the authors' earlier *To Not to Die,* and some parts of Gins's *Helen Keller, or Arakawa,* about regeneration and the ultimate vanquishing of mortality.

Helen Keller, or Arakawa celebrates an originary or "initial sense of ubiquitous site" (253) ingrained in humans—and the present architectural undertaking in its enormity re-creates just that.[14] How are we to deal with this creative thought? The genre of the art essay falls flat before it; the fictional will not do, even if we believe in fiction; poetry has no grip here. Let me try one of the quirks of tradition: the dialogue form.

Always, dialogues—Plato, Rousseau, Diderot, Valéry, Suarès—have been difficult, mind-splitting. Let me try to converse with myself, inventing a dialogue with my memory of *The Mechanism of Meaning,* its development to the present, and the mark it has made on my ordinary reader's mind. Do I have to obey instructions? Do I have to keep my eyes open or closed, as I am told? Do I have to hear the lullaby sung over the audiophone? What can I turn off and still be part of the experiment? SLOW DOWN, says a sign somewhere. What do I do as a fast reader? The thing is aimed not at me. And yet . . .

Two kinds of architecture are being thought of here. One kind has meaning; it is extensible and reversible, it is a *helter-skelter-shelter,* and it performs. It performs ellipsis, being—in both architecture and life—short on one side and long on the other. The other kind is self-sufficient, stable; it represents mortality, and it is ultimately boring. *Reversible Destiny* participates in the first kind of action, but must we let the other action go? I cannot read them at the same speed. I cannot read and listen and see all at once. Limits of mind are my concern here.

But how *do* I read this kind of architectural diagram, green and brown, with figures indistinguishable one from the next, and believe it? How *do* I put any of this on paper, or in my mind, at the changing rhythm it requires: slow, fast-perceive, slow, fast-perceive? The diagrams are for instant understanding, the captions for lingering. The aural reception would like to take account of both, since both speeds are necessary to undertake this or any project. There are mostly entrances here, few exits; slowly noticing that, I point it out to my neighbors, who are seeing something else. Without the verbal component, the visual makes less sense. As for the auditory, it has its use: *I/you do not want to forgo any component of what I am/you are given in an exhibition.* Hence, the problem.

Does boredom enter in? Is that not part of the point? Part of our consideration of textual time must surely include our capacity for getting annoyed, bored, irritated, diverted. And yet, as the preface to *Reversible Destiny* puts it, "Being a person is an astounding event or series of events." However we read or reread architectural texts, and not just blueprints for them, the specific skills the activity demands must be accounted for in our reexamination of our ways of imagining. The experience of experiencing this kind of work of thinking and rethinking forces us to reexamine our textual timing, and our vision of what we can think, in "real" presence as in "virtual" presence. Let us rethink thinking right now.

Some things in textual thinking and building will last longer than others, and among them are the possible ways of visualizing meaning's meanings in their radically different speeds. We have to adjust how we see to what we read. Whose choice is it, anyway?

Ours. What we need is practice. Computer graphics, dare I say it, are not the same as paintings out there in the world, in museums, galleries, the visual works. We have to learn to linger, even in our hurried days and ways, over the painting or the sketch, finished or unfinished. (We have learned, some of us, to prefer the latter, since we can participate in the mental work of it.) Lecturers on art have always known that their patter serves the purpose of getting the mind to dwell on what the eyes have to learn not to turn away from in haste. That is one reason why artists copy: that is how they learn to slow down, in order to see.

Finally, we should insist on inserting ourselves in a visual time preparatory to, simultaneous with, and enduring as long as the time of the text, actual and virtual. John Ruskin was a seer: "The greatest thing a human soul ever does in this world is to *see* something, and tell what it *saw* in a plain way. Hundreds of people can talk for one who can think, but thousands can think for one who can see. To see clearly is poetry, prophecy, and religion—all in one."[15]

We are complex readers; we have not learned, most of us, to be complex viewers. We do not have the time, in whatever costume we may attend the temple of virtuality and its time-consuming rituals. The business of art has been set over against the business of text, and we have done a sketchy job of bringing them together. All of us—even those who have spent the most time trying to find a discourse for dealing with difference (that difference) and with resemblance (that resemblance)—find ourselves stymied when all the subtle stuff feels as if it is on the side we are not on. *Can we slow ourselves down?* It is the speeding by, the turning away from (excuse me for a moment) the real to the virtual, that ties us up and does us in. How can we best focus on what Bergson called "the inner becoming of things"? For what finally matters, in the long stretch at whatever pace, is not just what we give but what we learn to take: it's about time.

Notes

1. About "mind," consider the Wittgensteinian attitude, described by Richard Rorty in *Contingency, Irony, and Solidarity* (New York and Cambridge: Cambridge University Press, 1989), and associated with Ryle, Dennett, and Davidson: that mentalistic terminology is just a vocabulary that works, "predicting what an organism is likely to do or say under various sets of circumstances. . . . Think of the term 'mind' or 'language' not as the name of a medium between self and reality but simply as a flag which signals the desirability of using a certain vocabulary when trying to cope with certain kinds of organisms. . . . It makes perfectly good sense to ask how we got from the relative mindlessness of the monkey to the full-fledged mindedness of the human, or from speaking Neanderthal to speaking postmodern, if these are construed as straightforward causal questions" (15). For Wittgenstein, see Marjorie Perloff, *Wittgenstein's Ladder: Poetic Language and the Strangeness of the Ordinary* (Chicago: University of Chicago Press, 1996). One of the few mesmerizing biographies that measure up to the mind of the subject is Ray Monk, *Ludwig Wittgenstein: The Duty of Genius* (Harmondsworth: Penguin, 1990). For a little more on thinking via Wittgenstein, see the chapter entitled "Thinking" in the *Wittgenstein Reader*, ed. Anthony Kenny (Oxford: Blackwell, 1994), 111–25.

2. A reference to David Greetham's reference in this collection to Richard Rorty, the most sophisticated ironist of them all. See note 1, and other works by Rorty.

3. The true verb would probably be "writing," but in principle, *r* comes before *w*.

4. My thanks to Matthew Caws for his interception of Eco's method from a wire service.

5. I refer, of course, to David Greetham's comment on the "shabby" discourse of modernity, among the multitude of possible discourses (see p. 32). "Shabby" is good.

6. Charles Bernstein, in collaboration with Susan Bee, "Meaning the Meaning: Arakawa's Critique of Space," in *Content's Dream: Essays 1975–1984* (Los Angeles: Sun and Moon, 1984), 186.

7. See also Bernstein's *Artifice of Absorption* (Philadelphia: Singing Horse Press, 1987); and Michael Fried, *Absorption and Theatricality: Painting and Beholder in the Age of Diderot* (Berkeley: University of California Press, 1980).

8. Shusaku Arakawa and Madeline Gins, *The Mechanism of Meaning*, 3d ed. (New York: Abbeville, 1988), 67. (1st ed. [Minneapolis: Minneapolis Institute of Arts, 1979]; 2d ed. [New York: Harry N. Abrams, 1979].) Citations in this essay are from the third edition, abbreviated *MM*.

9. For example, in the texts of Antonin Artaud, famously constipated and unable to get out, as he put it both physically and metaphorically—two ideas at once, except through the same words—I discovered long ago various extraordinary subtexts reinforcing the ideas of struggle, the notions of incompatibility and impossibility. See my "Antonin Artaud: Suppression and Sub-Text," in *About French Poetry from*

DADA to "Tel Quel": Text and Theory, ed. Mary Ann Caws (Detroit: Wayne State University Press, 1974), 254–72.

10. See also Jacques Derrida, *Mémoire d'aveugle* (Paris: Réunion des Musées Nationaux, 1994); and Martin Jay, *Downcast Eyes: The Denigration of Vision in Twentieth-Century French Thought* (Berkeley: University of California Press, 1993).

11. See my *Metapoetics of the Passage: Architextures in Surrealism and After* (Hanover, N.H.: University Press of New England, 1981).

12. This refers to Alain de Botton's *How Proust Can Change Your Life* (New York: Pantheon, 1997).

13. Mieke Bal, *The Mottled Screen: Reading Proust Visually* (Stanford: Stanford University Press, 1997).

14. See the following books by Madeleine Gins: *Word Rain; or, A Discursive Introduction to the Intimate Philosophical Investigatations of G, r, e, t, a G, a, r, b, o, It Says* (New York: Grossman, 1969); *Helen Keller, or Arakawa* (Santa Fe: Burning Books; New York: East-West Cultural Studies, 1994). See also her works with Arakawa: *The Mechanism of Meaning*; and *Pour ne pas mourir/To Not to Die,* trans. François Rosso (Paris: Éditions de la Différence, 1987); *Architecture: Sites of Reversible Destiny* (London: Academy Editions, 1994); and *Reversible Destiny* (New York: Guggenheim Museum, 1997).

15. *The Works of John Ruskin,* 39 vols., ed. E. T. Cook and Alexander Wedderburn (London: George Allen, 1903–12), 5:333.

Johanna Drucker

Intimations of Immateriality
Graphical Form, Textual Sense, and the Electronic Environment

In the electronic environment, new forms such as hypertext, hypercard stacks, and the rhizomatous, interconnecting threads that link one website to another in the vastly amorphous and seemingly unbounded field of the Internet have all generated critical speculation. The structure and form of the traditional, linear-seeming print media have been reinvestigated, resulting in the insight that many features of hypertext have precedents in conventional formats, while other features are significantly transformed by electronic technology. But are there even more fundamental issues about the nature of textuality that come into focus in the electronic environment? Textual studies have brought attention to the ways various aspects of materiality (type, format, paper, book structure) participate in the production of meaning, just as the "immaterial" text of the electronic environment has become a fixture within the popular imagination. To understand what portion of the actual message and meaning a text communicates is challenged, intensified, or lost in this electronic environment, we must ask the basic question, "What constitutes the information of a text?" In particular, does the structure or configuration of a text (its schematic organization), an increasingly self-conscious feature of electronic texts and website "interfaces," actually function as information at the level of textual production?

To answer these questions, it is useful to start at the most basic level— that of the letter—since it is at this level that the first link between electronic storage and textual information is made. Considering what the identity of a letter contributes to a text—as a visual form, a graphical form, and an element of a finite sign system—leads quickly to philosophical speculation about the basic relation between form and information in letters themselves. Does the letter *have* a body? Or, does the letter *need* a body?[1] The assumptions underlying these two questions are quite distinct. If we assume that a letter *has* a body, then its identity is bound up in some *essential* way with that form. If the letter merely *needs* a body, then the implication is that the letter could function simply by having any form that is sufficiently distinguishable for it to be recognized and read. The first identity can be characterized as phenomenological: it assumes an inherent essence to any form (graphical, visual, metaphysical), and further, that such an essence constitutes substantive information which would be irrevocably lost if the letter's form were altered past all recognition (as in fact occurs when a letter is stored electronically). The second concept of identity is more clearly semiotic: it assumes that identity relies on systematicity and difference, so that the letter has to be a distinct element in a system of signs. In an electronic situation, this means that its encoded form (binary sequence) is distinct from that of any other letter; the letter is considered functional rather than visual, and any notion of essence or substance is discounted. The question of whether graphic form is substantive *information* replays in the electronic environment at every level of textual production: What is lost in the encoding of the discrete elements of written language (the transformation of letters into binary code and/or algorithms)? To what extent can the "material" information in document formats be translated into such binary storage? And does the format design of graphical interfaces for the display of information in every area of communication (including poetic expression) actually contribute substantively to the text? Philosophical questions, linguistic histories, technical issues, and design concerns can all be brought to bear on the question of which graphical and visual features are to be considered textual "information" in an electronic environment.

Electronic media push the examination of form to the very limit of its existence as binary code. At a philosophical level, the question is whether information stored as code has been pared down to its inherent, essential identity as data, or whether, on the contrary, code is always, and merely, an inscription of difference that produces meaning in a system. (Since "difference" by definition cannot be substantive, one could suggest that binary code, the fundamental condition of all electronic information storage, can never constitute an essence, a substance, or inherent form.) Many questions arise from this fundamental consideration of the "ontology" of the text in "code storage," and from consideration of the way graphical features of a preexisting print text are affected by the process of encoding into electronic format for storage. These considerations open a rift in relations between form and meaning, between a letter and its graphical identity, between a text and its configured format—relations that seem inextricably intertwined in print media. In the electronic environment, these distinctions are newly conceivable because it is possible to imagine (and encounter) a letter or a text outside or independent of any specific embodied form—not as an abstraction, but as a daily reality.[2] For instance, there is no longer any necessity that a text be inscribed within a material substrate: a document can be stored in an electronic form and then output through a variety of devices to produce musical notes, graphical forms, patterns of lights in a theatrical stage, or letters on a page. There is no *necessary relation* between the material form of input and the material form of output in electronic media. The mutable condition of "code storage" can transform the identity of the written text. This introduces a new self-consciousness about writing's past functions, dependencies, and relations to materiality. Code scintillates between material and immaterial conditions long enough to let us ask what (and how) the substantive content of material might mean, and what an *immaterial* text might be.

This essay traces these issues through different levels of investigation, beginning with the question of the letter posed above and its fundamental identity in the electronic environment. In philosophical terms, this question is posed as an investigation of the "ideality" of form (or form as cognitive sense, an idea, or an idea that appears to consciousness as a form but without materiality). In the electronic environment, this "ideality" becomes problematic when considered with respect to the identity of the letter and other visual features of a text, because the basic investigation of whether a letter *has* or *needs* a body already questions whether a letter's identity may be bound up in its material form or whether it exists without materiality. If form is determined in part by the transformation that takes place between a stored file and an output device (if a keystroke of input becomes a musical note as output), then to what extent is the "information" of that output actually a substantive part of the text? I will investigate this question here by looking at the graphical organization of various documents—print media to electronic, with a special focus on poetic works and their use of the spatial and temporal potential unique to the electronic domain. If graphical format (at any level from letter to document) *is* an integral part of textual information, then how does the stored condition and mutability of that information in the immaterial environment transform, alter, or threaten the substantive content of an electronic text?

The curious history of language in its relation to electronic media enters into critical consideration here. That history involves a basic split between the logical language used to interface human communication with machine function and the analysis/interpretation of "natural," data-rich language by the machine. In each case, the concept of what constitutes "information" is subject to different constraints and limitations or meets different kinds of problems in machine processing. The development of logical languages progressed as programming languages proliferated after the mid-twentieth century, spawning a veritable Babel of dialects for specialized purposes. But such "languages" are more mathematical than linguistic: highly constrained and specific, basically aiming to eliminate ambiguity, nuance, or variable interpretation. Meanwhile, natural language reached certain impasses in its relation to computers: early (1960s) optimism about the capacity to parse natural grammar into machine-readable and machine-usable forms foundered on the problem of the context-dependent character of linguistic meaning.[3] The two trajectories by which language and machine interact remain fundamentally at odds, splitting along the line that divides two belief systems (top-down programming or bottom-up data processing) on which rival concepts of artificial intelligence came to be based.[4] Current debates about whether *either* a logical *or* a data-rich system of representation adequately mirrors *thought* (basic cognitive processes) continue to test their positions in and through functions of language(s).[5] But this leaves open the question of how aesthetics and form function as components of meaning. Therefore, I suggest that in addition to logical and natural language, we consider *configured* language (that is, language in documents where format, graphical organization, or other structural relations contribute substantively to textuality) in the electronic context. The properties of configured language are not the same as either an algorithmically programmable statement with its logical, mathematical premises, or the replete, complex, context-dependent, mutable utterances of natural language familiar from daily usage. Configured meaning is an aesthetic, structural, and substantive part of linguistic form. Consideration of configured meaning (in which configuration is taken to be part of textual information) allows us to revive the philosophical inquiry into the relation between sense and form. This can be explored initially in the interrogation of the identity of the letter, and then at the level of text, document, and archive. The exploration always asks how the visual forms of language inform the production of meaning in the electronic environment, and, in turn, how the apparently "immaterial" text of the electronic domain offers the possibility to interrogate the fundamentals of "ideality" of sense in relation to visual, graphical form through an examination of configured meaning at the level of the text.[6]

The Identity of Letters as Forms

The process by which any text can become stripped of its materiality as it enters the electronic environment is readily illustrated. Imagine the dilemma of the archivist or librarian deciding on the appropriate mode for storage of a handwritten work or a printed document that has as much visual information as it has textual information.[7] The document can be saved as a text file, such as an ASCII file, in which the sequence of strokes on a keyboard will be all that is left of the visual information of the original document as it becomes a bare record of linguistic fact. The other choice is to save the document as an image, a picture of the document itself—at much greater cost, with much greater memory requirement, and without benefit of access through text-based search engines. The question of what is lost (and gained) in the process of turning a text into the stripped-down, letter-by-letter-only form of an ASCII file immediately calls attention to the rich materiality of visual information that is an aspect of *any* text file. This is now familiar territory in the work of bibliographers, literary critics, and poets who pay attention to "materiality" in the production of textual meaning.[8]

For a specific example, one has only to think of turning the Pythagorean "Y" and its emblematic visual symbolism into the keyboard stroke for the letter to realize how much "meaning" is lost in the translation. In the version designed by the Renaissance typographer and printer Geofroy Tory, this "Y" (fig. 1) contains considerable "extra" visual information to make its metaphoric moral point about the choice between the difficult path of virtue and the easy path of vice. In such an extreme case, the loss of "information" is not purely textual, but the spectrum that stretches from this example through the full gamut of illuminated and engraved letters to display faces, fancy script fonts, and utilitarian-seeming (but nonetheless historically specific) type designs is a continuous one. The question of the point at which such "visual" information is fully contained within the "textual" is moot if one realizes that any transformation of the material form of a written document alters and often diminishes the actual information in a piece. The crucial question is which aspects of information are lost in the encoding—and whether they merely need a higher level of code or programming in order to be recorded, or whether the very process of transformation from material to immaterial condition is an intervention in the ontological identity of a text.

To frame the argument, I want to return to the questions of the letter and its relation to a "body" or a form through the concerns faced by practitioners in trying to understand what a letter *is* so that it can be translated into electronic form. In the late 1970s and early 1980s, the mathematician Donald Knuth attempted to make a program for the alphabet.[9] This immediately brought him up against the heart of the problem: Is there an algorithm specific to each letter of the alphabet such that any and every instance of that letter conforms to and is describable by that algorithm?[10] Or are letters merely elements of a set which only have to be distinguishable from one another? In the first case, the assumption is that the form of a letter is part of

Figure 1. Geofroy Tory, Pythagorean "Y," in *Champ Fleury* (1529, Paris).

its identity (as noted above, it *has* a body). In the second, the assumption is that a letter may take any form as long as it can be recognized within a finite set of other symbols (it *needs* a body to distinguish it from the twenty-five or fifty-one other letters, plus numerals and signs of punctuation). The either/or nature of this distinction—the idea of a letter's essence being describable as a mathematical formula which always and only results in a form of that letter or, by contrast, the idea of a letter as a mere place-holder whose form is utterly without significance—gets blurred in the nuancing of the nature of the set that is comprised by all letters. This is, as Douglas Hofstadter describes it, not a fixed, closed set but an open set, one in which every and any instance of occurrence adds to the set without distorting its defining parameters.[11] (He compares the letters to chairs as a set: they are not describable in a single, highly constrained, and specific mathematical formula, but nonetheless, they are distinguishable from other items of furniture by definite characteristics, and every instance of new chair-ness simply expands the set to include new members.) This elasticity confounds the reductive requirement of the algorithmic identity. To a common-sense perception, letters *seem* to have an essential form that would lend itself to an algorithmic description. But in actuality, the means by which we regularly read/process their forms are system-dependent, relying on convention, and not inherent.

Knuth's dilemma becomes even clearer when the problems of generating letterforms are contrasted with those of recognizing letterforms. Programs for optical character recognition (OCR) have to assess the symbol set, either according to primary characteristics (the basic-what-to-look-for of a crossbar, number of loops, ascender/descender characteristics used in sorting any set of symbols by distinctive visual features) or by making a match between the number of elements (whatever they are) and the number of letters/symbols in the notational system. By probability, distribution, and other statistical phenomena, the program attempts a one-to-one match and translation.

The practical dilemmas faced by designers (and technicians) in the display of letterforms within the electronic environment also touch on these issues. If a letter were in fact fundamentally algorithmic, its shape and distinctive graphical features could be prescribed as variations on a single formula. In scalable, multi-sized fonts, letters *are* described as objects. That is, they are stored as a set of instructions about shape, form, openings, and closings—as complex images whose patterns of line are recorded in mathematical descriptions as curves, straight lines, or connections among points on a bezier curve or a grid. This "object" can be treated in many ways—sloped, thickened, stretched—without losing the fineness of resolution essential to communicating its form. But fundamental, geometric form is not reducible to an *essential, prescriptive* algorithm, though it can be stored as one that is *nonessential* and *descriptive.* The latter algorithm does not constitute the *identity* of the letter, but it creates an adequate description of a designer's drawn pathways, vectors, and shapes as visual information.[12]

Letterforms can also be described and displayed as patterns of pixels, or screen lines, and then output as points in a grid or as the start/stop of raster

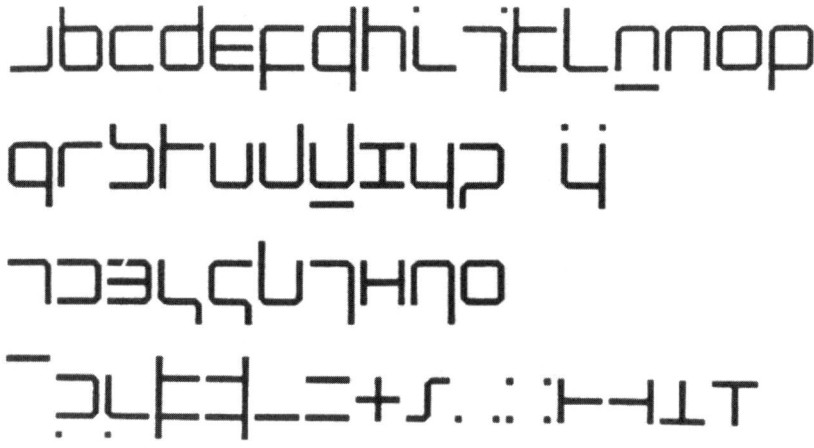

Figure 2. Wim Crouwel's "New Alphabet" (1967, Utrecht). (Courtesy of Crouwel)

lines. Display modes (whether on-screen or as output) that use this approach merely map a shape (the metaphor is of a hooked rug or needlework tapestry in which the fineness of resolution depends on the fineness of the screen or scrim pattern). No information about the way the image is arrived at is stored — merely the shape it makes. The letter is not an "object"; it is only a footprint in the grid.[13] In this approach, no attempt has been made to construe the "identity" of the letter; there is no "inherent" form, merely a drawn pattern.

The technical requirements of screen displays (and early, low-resolution output devices) are such that the question arose of the *essence* of each letter as a shape. In a font like the machine-friendly "New Alphabet" designed by Wim Crouwel in 1967, the identity of the letters resides as much in their distinction from one another as in their continuity of letterform traditions. (One has only to isolate one or two of the characters from the others to realize the extent to which recognition depends on the set; see fig. 2.) The issue of *essence* comes to the fore when low-resolution or reductive display mechanisms require compromises in the conventional forms of letters. The question of whether the *A*-ness of the *A* resides in its capacity to be differentiated from the *B* or in some inherent property recognizable in a crude pattern of "jaggy" pixels is cast as a very practical one.

As letterforms have evolved and proliferated in the era of electronic type design, liberties with conventions have been taken to new extremes. Freed from the requirement of arduous, tedious, and expensive cutting of steel punches, type can be designed on the screen to function in the electronic environment or to be output photographically. The chimerical search for an inherent form of the letter proved elusive, a holy grail of a pseudo-mystical belief in essences, a sometimes too persistent remnant of the kabbalistic tendency to ascribe cosmic, universal values to the alphabetic code. But in a sense, this realization only revives the question of materiality with a vengeance: it is in the inscription of letters into forms, shapes, in accord with the whims and styles of a historical and cultural moment, that allows them to realize what might be termed the *affective massage coefficient of form*. That is the property whereby the graphical and visual properties inflect the text with a meaning that is not separate from its linguistic content, nor exactly proper to it, but interpenetrated with the text itself as its fundamental expression (thus the "massage" of meaning, a bending, flexing, of its "message").

Configured Texts: Historical Precedents and Electronic Possibilities

At the secondary and tertiary levels of organization (above the letter, at the level of text and the document), language contains information as format, using spatial arrangements as a way of constituting meaning. A familiar example is the outline form, in which headings, subheads, and sub-subheads demarcate a discourse into conceptual spaces and territories. Elaborately structured descriptive systems of cosmological breadth and ambition developed graphical form in the Middle Ages and blossomed in the Renaissance work of such ambitious polymath scholars as Athanasius Kircher and Bishop John Wilkins. Wilkins's monumental *Essay towards a Real Character and Philosophical Language* (1668) includes a full outline of all aspects of the universe—part of his scheme to represent all of knowledge/the world (in his work, collapsed without argument) in a corresponding system of notation. Throughout Kircher's many volumes, his hierarchical diagrams chart the structure of a full cosmology in graphic form (fig. 3). This may sound quaint and recall ideas that stretch back into antiquity and link language and knowledge in a guaranteed system (whether according to an atomistic logic or adamic naming), but those elaborately "configured" visualizations of the order of things, of knowledge, and of calculable relations possess a sense of the potential for communicating complex hierarchies of information through graphic form. At the moment at which Kircher (at the end of his long career) and Wilkins (at the start) overlap—the 1660s—the late medieval tendency to diagrammatic exhaustive detail combined with a

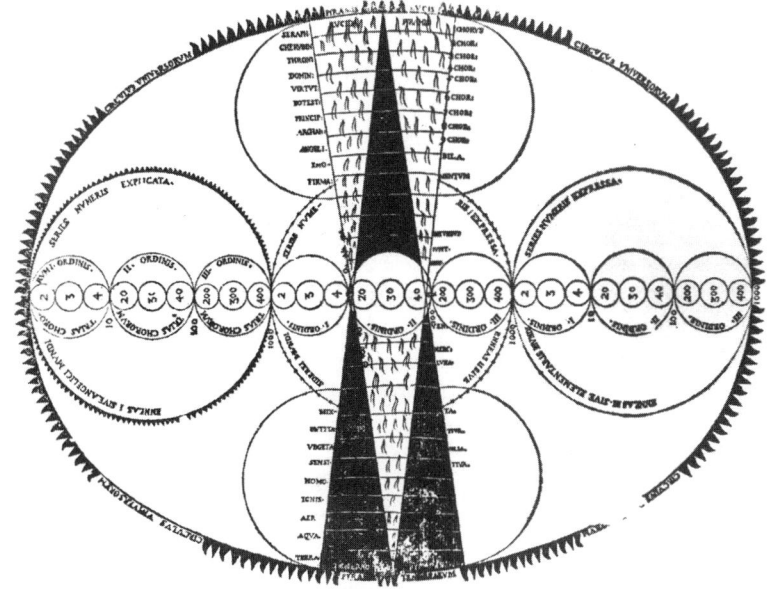

Figure 3. Athanasius Kircher, the three worlds, from *Musurgia Universalis* (angelic, sidereal, and elemental worlds in a hierarchy from top to bottom) (1650, Rome).

modern schematic system of categorization. The visual domain, particularly the graphical domain of print production, permitted elaborate pictorial realizations of knowledge as system in which format was clearly articulated as the substance, not merely the display, of information.

This relational, structural, aspect of materiality uses spatial relations as *significant,* as part of meaning. The old memory theaters, also devised in antiquity and perfected in conceptual and practical terms in the Renaissance, serve as another instance of intertwining meaning and spatialized relations. Such theaters used mental images of specific architectural spaces as a mnemonic structure, enabling elaborate recall of objects or information "placed" in them. In these systems, "space" is meant as something schematic, metaphoric, and abstract simultaneously. Relations among linguistic components can be mapped in a variety of ways which build on the conventions of spatialized organization: hierarchically in an outline, in tree diagrams, in grids, in various indexed charts, in two-dimensional graphs, or according to an iconographic or pictorial form (as in the case of certain concrete poems using shape to contribute to meaning), and spatially according to the descriptive coordinates of solid geometry (with a fourth dimension in electronic media). When these concepts of schematicization and spatialization intersect with electronic media, they can expand into the multidimensional structures available in hypertext and Internet architecture. The challenge is to make spatial organization clear enough—logically, conceptually, metaphorically, and visually—for it to be useful rather than confusing. Positing the value of this graphical quality forces the issue of the information of configured texts.

As a text is put into binary code storage or made into an element of a software program, should its typeface, style, and format be encoded as well? This question was answered in the negative by the original designers of HTML (hypertext markup language), the design software used to give graphical expression to texts, images, and websites. In effect, the decision that was made was that typography was *not information* in any *fundamental* sense. This decision was made for practical reasons: if, hypothetically, a text had to be capable of being displayed on any platform, system, or monitor, and if the HTML file had to be readable by any browser, then including the specific information of a typeface would restrict readability (the machine/browser/platform might not have that typeface) or would make the files too large to transport efficiently (they would have to contain the typeface, raising problems of copyright and sales control as well as file size). Recent moves to rethink this decision by modifying the capability of HTML (through development of DHTML, or Dynamic-HTML) and by including what are known as "cascading style sheets" (style sheets encoding typographic and format preferences for a file that are made available when the browser has the capability) have begun to redress this oversight. But the advantage of the "oversight" was to call attention to the dramatic significance that attaches to the material information included in type and format decisions in a document—whether designed in the electronic environment or merely stored there.

Whether any or all objects of thought can be reduced to a mathematical "configuration" as their ultimate and essential form is open to debate and speculation in mystical to mechanical modes. But it seems inarguable that configuration factors into the effective production of substantive linguistic meaning in electronic documents, as in print documents. The specific character of those factors is different in electronic media than in print media because of the presence of the additional factors of temporal, spatial, and linked manipulations. The dynamic capacity of display modes and the mutable nature of all files and browsers suggest a continual reconfiguration of most files in their reading and display, rather than a final, fixed, and static format. In either case—static/fixed or dynamic/mutable—configured information is meaning and contributes substantively to the "message" of the text.

Certain print conventions are readily adapted to electronic formats—for example, the now familiar form of the "front page" of a website or on-line document follows print conventions. The graphical form is essentially flat; the reading space is framed by the monitor as a "page"; and the links within a document are opened by clicking highlighted text. But once one moves beyond this graphical convention into spatialized modes of display, or confronts the difficulty involved in giving a visual gestalt to the interrelated documents of a complex archive, the electronic environment reveals its limits and potential simultaneously. Obviously, the absence of conventions not yet established is a limitation to "navigation"; the problem of "mapping" a course through linked archives (within a site/document/set of files or to outside sites) has yet to be given graphical form or consideration. Within a site—even within a document—there is the possibility of drawing on visual conventions such as mapping, perspectival schematically rendered space (in VRML or other spatial design programs), or drawing on a visual schematic that gives a graphical form to the hierarchical compartmentalization and interrelations of elements. The challenge of designing information interfaces that are at once intuitive, conventional, and adaptable to the dynamic activity of electronic materials tends to push designers either toward "cute" conventions—windows, doorways, desk drawers—or toward minimal but functional solutions (the "button" and highlighted text). The exploration of the configured text is in its infancy in this regard, though the interrelation between information architecture and user interface will become increasingly sophisticated as capacities evolve for representing conceptualizations within these structural modes.

The notion of configured text has been explored in a preliminary manner in the work of a number of poets for whom the electronic medium offers new possibilities of using a configured format. Works by Loss Pequeño Glazier and Jim Rosenberg give a concrete sense of this potential, while Charles Bernstein's work *Veil* illumines the translation between print and electronic media in an exploration of the distinctive properties of each.[14]

Both Glazier and Rosenberg make use of the screen as a "flat" space of display. In this regard, both observe certain print media conventions: the plane of reading is more or less perpendicular to the line of sight, and the type lies on that plane without dimensional distortion. Both, however, make use of the dynamic properties of the electronic medium. Glazier's work has a self-regulated rate of display. "Command: Change Folder" (1996), for instance, is a poem self-referentially concerned with the electronic document (fig. 4). As it loads on the screen, it scrolls down. The timing of the screen's rewriting and the timing of the poem's display are the same. Once into the second "verse" or section of the work, a screen appears in which there is an alternating sequence of words and phrases. These are dispersed in constellationary format, so that the words which appear in alternating intervals fill in the blank spaces, transforming the text in an on/off

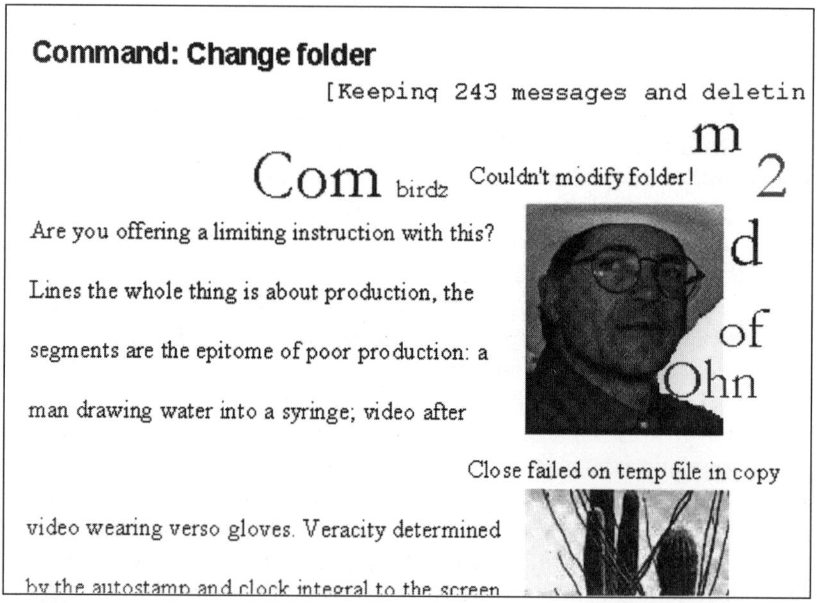

Figure 4. Loss Pequeño Glazier, "Command: Change Folder" (1996, Buffalo, N.Y.), a static image of a dynamic configuration. (Courtesy of Glazier)

binarism of linguistic production which takes full advantage of electronic dynamics and textual conventions. The text is configured spatially as well as temporally, and the material properties of a static text are either extended or subverted (depending on one's point of view) by this activity. Into the open holes of one text appears another which transforms the whole in a blinking alternation. It is the "immaterial" unfixedness of the text that allows its full configuration to be dispersed over a temporal axis. There is no single static state in the phenomenological perception of the work, though the ontological condition of the programmed GIF (graphical interchange format) files is also stable. Configuration is structured within the text display through a temporal articulation uniquely suited to work in the electronic environment.

Jim Rosenberg's work layers texts in hypercard stacks, one of the basic building blocks of nonlinear text models in electronic documents. The apparent layering, which makes the texts cancel one another in a dense palimpsest, can be undone, pulled apart, by the reader/viewer. Each successive layer of "Intergrams" (1993) can be selected independently, or it can be displayed in a mode of replete simultaneity (fig. 5).[15] Rosenberg's schematic diagrams of relations among text elements are key to his work. The

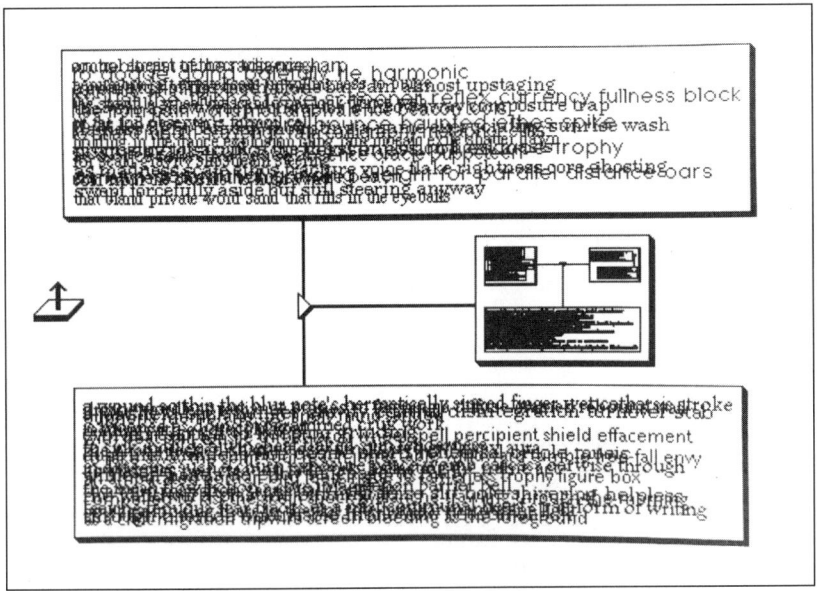

Figure 5. Jim Rosenberg, from "Intergrams" (1993, Watertown, Mass.). (Courtesy of Rosenberg)

visual configuration of the text *is* the text; its graphical organization and layout parse its conceptual and linguistic structure. One could debate the effectiveness of this structuring, but the usefulness of such a process in the interlocking of elaborate archives or documents would function informatively in the same way as flow charts, engineering diagrams, or other specific schemata for structuring relations among elements of a system. Although such infrastructure is evidently substantive, it is not, strictly speaking, linguistic. The relations *among* linguistic elements, however, do determine sense to a very real degree. Just as sequence determines meaning in English sentences ("Jane bit the dog." vs. "The dog bit Jane."), an expansion to other dimensions of relational possibilities factors into linguistic meaning production in ways that are not necessarily fully capable of being translated. Still, reading a table, a chart, or a graph requires that *position* and *sequence* be granted their full force of signification. Rosenberg's poetic works point toward the creative exploration of these dimensions of configured text, pushing structure to the foreground with insistence on its semantic contribution.

Charles Bernstein's two versions of his work *Veil,* produced in 1976, first published in print form in 1987 (Xexoxial Editions), and in electronic format in 1996, offer a useful contrast between two modes of materiality.[16] The printed *Veil* is a typewriter poem, produced on an IBM Selectric, in which overprinting line after line creates a scrim or screen effect of language which renders the text almost illegible (fig. 6). Like Rosenberg's "Intergrams" in their simultaneous mode of display, *Veil* is nearly illegible in print form. But this illegibility is the point of the text: its porosity permits scraps of meaning to surface through the dense field of letters, the fine mesh of its own self-produced screen *veil*ing the linguistic transparency of language with the effects of a layered text. The materiality of print form is inherent in the visual and verbal value of the work; they interpenetrate in a dialogic synthesis, the two aspects of the *writing*—visual and verbal—playing equal parts in the production of the whole.

In transposing *Veil* into an electronic format, Bernstein modified the text and the visual production (fig. 7). The layered effects on the screen take advantage of the possibility for bleed-through rather than cancellation. Where the letters in the printed *Veil* are always fully and entirely present, each layering upon the next in an irrefutable maximization of information, the letters and blocks of texts in the electronic version merge. For each point on the screen there is a final value in the gray scale of the image's display, which is in some cases an average on account of overlap. Unusual effects are produced that would not occur in a print environment, such as the lightening of an area where a letter makes a light opening in a dark field rather than closing or covering another. There is, in some sense, more transparency in this *Veil* than in the other, but the texts no longer retain their replete autonomy. Even if they are unrecoverable, unreadable, in the printed *Veil,* they are fully present in some ontological sense. In the electronic *Veil,* this is not the case. There is a history of placement/displacement in the layering of one block of electronic text after another; one can discern the "top" frame by the fact that its autonomy is not disturbed by intruding texts. In a page-description language, this history might be encoded. In a GIF or TIFF file, it is completely lost. The immaterial substrate, a mere display of code, has eliminated the production history and process, thus configuring a loss of information as its imaged form. This is a new *Veil*—the screen between production and display, between a history of production and its immaterial encoding, between a text-as-image and the graphical end result of a series of now fully absent manipulations whose trace is the result but which are not recorded in the material of the text. The palimpsest is both real and illusory. In the immaterial condition, it lacks all recoverable dimensionality. The text is configured as patterns, not object (in direct contrast to Glazier and Rosenberg), creating a veil which screens and filters the linguistic sense through immaterial means. What is the "essence" of the language in this

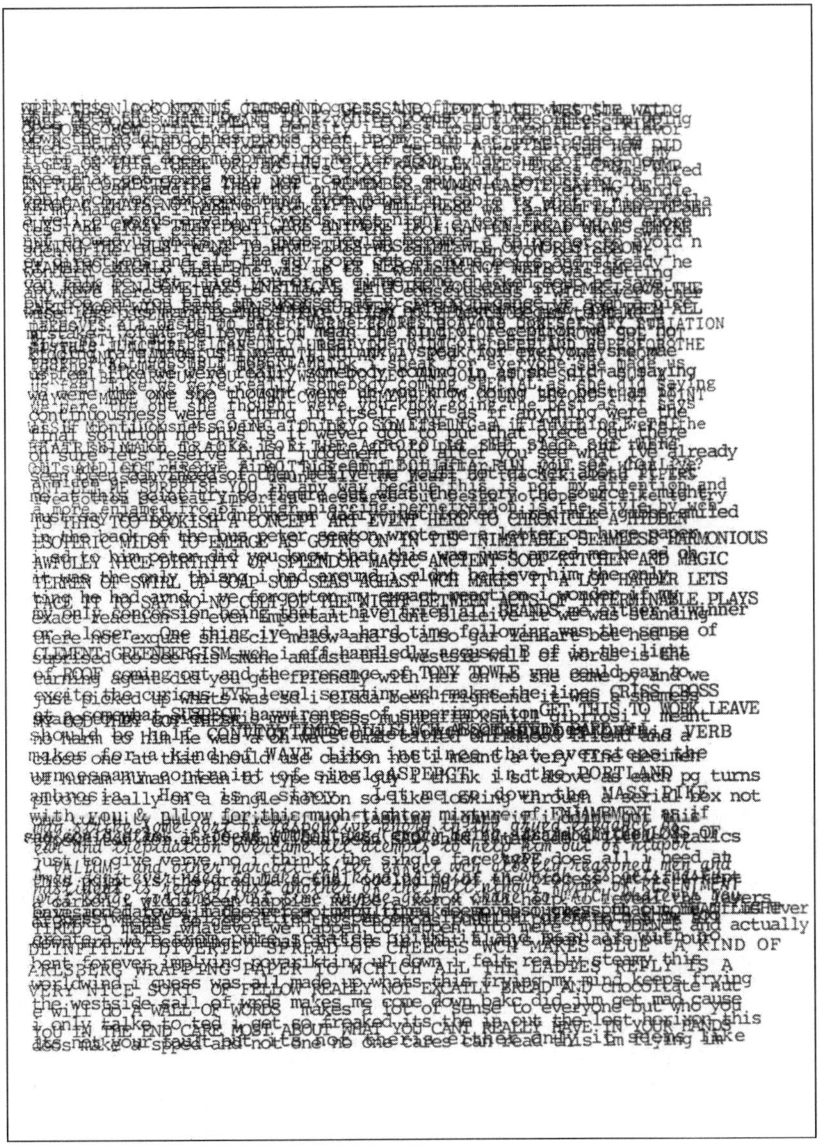

Figure 6. Charles Bernstein, from *Veil* (1976; Xexoxial Editions, 1987, Madison, Wis.), print version from typewriter script. (Courtesy of Bernstein)

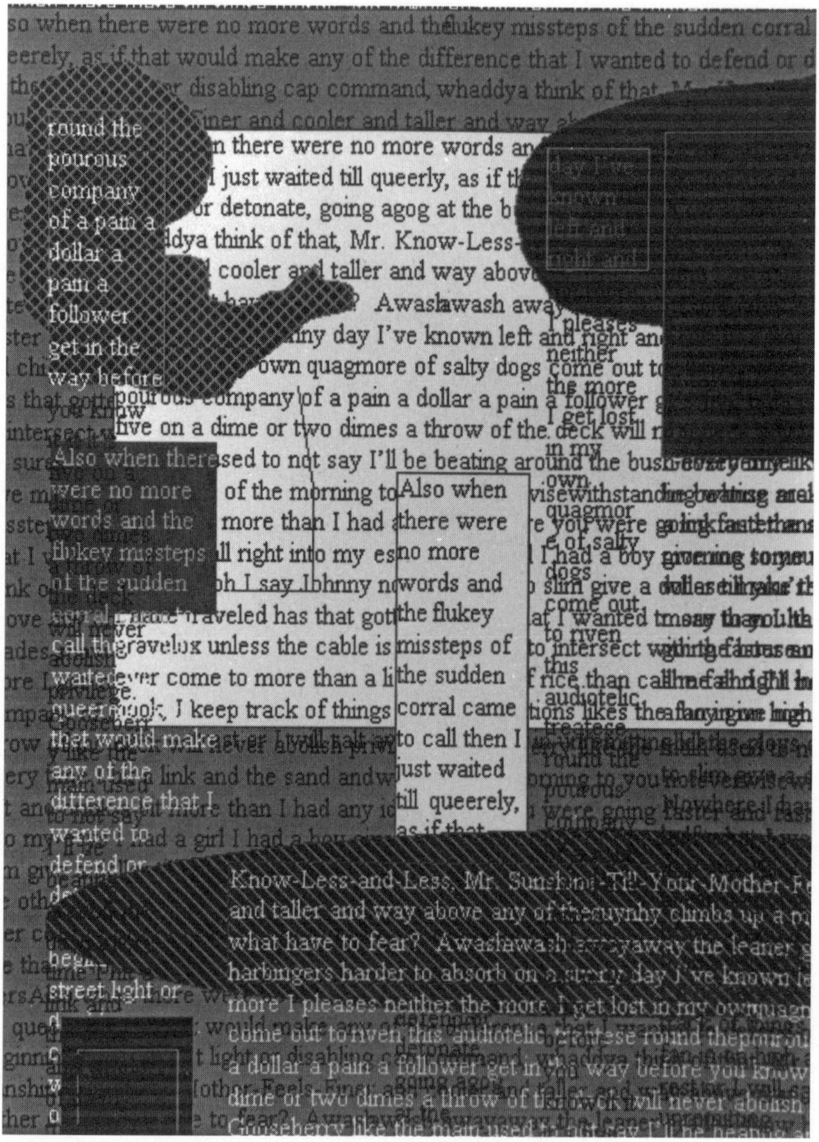

Figure 7. Charles Bernstein, from *Veil* (1996, Buffalo, N.Y.), on-line version. (Courtesy of Bernstein)

case: its lost or unrecoverable form, its inherent but unreadable meaning, or its newly configured form as visual effect?

The challenge of three-dimensional display modes introduces a problem of legibility, in that the visual distortion of typographic form is ill suited to the eye trained to recognize the shapes of letters on a page. The manipulations, though interesting as graphical effects, seem to struggle for effect at the expense of increased meaning value. So much programming is required to manipulate the texts as dimensional forms that most modeled "virtual" poems (e.g., the holograms of Eduardo Kac or the entropic works of Ladislao Pablo Györgi[17]) are still more intriguing as novelties than as poetic works. However, the idea of a schematic "topography" as elaborate as a clinical storage cabinet or a detailed map—or an architectural diagram for a highly organized series of spaces—seems a more promising possibility for graphical schemata for virtual documents and archives than is the dimensional modeling of letterforms and text. VRML models of spatialized imagery have potential as models of archival storage and structure because they offer complex organization in a visual form that is sufficiently familiar to be navigated intuitively while taking advantage of the way space can be read as logical order. Such spaces need not be simply schematic or sterile; the detailed topography of surface maps or dimensional models can be rendered lucid by following familiar pictorial conventions.

The question of whether a letter's identity is an essential or differential attribute of its form, and the question of configured graphical meaning, are not the same as the question of "ideality" of meaning in a linguistic text (the arbitrary nature of the linguistic sign is a long-resolved issue, and assessing the "form" of a linguistic sign in relation to the notion of transcendent meaning is not the same as assessing the inherent form of a visual alphabetic symbol). But all these questions are concerned with the functional link between form as it appears to cognitive consciousness and the "sense" produced in grasping that form. The "configured" logic of thought is not a priori, or anterior to the formation of symbols, but is made in the process of their being inscribed in consciousness as forms. The twentieth-century philosophical extension of inquiries into the logical potential of language initiated in Gottfried Leibniz's search for a "calculus of thought" continues the investigation wherein logical, mathematical formulation tends to be conceived of as closer to an "ideal" than is quotidian language with its ambiguous, subjective character. Although the "ideal" objects of mathematics are obviously different from the imprecise and culturally dependent objects of language, at the level of *sense* the same questions can be asked of each. How is sense *form* in some fundamental way, such that an idea is grasped in form-as-sense in cognitive terms? Configured meaning draws both on ideal mathematical form and on contextualized cultural elements of language because it is precise (as structure) but impure (not readily translated into either binary code or computer program language). A quick history of natural and machine languages in the electronic environment will help to explain this combination of properties.

Language(s) in the Electronic Environment

In electronic media, "language" has evolved along two distinct trajectories with overlapping agendas, and neither has taken into account the way graphical configuration factors into the production of linguistic meaning. These trajectories are, first, the evolution of highly constrained, rule-bound, and logical forms of "language" which are instructions readily translatable into machine code (logical statements which ultimately can be stored as binary signals), and, second, the attempt to make machines understand "natural" language. In the history of computational devices, the leap from gears connected to cogs and axles (the basis of Blaise Pascal's calculating device) to sequences of interconnected switches would have had very little impact were it not for two things: the possibility of logic, using "natural" language in constrained form to function as a set of precise instructions translatable into mathematical equivalents; and the possibility of encoding these mathematical equivalents in a binary form corresponding to the fundamental on/off of current in an electrical gate/synapse/circuit. Curiously, both of these lend themselves to configurable form—to representation in the diagrammatic languages of logical statements, themselves largely translatable into the visual schemata of set theory diagrams (the familiar Venn diagrams). The fundamental terms of logical constraint—commands such as AND, OR, NOT, NAND, and NOR—can be visualized. Their elaboration into more complex sets of instructions quickly moves the logical configuration of the program out of the realm of any practically realizable visualization—but only in practice, not in theory.

The linguistic properties of the lineage stretching from Gottfried Leibniz in the eighteenth century to George Boole in the nineteenth and Gottlob Frege and Rudolf Carnap in the twentieth provided a means whereby linguistic terms could be made compatible with computational acts, and even their basis. It was this basic rule-boundedness that allowed Alan Turing and John von Neumann to interlink the concepts of "reasoning calculus" with that of the "automata" of computational machines, as Turing realized that logical/mathematical symbols could be made to represent any kind of information through the effect of translation into machine code. This, of course, is the key. In computer programming, ultimately *all* computer languages have to translate into machine language, binary sequences that give specific instructions to data stored in various address locations to perform particular tasks in a particular sequence.[18] Even a quick reading of a line of machine language shows how little these strings resemble "language" as we know it, and this is just the point. Machine language, computer language, and programming languages are all able to contain information—to function as a descriptive metalanguage that is not information, but rather a highly constrained and specific means to encode it outside of material form.

Natural language and the parsing of syntax resist the algorithmic and logical translation. The first peak of enthusiasm for the project of a direct interface between natural language and computers occurred in the late 1960s and early 1970s. Noam Chomsky and a generation of structural linguists working in computer science, information science, and linguistics proper struggled to discover rules of syntactic and semantic functioning which could, in turn, be programmed into a machine. Since these rules were necessarily simple enough that a child could learn them, the rules of language must be able to be systematically described and understood. The deceptive simplicity of the problem turned out to conceal pitfalls and conceptual flaws so profound that they could not be overcome. It became apparent that the "sense" of a simple English sentence relied to a great extent on the experiential database of the speaker. The resources of linguistic computing were inadequate to solve the problem of programming comprehension as a set of algorithms—a set of procedures that could be carried out without any information beyond what was needed to perform the operations in a procedural sense. Was this attempt to analyze natural language foundering merely because it required too much in the refinement of a programming apparatus? Were the crudeness of result and the impasse reached in these early struggles merely a result of the conceptual jags in a model too gross to imitate so complex a process? Ongoing experiments in this area take as a point of departure the premise that a sufficient exposure to language will eventually create the context necessary for comprehension—a rich, replete verbal field. In the interim, however, we are left with the philosophical issue that natural language is not merely machine-incompatible, but also that basic properties of syntax which operate within natural language cannot be translated into fully logical principles.[19]

Code, Immateriality, and Configuration

When we consider language in the electronic environment, it becomes evident that, in one sense, the assumption that the electronic environment and the condition of pure, binary code are themselves "immaterial" is false. There is an apparent paradox, which Matthew Kirschenbaum has described as that between the "phenomenological materiality" of the text and the "ontological immateriality" of its existence.[20] We perceive the visual form of the letter on the screen as fully material—replete with characteristics, font specifications, scale, and even color—even though the "letter" exists as a stored sequence of binary digits with no tactile, material apparency to it in that fundamental condition. The paradox can be inverted as well: electronic current, hardware, and the support systems of the code are materially more complex than any pen and pencil on paper. And even at a fundamental level, the nature of code is not immaterial; it functions as a temporarily fixed and infinitely mutable binary sequence which must and always does refer to place within the structure of the machine to allow the program or protocol to operate. "Code" always contains a stored electronic sequence that includes the address of any particular piece of information. Thus, the binary sequence, the ultimate "difference" that constitutes the identity of any data in code storage, is also always topographic, place-specific, sited, and therefore a location within the mapped territory of the machine's circuit/real estate. Or, to cite the historian of computer science René Moreau, "No item of information can have any existence in the machine unless there is some device in which its physical representation can be held."[21] Code is material, and its materiality has implications at the most basic level of the inscription of that difference for a notion of *configuration as information*. Though not inherently or specifically visual in and of itself, this "configured" condition *is* fundamentally *visualizable*. Both binary sequence and the topographic location of code storage/machine address are representable in diagrammatic form as images, maps, or locations.

What does this mean? On a fundamental, binary level, code is linked to configuration—literally, schematically, and metaphorically. Whether it is organized into computer language, or controlling protocol, describing the paths of data gates, of logical circuits, or schematizing set theory from instructions and constraints in programs, the configured character of electronic information is fundamental to its identity at this most basic ontological and functional level. But this realization immediately raises another set of questions: To what extent can such "forms" (visual and graphical in their manifestation, mathematical and electronic in their ontology) be "read" as sense? At what point does the relation between form and sense get formulated? Where does "form" emerge and come into "sense" in the most basic operation of machine process, and how does this relate to the human cognitive process in which such forms are originally conceived? The electronic condition of form seems to return immediately to these fundamental and original questions. The very idea that one might get at the essence of form, at the essence of meaning in some mathematical/configured sense, and thus to the basis of cognition/thought as mathematics is part of the mystique of the electronic environment. Metaphors of brain and computer similarity, of the mind as machine, and of thought as a programmable set of algorithms or as a product of neural networks processing data all inspire immediate fantasies. But under the sci-fi and popular culture imaginings that spring from this source is a philosophical issue that can be approached more seriously. Jacques Derrida's reading of Edmund Husserl's *Origin of Geometry* addresses the essential question of how form—particularly "ideal," mathematical form, in the instance of the "first" geometer—arises to cognition, and then establishes the basis on which the possibility of historicity can be premised. The problem of form coming into sense within cognition is the area in which the issue of configured meaning first arises (if "first" is thought of as necessary to what follows rather than primary or temporally precedent).

It is useful to backtrack into classical philosophy for a platform on which to consider this problem. Aristotle's description of "sense" was linked to form. He suggested that form was what allowed "sense" to be grasped, to be perceptible to sentience. There might be any number of things—from sensations to objects to stuff in the world—that did not find their way into form. But these were merely, de facto, whatever was not graspable as form; this "other" to form was not chaos, void, nothingness, or some other stigmatized *informe*. Aristotle's concern was with what made "sense" possible to human consciousness, and that was the "coming into form" of that sense. And this was the point at which it could be understood, at which there was "sense" and cognitive intelligibility. Husserl focused on those forms that, by their "ideality," exist independent of human cognition (geometric and mathematical forms, in his essay, are the exemplary and perhaps unique instance). Yet his consideration of their "ideal" existence, in contradiction to the Platonic tradition, has no particular meaning or value until it is grasped by human consciousness—the mythic "first geometer"—in such a way that this understanding can then be communicated. The ideal condition of being of a mathematical form poses a problem: Where does the form exist? Rejecting the idea of its residing in a spiritual mind (theologically or otherwise conceived), Husserl is intent on the problem of the way an ideal form appears to consciousness, as *ideal,* and as *specific,* and as a *form.* How is its ideality recognized? How is its form grasped, understood, and then communicated? In the case of geometry, this takes into account both the independence of the form from human cognition and its interdependence with cognitive apperception. Language, of course, raises other questions because the "ideal" aspects of its forms are less apparent.

In a footnote in the introduction to *The Origin of Geometry,* Husserl raises the question of whether mathematical form can be taken to be exceptional, or whether it is instead the actual condition of *all* form at some fundamental level.[22] This note opens the loophole through which the electronic configuration of information as meaning enters. For if the sensible forms that appear to consciousness are in some (however metaphoric) sense actually *forms*—configurable, mathematical, and specific—and if it is as forms that they provide the basis of sense, then are the forms in which electronic configurations occur "readable" and intelligible? And does the interchange between "code" and the topographically configured form of storage translate into an essential or a differential form?

It is perhaps a mistake, but at least an interestingly suggestive one, to conflate the notions of an "originary" grasping of sense—that which occurs as idea comes into form, inscribing a form through the process of *différance,* the differentiating that allows form to become specific—and of the initial inscription into code of the binary processes of electronic memory. It is equally facile to map the notion of "form" as a configured shape (mathematical and visual) onto the notion of the "topography" of the machine's physical structure. Nonetheless, making these connections at least allows a metalanguage of the code to emerge as a possibility. Eschewing any ultimate metaphysics, however, seems an important caveat in making these elisions; the "code" should not be read as transcendent, as "ideal," as a set of universal, independent, and autonomous symbols (any more than the alphabet should be construed as the fundamental elements of the cosmos). Rather, the nature of configured meaning within code (again, at the fundamental level of stored, binary sequences) should be read back into the material world in its variously layered interpretations: the first, meta-level of idea coming into being as form and grasped as sense, which I take to be the originary inscription of code; the secondary level, in which form is read as meaning, with all the complexities of iconography, symbolic imagery, and aesthetic inflection; and a third level in which style and specificity engage with ideology, with the specific historical, cultural, and institutional discourses of power.

When meaning is treated as transparent and materiality dismissed in the name of transcendent ideals, then the implications of these historical and cultural discourses are rendered unavailable, their full significance concealed behind dismissal and the characterization of triviality. I would argue, here as before and elsewhere, for the nontriviality of materiality in the visual, graphical information of the text—even (and maybe *especially*) within its (mis)perceived condition as *immaterial* in the electronic environment.[23] The "immaterial" is the gap of transformation, like what used to exist for the typesetter between the reading of a line in memory and its setting into a line of lead type, and what also exists between the material of text and its becoming that of sound, from sound to mind, from eye to voice, from hand to writing; this is also a basic characteristic of the way language *is* information in electronic form. It always precipitates back into material—mutated, trans*formed,* rewrit, as it were. Language is not ever *only* an ideal form. It always exists in some phenomenal form. In many previous works, I have insisted on the value of materiality, but I am also interested in the freedom from fixed relations of materiality. Ultimately, one of the intimations of immateriality is the way it promises to change material form—and, as such, offers possibilities for reconceptualization of language as information in the traditional media as well as in hypertext and electronic formats. The configured features of language seem poised to play an ever more significant role in these formats. From the level of code to that of program languages and then document structures and interfaces, the configured elements have a graphical aspect that contributes to the structured production of linguistic meaning.

Notes

1. Marisa Januzzi deserves credit for these two questions, which she asked following my presentation of a much earlier version of this essay at the meeting of the MLA in Washington, D.C., December 1996, at a panel organized by Mike Groden with Jay Bolter and myself. That version was published in my *Figuring the Word: Essays on Books, Writing, and Visual Poetics* (New York: Granary, 1998), 212–20.

2. If one thinks of an *A* in any mental image, the visual properties may be vague, but the *A*-ness of the letter remains linked, however weakly, to that visual icon and its specific characteristics. In the electronic environment, the letters of any particular keyboarded sequence retain nothing of their iconic value. The search for a font, a now familiar element of the writing task, used to be a specialist choice made by typographers or designers. The increasing familiarity of this task has sensitized a wider public to the implications of typographic style, though not necessarily to the truly peculiar condition of the text without alphabet or without written form which is its code condition.

3. Karen Sparck Jones and Martin Kay's *Linguistics and Information Science* (New York and London: Academic Press, 1973) is an example of the peak period of this sort of research in the field of linguistics; heavily influenced by the work of Noam Chomsky, it reflects the effort to analyze natural language systematically into mechanistic operations.

4. Daniel Crevier's *AI* (New York: Harper Basic Books, 1993) is a useful introduction.

5. "Language(s)" refers to natural and programming languages.

6. The notion of "ideality" of sense that I am invoking here is rooted in Jacques Derrida's reading of Edmund Husserl's *Origin of Geometry*. In using the term "ideality," I am trying to open consideration of the notion that an idea comes into form, becomes available to cognition, and thus participates in meaning production. "Ideality" is the condition of form when it is available to cognition but without materiality. See Jacques Derrida, *Edmund Husserl's "The Origin of Geometry": An Introduction,* trans. John P. Leavey (Lincoln: University of Nebraska Press, 1978 [1962]).

7. The idea for this as an example comes from Howard Besser's presentation at the Mixed Messages conference, University of North Carolina at Charlotte, October 1997, in which he stressed the difficult choices faced by librarians in the preservation of information.

8. Jerome McGann, Marjorie Perloff, Michael Davidson, Susan Howe, Steve McCaffery, John Byrum, Spencer Selby, Thomas Tanselle, Marisa Januzzi, Charles Bernstein, Matthew Kirschenbaum, Nick Piombino, and Rosmarie Waldrop, to name just a crucial few.

9. Donald Knuth, *Text and Metafont* (Bedford, Mass.: American Mathematical Society and Digital Press, 1979). Knuth, or so the possibly apocryphal tale goes, was attempting to resolve problems in typesetting mathematical texts which had made his publication projects prohibitively expensive. In trying to design faces he could use for setting mathematical equations, he quickly encountered the basic issue discussed here.

10. René Moreau, in *The Computer Comes of Age* (Cambridge, Mass.: MIT Press, 1984), defines an algorithm as follows: "A procedure for solving a problem when it came to be expressed as a sequence of statements of operations to be performed and when no knowledge or intelligence is required beyond what is strictly necessary for those operations to be performed" (3).

11. Douglas Hofstadter, *Metamagical Themas* (New York: Basic Books, 1985).

12. Adobe Type Manager and PostScript fonts are "managed" in this way; the various stages of drawing/designing fonts in Fontographer or Font Studio and other design programs use these principles. This still stops short of arriving at a single mathematical formula for an *A* or a *B* that would resemble a formula for a circle, a square, or a triangle of specified angles in which the formula and the "ideal" geometric form are identical, interchangeable, and unique, each containing the distinguishing characteristics of the form. Thanks to Gino Lee for input on this.

13. The word "object" has a specific meaning within computer science in that "object" programs are those in machine language (generally arrived at when "source" programs are "translated"). Thus, the "object" of an object-oriented graphics program contains very different information than does a stored image tapestry. The first is structural, the second merely a pattern.

14. Loss Glazier, "Command: Change Folder" (1996) URL: http://epc.buffalo.edu/authors/glazier/viz/command/command.html; Jim Rosenberg, "Intergrams" (Watertown Mass.: Eastgate Systems, 1993); Charles Bernstein, *Veil* (Madison, Wis.: Xexoxial Editions, 1987), on-line version URL: http://epc.buffalo.edu/authors/Bernstein.

15. Rosenberg, "Intergrams."

16. Bernstein, *Veil*, print and electronic versions.

17. Eduardo Kac, "Holopoetry," and Ladislao Pablo Györgi, "Virtual Poetry," both in *New Media Poetry, Visible Language* 30, no. 2 (1996): 184–213 and 158–163 respectively.

18. Compiled and interpreted languages each organize the relation between commands and data according to distinct specifications, but an assembly language is required to translate program code to the correct machine address so that the data can

be located and the functions performed. Such symbolic assembly languages evolved in the mid-1950s, but it took until the 1960s for higher-level interpreted languages (mainly descended from FORTRAN, which debuted in 1954) to evolve. Compiled languages allow for little intervention in the course of the carrying out of the program. By contrast, interpreted languages are not entirely in machine code—they have a front-end interface that can be manipulated by the user throughout. These higher-level languages allow users to take advantage of interpretive techniques to build the concepts as they go. But all these levels of accessibility are illusory in the sense that they are all equally constrained. If today a high-level language contains a simple "Delete" command, then ten years ago that read as "Execute Command D on Files G, H," and/or something like "del.exe.bat* to *." At that point, the combination of syntactics and mnemonics (that is, sequence and terms) involved is hardly more flexible, even if slightly more user-friendly, than the assembly level (L 3,x, M 2,y, A 3,w, ST 3,2) or the machine level (41 2 OC1A4 3A 2 OC1A8 1A 3 OC1AO and 50 3 OC1 A 4).

19. Library and information science research in this area continues to refine the search engines that make use of natural language syntax in an increasingly good simulation of syntactic understanding, but they still stop a long way short of full linguistic competence in any machine interface. A fictional version of this problem is presented in Richard Powers, *Galatea 2.2* (London: Abacus, 1991).

20. Matthew Kirschenbaum, *Lines for a Virtual T/y/o/pography,* URL: http://www.rch.uky.edu/~mgk/

21. Moreau, *The Computer Comes of Age,* 30.

22. Derrida, *Edmund Husserl's "The Origin of Geometry,"* 27: "whether the mathematical mode is the mode of every objects' constitution."

23. Johanna Drucker, *The Visible Word: Typography and Modern Art Practice* (Chicago: University of Chicago Press, 1994) and *The Alphabetic Labyrinth* (New York and London: Thames and Hudson, 1995).

Charles Bernstein

Response
Every Which Way but Loose

I am writing this sentence in Word for Windows 95: the twelve-point Times New Roman letters are white drop-out against a blue background and when I first typed "blackground" a wavy red line automatically appeared under it until I corrected it with a word found in the Microsoft vocabulary list that comes with the program.

In the book, the one I imagine you to be holding in your hands, the text is printed in black ink on white-like sheets and the light needed to read the letters is coming from above or to the side of the book and is reflected off the opaque surface of the paper.

But is it even the "same" text?

If I chose to put this piece up on the Web (but not without the editors' permission in writing, for which a signed fax would be okay but e-mail would not), the light would come from the back, toward you as you read the text on (or is it off?) the screen. For an HTML version, I would need to make a number of additional decisions. First I would need to choose a background color or image—something few writers have had much choice about in the past five hundred years. If I pick an image—say a blowup of the holograph text of Blake's *Jerusalem*—I risk making my text illegible, or, to put it a different way, risk making my text into an image as I efface the contrast between figure (that is, the text) and ground (that is, the underlying image). As much as I want to tease at the idea of the text melting into an image, I also want each of my words to be identifiable, so I take the image into Photoshop and tone it down, ensuring that the letters I superimpose on it will be readable. Although I am interested in the merging of text and image in HTML, the markup language itself allows for clear differentiation between the two, treating the text as a layer separable from the background. Even if a text is illegible in the browser view, I can copy it and paste it into another field with a neutral background and read it, now without interference (or was it enhancement?). If I want to fuse the text and image I need to make a single graphic file of the layers, "flatten" them is the term of art, but then the text loses many of its unique user-friendly digital features: the reader/viewer can't change the font or size or color, can't copy it and paste it into another document—can't, that is, treat the text as we have come to expect texts to be treatable in an electronic environment. Ironically, converting (or is it translating?) a text into an image file re-creates just the immutability (materiality?) of text that we assumed before the advent of electronic textuality.

The new computer technology—both desktop publishing and electronic publishing—has radically altered the material, specifically visual, presentation of text. It begins to seem as natural to think of composing screen by screen or link by link as page by page. Many text-based works now exist primarily for the screen rather than as transcriptions from another medium. The printed versions of such works might be considered the reproduction and not the other way around, though reciprocity is a better way than hierarchy to understand the relations among textual media.

For the generation now learning to read and write on computers, the medium of writing has radically and inalterably changed in ways that can be called hyperalphabetic if not postalphabetic. The association of picture, font, color, sound, link, and design creates a writing space that is closer to William Blake's or Arakawa and Madeline Gins's or Johanna Drucker's practice than it is to the school notebooks I grew up with. Their primary pictorial feature was the tiny holes I created in the paper from rubbing the eraser too hard in one spot (or maybe from just making the same correction over and over and never getting it right). The ineradicable stubbornness of writing is one of the most powerful qualities of nonelectronic writing media and it is therefore understandable that with the partial eclipse of these media we have come to appreciate this feature of writing more and more.

In her essay in this collection, Drucker explores the implications of the premise that electronic textuality may be a technical realization of what had previously been an idealization of the literary work (for example, in G. Thomas Tanselle's textual theory, as discussed in this book by Morris Eaves) or geometry (for example, in Husserl's philosophy, as discussed by Drucker), because digitalized text appears to exist in a form that is separate from and prior to any given embodiment. Insofar as binary coding produces virtual texts, alphabetic sequences exist in an immaterial form for which any visible manifestation displayed on screen or printed "out" on paper is a second-order phenomenon. After thinking through these textual conditions, Drucker rejects the dematerialization of electronic textuality, pointing to the materiality not only of format and configuration but also of the emplacement of the digital code. The coding is not the antecedent original but an anoriginal source from which multiple versions emerge (to pursue a concept I develop in *Close Listening: Poetry and the Performed Word*).[1]

Drucker's speculations make for some suggestive parallels between analphabetic and postalphabetic language environments. Like oral performance, virtual textuality creates an original material work in each presentation. The computer screen provides a stage for the transformation of texts into works. Writers become language environment designers—textual architects—who need to foresee how the texts they write will be brought to life in particularized enactments. This entails anticipating the inevitable variances made by the different systems on which the work will be displayed. It also allows for creating variants in the configuration of the work; for example, randomizing the sequence of a hypertext so that each time it is viewed it is read in a different order. Moreover, readers can participate in the constitution of the work (and not only in its interpretation) by taking advantage of options for determining the graphic and acoustic environment in which they experience a work and for altering the text of works whose configuration allows for, or indeed mandates, variance.

Electronic textuality is expanding the pool of linguistic signs while at the same time "flattening" the alphabetic into an intensely and undeniably visual medium. In the West, alphabets replaced more icon-heavy writing systems because of their technical efficiency: alphabets utilizing twenty-six or a few more characters replaced writing systems that required memorizing dozens of characters. With electronic textuality, however, icons can once again proliferate because there is almost no limit on the capacity of the computer to unzip (decode, translate) these icons to meet the needs of particular readers (one example of this is the context-sensitive help provided by right-clicking your mouse on an unfamiliar pictogram on your screen). James Sherry recently pointed out to me that in the world of financial computing words are beginning to be characterized as too slow, at least in comparison with the amount of information that can be transmitted with semiotically packed icons. Twenty-five hundred years ago, the verdict was in: the alphabet is swifter than the hieroglyph. In 1999, the reverse appears possibly the case. In *Briggflats,* Basil Bunting laments, "Pens are too light / Take a chisel to write."[2] Is this something we are now in a position to understand? Or is it just another modernist shibboleth, as in pens are not light enough?

In any case, the more disembodied our language environment becomes, the more we may learn to value the materiality of writing. The aura of the prior stages of linguistic production and reproduction increases as each is displaced.

Art media emerge from culture and from the activities of the producers of culture; they are not intrinsic projections of materials or technologies. Pigment and canvas (or cave walls) do not necessitate the invention of painting as an art medium, any more than the alphabet prescribes the emergence of writing as a medium of art.

As a poet interested in the material and social dimension (you might also say social material) of writing, I find many of the most exciting ideas suggested by the new explorers of hypertext well worked out in the radically paratactic explorations of both modernist and contemporary work that have been aversive to the "humanist" ideology dominant within the university and also in the mass media. To be reductive about it: On the level of mass culture, humanist values emphasize mimesis of human presence and conventional modes of "realistic" representation as a means of maximizing the audience for cultural products by maximizing consumer passivity. On the level of high culture, humanist ideology works to maintain control of those free-floating value sectors not determined by market dominance. In this sense, the radical art of the modernist and contemporary periods is both anti–mass consumer art—trying instead to create works that require the active participation and critical reflection of viewers and readers—and anti–high art, critiquing the ideological assumptions and cultural biases behind the valuation of the Great Books, the Core Curriculums, Cultural Literacy, and the like. For this reason, it is fascinating that John Unsworth, in his essay "Electronic Scholarship or, Scholarly Publishing and the Public" devotes so much of his space to a critique of Sven Birkerts as representative of the criticism of scholarly work in the electronic medium.[3] Unsworth underscores Birkerts's fear of the new computer technology as engendering "depersonalization, of inauthenticity, of substitution to the mechanical, and . . . substitution of quantity for quality"—exactly the charges that Birkerts and others typically make against the sort of poetry and art to which I am alluding. Indeed, a version of Birkerts's critique that Unsworth cites was featured in the newsletter of the Associated Writing Programs, the home of the self-styled "anti-theoretical" imaginative writing so much at odds with those poetries that foreground their materiality and social construction. I bring this up as a way of noting that fears associated with computer media, including the often-stated concern about a loss of materiality, are often in the service of an intensively anti-materialist, which is to say idealist, assertion of cultural authority and legitimacy.

In his essay in this volume, Eaves shows that a continuing value of Blake's work is the anxiety it has caused over issues like this, issues we are just now, it sometimes seems, confronting for the first time. Swinburne's book on Blake was instrumental in gaining recognition of Blake's significance and, as a result, preserving his work. But Eaves has another story to tell, one that in many ways brings to mind Harold Bloom's thesis in *The Anxiety of Influence*.[4] For Blake's work is designed to be misread, but its singular value is manifest only when we come to recognize the misreading, albeit with yet another misreading. Eaves's discussion of Blake points to our culture's need to assimilate an artist's work into a well-established art medium: painter or poet but not, as Blake insisted, painter and poet. Swinburne the poet claimed Blake for poetry, inducting him into an insurgent literary tradition at the apparent expense of adequately acknowledging the graphical body of his work. The burden of Swinburne's *Critical Essay* was to associate Blake with Whitman and Baudelaire, and implicitly with Swinburne's own poetry—all aesthetically revolutionary projects marked by a refusal to be absorbed into the norms of the contemporary moral order. Blake's verbo-visual excess is Swinburne's exalted example of a visionary art unconstrained by the shackles of propriety (including the constraints of genre). Yet because Blake's project involves redundancy and contradiction, both within and between the layers of his work, much of the force of his aesthetic is evident even in monodimensional samplings. Nonetheless, the full complexity of his work can be experienced only cross-sectionally—not as a synthesis or flattening of levels but, on the contrary, in the clash of levels. Blake's work is not a singular whole, a totality, but a complex of incommensurable layers.

It has never been easier to find graphical reproductions of Blake's work than now, when they can be downloaded from the Web as JPEG files. These files allow for a viewing that in some ways exceeds what is possible with the originals because of the ability to enlarge small sections of a page in order to see more clearly the ravishing details that comprise these works. In the past, the cost and accuracy of color reproduction limited access to the pictorial dimension of Blake's work, at least in comparison with the ubiquitous text-only dubs. Yet even as these images become more available, they will not replace those textual dubs. For who among us has not secretly read our paperback, graphics-expurgated, Blake with the glee of a schoolchild high on Cliff Notes, even after many professions of born-again faith in the only truth of his visualized hypermedia? Not to mention giving one too many lectures starting "You haven't read it at all if you've read it without the pictures"—the most recent, in my case, pressed on one of three Japanese tourists asking for directions to Niagara Falls, whom I stopped with just this message on a foggy night not long ago, only to be spurned—"Now get thee hence, though grey-beard Loon! / Or my Staff shall make thee skip."

The question of misleading editions of Blake (or Dickinson) turns us all into loons, whether we hold out for extra-lexical meaning or tenaciously insist that words are words. Or if not loons then cormorants, diving into the inky waters of our deep blue amnesias. As if we could be woken to words while asleep to language. If we imagine (begin to reimagine) that works of poetry always exist as versions, that there is no singular original but an array of realizations, then the relations between versions is not a moral one of right and wrong but an ethical one of reciprocity. Versions become translations in the sense that all works of poetry are translations, which is to say that writing itself is a form of translation and transformation, spinning and respinning, positioning and repositioning, transcribing and eliding. Editions may redress the wrongs of previous editions but they also address the songs those editions set in time.

It's not that words exist prior to or independently from the world but rather that we know the world through the words that initiate us into it. Just as we know words through the world in which we learned them. Poets actualize these potentialities: the worldness of words, the wordness of the world. This is why poetry is not a matter of "understanding": one does not wish to stand under, and in that sense outside, but to move into, within; or perhaps move back and forth: under, inside, on top.

Translation implies a conversion from one set of terms to another. This is a process that is continuous within one's own language and its many layers as well as between different languages. The process is less atomic than contextual: not a matter of identifying individual words or even individual meanings but a matter of attuning oneself to systems of meaning, clusters of signs, contexts of utterances: to scale and shape as much as format and configuration; to sounds and sights as much as lexicon.

In his *Critical Essay,* Swinburne writes, "All that was accepted for art, all that was taken for poetry, [Blake] rejected as barren symbols, and would fain have broken up as mendacious idols."[5] Much the same could be said of Arakawa and Gins, the focus of Mary Ann Caws's essay in this book. Arakawa and Gins have resisted, with increasing scale, the ability of readers/viewers to absorb their work as painting or poetry—or indeed as art. While they may be described as architects of the *Reversible Destiny* projects, the point is not to make aesthetic objects to be appreciated but to construct "stations" that will transform perception. Caws details the temporal modeling of Arakawa and Gins's visual and architectural projects, showing how they are configured to warp and reform the space–time continuum. Language is embedded into these works not as something to be read, as on a page or even a screen, but as something to interact with in an unfolding/enfolding web. The constructed "landing sites" of *Reversible Destiny* challenge rote perceptual patterns and activate underutilized cognitive paths.

The idea that genres, if not the aesthetic itself, are a barrier to perceptual transformation connects the projects of Arakawa and Gins and Blake to a range of practitioners from Mallarmé and Williams to Duchamp and Cage, all of whose antifoundational investigations have a visual and verbal component. In retrospect, we might say that these artists do not so much abolish the aesthetic as extend and transform it, partly because the boundaries of the aesthetic—our willingness or ability to see something as a work of art—are surprisingly mobile. But if the aesthetic is not a static category, then it may be possible for the "same" object to be viewed, alternately, as aesthetic and not aesthetic. Indeed, aesthetic oscillation is potentially a rhythmic dynamic in a work; that is, a work may be configured in a way that pops out of the aesthetic and then is sucked back in, creating a "hyperaesthetic" environment, to extend an idea of Misko Suvakovic.[6] Such a work would be as far from the heightened aestheticism of Mallarmé as from the postaesthetic of Conceptualism. In the case of *Reversible Destiny*, the goal is neither to aestheticize the nonaesthetic nor to deaestheticize the aesthetic but rather to create a zone that is no longer subject to this oscillation.

We used to say the artist would drop away and there would just be the work. With *Reversible Destiny*, can we go further and say the work drops away and there is just the station, a nonplace or point blank of radical metamorphosis? Only when we experience this as an emplacement of textuality into concrete sensory-perceptual fields—turning ever further away from ideality in the pursuit of an ultimate concretion.

Art is made not of essences but of husks. Hazard will never be abolished by a declaration of independence from causality. But such a declaration, as of reversible destiny, may change how hazard is inscribed in our everyday lives.

Arakawa and Gins create not texts but pictures, not pictures but textures, not textures but models, not models but plans, not plans but landing sites, not landing sites but perceptual encounters, not perceptual encounters but live experience, not live experience but three-dimensional conundrums, not three-dimensional conundrums but philosophical buildings, not philosophical buildings but blank writing, not blank writing but virtual structures, not virtual structures but impossible necessities, not impossible necessities but pitchers, not pitchers but moldings, not moldings but pageants, not pageants but straddling heights, not straddling heights but conceptual rejoinders, not conceptual rejoinders but livid exponents, not livid exponents but cross-interventional convocations, not cross-interventional convocations but philosomatic trillings, not philosomatic trillings but blinking sensors, not blinking sensors but curtained encapsulations, not curtained encapsulations but plausibly deniable links, not plausibly deniable links but pillars, not pillars but mouthings, not mouthings but plasma, not plasma but branding lights, not branding lights but invented enclosures, not invented enclosures but sifting exposés, not sifting exposés but torque-topped initiations, not torque-topped initiations but philanderous moorings, not philanderous moorings but blurted secrets, not blurted secrets but curling capacities, not curling capacities but prismatic illocutions, not prismatic illocutions but pantomime, not pantomime but mourning, not mourning but placebos, not placebos but blistered ratiocination, not blistered ratiocination but inverting domination, not inverting domination but shifting fabrications, not shifting fabrications but tongue-tooled emanations, not tongue-tooled emanations but philogenerative groundings, not philogenerative groundings but blanket riveting, not blanket riveting but invested *détournement,* not invested *détournement* but . . .

Notes

1. Charles Bernstein, ed., *Close Listening: Poetry and the Performed Word* (New York: Oxford University Press, 1998).
2. Basil Bunting, *Briggflatts* (London: Fulcrum Press, 1996), 14.
3. John Unsworth, "Electronic Scholarship or, Scholarly Publishing and the Public," accessed 9 March 2001 at http://www.village.virginia.edu/~jum2m/mla-94.html.
4. Harold Bloom, *The Anxiety of Influence: A Theory of Poetry* (New York: Oxford University Press, 1973).
5. Algernon Charles Swinburne, *William Blake: A Critical Essay* (1868; reprint, New York: Benjamin Bloom, 1986), 3.
6. Misko Suvakovic, *Pas Tout: Fragments on Art, Culture, Politics, Poetics and Art Theory, 1974–1994* (Buffalo, N.Y.: Meow Press, 1994).

TEXTUALITY AND CULTURE

Tim Hunt

The Muse Learns to Tape

A Preface of Sorts

Even for country kids like us, attending "Calistoga Joint Union High School" seemed a joke to savor, at least in 1966 with San Francisco in driving range. On weekends we'd pool our money and head to the ballrooms for the lights and bands, and maybe even dance a little—in spite of our pretty short hair and lack of costume. We heard bluesmen like Jimmie Reed and John Lee Hooker, jazzmen like Yusef Lateef, and an odd array of the soon-to-be-famous and never-to-be-heard-of-again (Cream to Sons of Champlin, by way of Aum and Sanpaku)—and, yes, the Dead and the Airplane; and when Jerry Garcia trucked on to that great Fillmore in the sky, I found myself thinking that those evenings had something to do with the nature of textuality.

Mostly, we heard the San Francisco bands perform before we heard their records. We assumed—so did the musicians, I think—that the performances were the "real" music. (One reason for Bill Graham's success may have been that his "dance-concerts" felt more like louder, more kinetic coffeehouse readings than like the rock shows where teens came to watch their treasured 45s acted out). When one of our bands signed the contract that made them stars, we were pleased (we thought of the musicians as friends we just hadn't met), but the recordings that followed struck us as inferior to the performances and the performing. If they were more disciplined and more realized than what we heard on the weekends, they were also safer and more abstract. We were spared Country Joe, too ripped to tune his dangling guitar, weeping over the invasion of the DMZ as the Fish swam on; but we missed the risk and glee of Marty Balin and Grace Slick spinning multiple choruses of "It's No Secret."

A music that stressed communal creation and consumption, spontaneity and individualism, and the rejection of social and musical conventions might have a great deal of vitality, even a certain authenticity, but record companies had little choice except to distill what we valued—the fluidity of performance—if they were to construct marketable products. And we were too naive (for all our left-leaning politics) to respond with Gramscian critiques of this commodification of "our" music. We just assumed that music that was packaged to fulfill commercial conventions was somehow inferior, and we skipped the pleasures of Beach Boys and Motown acts—the costumes *qua* uniforms, the choreography, the ability to replicate in performance every note so precisely placed on those wonderfully realized recordings. And while our taste (or lack of it) may say more about our assumptions about race, class, and region than I might like today, our reactions also point to a dichotomy between music as performance and music as composition—between music as a process and music as sound constructed into a preservable object. And it is here that Jerry Garcia and "textuality" begin to bear on each other.

A few days after his death, I saw a clip of the young Jerry describing the bluegrass festivals of his folkie days—family affairs of picking tunes around the pickup tailgates and savoring the locals and a headlining star—say, the Stanleys. These festivals-as-occasions-for-community seemed precursors to his own aesthetic, and he noted that the promoters used to put electrical outlets along the stage for fans who wanted to tape the music (early-1960s tape recorders weren't as portable as today's gear). He didn't mention what Decca Records thought about fans bootlegging Bill Monroe, but he assumes it was square with Bill. To Garcia, anyway, the point was to perform for an audience, and he apparently thought the point for the audience was to participate in the music as it happened—each unique performance fully "real" only as it was unfolding. The reel a fan might carry away wasn't the music, just a representation of an instance of it. The music was the performance: the being there, the matrix of performer, sound, circumstance, and audience. The fan's tape would increase the desire to attend another performance; that it might reduce the demand for a commercially produced recording of the music was to Garcia, it seems, simply beside the point.

For Garcia, then, there could be no adequate text of his songs "Dark Star" or "St. Stephen," if by "text" we mean a pure, final, fully realized, storable, and reproducible representation of the "work." The music is either a possibility (the skills, motifs, and patterns of interaction a set of performers use to enact a "work" by a semi-improvisational blend of creation and re-creation), an actual moment of performance, or a memory of an array of performances (some documented, some not), among which one might have favorites but where none is the definitive representation—the work's text. It is hardly surprising, then, that the Dead seem initially to have been unsure how to represent their performing on their records, and that the group's early albums explore different strategies for managing—or resisting—the seeming fixity, the seeming definitiveness, and the pressure to distill introduced by the decision to "make" a record as opposed to "playing" music.[1]

The Almost Theory Blues

For the most part, contemporary debates about editorial theory derive from and reflect the typical occasion of our practice: works that now have their primary existence in scripted or printed language. Textuality, as we have debated it, is intertwined with writing. Even with such pieces as *The Iliad* and the Bible's various books, we work primarily from (or toward) the moment they were given written shape. For one thing, we have no access to their prior states. For another, their oral "form" was probably a historical succession of forms, each retelling a semi-improvisational reinvention that is only partly captured by writing's fixity and linearity. A Grimm tale, read from the printed page at bedtime, is not the same thing as the tale performed from memory before a particular cottage hearth.[2]

Our emphasis on written materials points to an axiom I think most of us share: that a work must be physically embodied to be textual; it must have a preservable form apart from its creator or performer. This storage of the work in a stable medium can take the form of chirographic script, print, or musical notation (representations that can be reproduced and transmitted), or the work can itself be a unique physical object such as a carving, painting, or building, which are also experienced long after their production. But unless the creative process yields some such physically preservable form, the work ceases to be even as it is being performed, since the performance leaves no record. Instead of a "text" or "work," there is only the potential (in the performers) to generate more or less equivalent or parallel instances of the particular tradition through new, unique performances from the terms of practice that happen to define the "tradition" at a particular moment. And even this potential survives only while the tradition continues to renew itself through succeeding generations of practitioners.

This axiom points to textuality's power and importance: unless practices and performances can be given physically preservable form and can be brought within the textual horizon, they fade from the cultural record—and much of the vernacular art of the past has clearly been lost. However, as the example of the Grimm tale suggests, giving nontextual materials textual form alters them in significant ways. At least using writing, historically the most powerful and pervasive textual medium, to preserve oral materials transforms the materials even as they are preserved. Textualizing extends the circulation of oral traditions and practices and prolongs their cultural life, but it also converts them from a set of elements, procedures, and occasions for performing a "work" into a single, fixed example of what those elements, procedures, and occasions might have produced. Valuable, even necessary, this textual recording and recasting replaces what was a cultural process or praxis with a cultural "artifact."[3]

In general, we recognize that the conditions of textuality have changed across time. The textual modes of Homer's *Iliad,* sixteenth-century manuscript culture, and our own world of print are not the same, and (reasonably enough) we approach the editing of ancient epics, poems circulated in manuscript, and nineteenth-century novels differently. That is, we recognize that textuality is historically conditioned and that its terms and processes are intertwined with both social and technological conditions. At times, however, we seem to forget (or at least take for granted) that textuality is "historical" in another sense as well. Most of the works we study and their textual representations were produced within and for textualized traditions, or they were textualized so long ago that it is difficult to imagine them as anything other than textual. Moreover, we are deeply enmeshed in the literacy that makes our textual practice possible. Both training and habit conspire to obscure not only that the textual dynamic changes fundamentally what it preserves but also that textuality is itself a historical development—that there was a time (pre- or post-lapsarian) prior to textuality.

To textual scholars, this pre-textual condition seems beside the point, but its existence (even if now past) poses a question: To what extent is textuality's transformational impact inherent in the nature of textuality itself, and to what extent does it change with (and reflect) particular textual media? Until recently, we might not have asked this question—at least in this form—but two factors bring it into view and offer ways of exploring it.

The first, implicit in much of what I have said, is the exploration—initiated by the Homeric scholar Milman Parry and since extended by Eric Havelock, Walter Ong, and others—of orality and literacy as counterpointed cultural modes. This research indicates not only that oral and literate cultures evolve different procedures for inventing and conserving verbal works, but also that "orality" and "literacy" encourage qualitatively different logics and styles of cognition. The oral performer (whether of epic or African American folk blues) relates to his materials and shapes his "work" in a fundamentally different manner than does the literate creator (whether John Milton or Barry Manilow).

The second factor is the development of new modes of storage—film, audio tape, video tape, and various digitized media. Like written language, these can be used to store, multiply, and circulate cultural products. They are, that is, "textual"; the boom in VCR movie rentals shows that they are used as such. These media, however, more nearly capture the actual texture and process of performance than does writing; they offer a degree of transparency, a neutrality, that writing cannot manage. Recording a work in these new media thus enforces less abstraction than writing does. Reading the score of an opera is not the same as listening to a recording of it is not the same as watching a film of it (and none of these is quite a front row seat at the Met). Perhaps more to the point, a videotape of a Homeric performance would bring us significantly closer to the dynamic of oral creation and practice than the recovery of even the earliest manuscript of *The Iliad*.

The greater transparency of these new textual modes highlights writing's transformational power; it also moves us closer to being able to give nontextual works (folk and vernacular performances of various sorts) textual form while yet preserving something of their original, pre-textual dynamic. If so, the impact (if any) of these new textual modes on the performances and performance traditions they preserve should help to clarify the extent to which textuality itself (not just written textuality) is transformational— and perhaps something of the way it is transformational, as well. The nature and process of these newer textual modes may even have some relevance for the ongoing debate over the meaning of "work" and "text" and their relationship to each other, since these are terms that we have tended to address within the historical and technological context of writing without really doing much to determine the general validity of this specific and contingent textual mode. At least within the textuality of recording (whether audio or video), the categories of "work," "text," and "performance" appear to be not simply interdependent but also relative; they seem to take their meaning from the specific structures and dynamics within which pieces are produced and consumed; they seem to be elements that both enact and derive from what might be termed a "textual rhetoric," of which our models for written productions are specific instances.

2:19 Blues

Recorded music offers numerous illustrations of the contrast between music as a textual practice (where we assume either that a particular notated score or a particular construction of sound preserved on tape or vinyl is the musical work) and music as a tradition of performance. It may be that Lennon and McCartney, Dylan, Garcia, Jagger and Richards, and some other musicians owe their relative creative longevity, their staying power, and their ability to catalyze other performers in part to their having sensed this dialectic early on and having chosen to exploit it. Thus, their work/ working can be "read" partly as an ongoing exploration of the collision between the pre-textual and the textual, between the flux of the oral and the stability of the constructed object, between the dynamics of folk practice and those of pop art. But rich as these examples are, they reflect what happens when performers whose heritage is primarily textual encounter practices that are essentially not textual and then try to accommodate to these new (actually old) possibilities; witness the first generation of British rockers collecting the 1950s blues 78s of Muddy Waters, Howlin' Wolf, or Slim Harpo; Dylan, Garcia, and others cutting their eyeteeth and molars on the compilations of 1920s rural white and black Southern performers from Dock Boggs and Uncle Dave Macon to Mississippi John Hurt and Blind Lemon Jefferson.[4] For clarifying the dynamics of textuality per se, the more significant question is what happens when performers whose practice is primarily oral have their music "textualized" by recording without necessarily having had to master a textual technology for themselves, and for this the early history of jazz offers a particularly suggestive set of examples.

Histories of jazz typically note that it is a hybrid music that amalgamates African American and western European materials and performance practices, and they often rehearse the probable terms of exchange in the twentieth century's first decades between those African American musicians in New Orleans who were musically literate (read music, had some knowledge of harmony, and had some training in how to play their instruments) and those who were musically illiterate (could not read music, developed instrumental technique by trial and error, and approached performing from the orality of African American folk musical practices). The politics and sociologies of this interaction are mostly beyond this essay's scope; the point here is that this was a collision not only between the aesthetics of two different African American communities, one more middle-class, one lower on the socio-economic ladder, and between two different musical traditions, but also between an art that was fully textual (composed, preserved, and transmitted in musical script) and one that was nontextual (oral and performative). It is also important that initially, at least, the nontextual dynamic seems to have been the force driving this transformation; since this re-oralizing of the compositional elements occurred prior to recording and the performances were neither fully nor easily notatable in conventional script, the amalgam that resulted had to depend initially for its preservation and transmission on the resources that typify oral folk practice—memory and semi-improvisational re-creation.

At the turn of the twentieth century, when ensemble jazz first developed in New Orleans, its explicit musical elements were the melodies and voicings of brass band marches, ragtime, and blues as these were borrowed and synthesized by amateur and semi-professional musicians whose small ensembles provided functional music for neighborhood dances and picnics, funeral processions, and the like. Some bands were as much social clubs as musical enterprises, and the musicians were essentially folk artists who evolved their practice through improvisational give-and-take. Initially, therefore, jazz seems to have been a performance tradition, a practice learned by imitation, in which no two performances would have been the same. It was not a textual art, and the fact that the ragtime and march strands used in much early jazz had a written basis does not really contradict this, if we consider how these elements probably entered the vocabulary of these seldom-recorded musicians: the way early jazz performers apparently recast these materials suggests that they learned them aurally rather than from notated arrangements, and that they circulated them aurally as well. Thus, these musically literate materials were functionally no different from the blues strands (oral material having no basis in written tradition) with which they mixed in practice.

Ironically, the musically literate jazz pianist Jelly Roll Morton (initially piano players were a tradition all but separate from the small brass and woodwind ensembles that played in parades) offers one of the clearer demonstrations of what might be termed the "oralizing" of written musical material. In his 1938 Library of Congress interviews, he talks about both his development as a musician and the way jazz coalesced from, and out of, various performance traditions.[5] Although his tendency to mythologize his own centrality (at times it seems he would have us think that his history and jazz history are one and the same) partly compromises his validity as a witness to early jazz, the musical demonstrations he offers with his tales still seem to convey something of the process by which he and others created the music.

Morton could read and write music, had been exposed to both opera and instrumental classical music, and could handle the written popular piano pieces that were a mainstay in polite, pre-Victrola middle-class parlors, both white and black. However, he was also a "professor" (a brothel piano player), pimp, hustler, and gambler, as occasion dictated. Operatic airs were not the musical currency of this realm; Chopin's harmonic intricacy was in less demand than the rhythmic drive of the rural piano stylings being developed in the barrelhouse joints by self-taught musicians who were adapting folk blues to the piano. For his Library of Congress sessions in 1938, Morton both recalled and demonstrated these two competing musical worlds—one written and polite, the other oral and improvisational. His key example was ragtime.

As elaborated by Scott Joplin and others, ragtime is a composed music with clearly defined sections, multiple melodic themes, and precise counterpoint. Its chief innovation was using mild syncopation (borrowed from folk practice) as an element in written compositions that still foregrounded melody, harmony, and counterpoint. Ragtime, that is, formalized and popularized an aspect of folk practice. Its compositions, published as sheet music, could be found next to such pieces as "Nola" and "After the Ball Is Over" on the pianos in those polite parlors. In the Library of Congress recordings, Morton plays Joplin's "Maple Leaf Rag" twice: first in a close approximation of the score, as he claims Joplin performed it, and then as he used to play it in the brothels and bars. Playing the piece à la Joplin, Morton articulates the melodic strands and counterpoint; he also carefully subordinates the syncopation to the melody and counterpoint. In this approach, the harmonic features are clearly ordinate and the rhythmic features subordinate, and the piece seems primarily something to listen to and appreciate for its formal yet sprightly elegance. In offering the piece à la Morton, though, Morton abstracts the melodies to their basic intervals and mostly ignores the counterpoint. He thus slights the elements that distinguish "Maple Leaf Rag" as composed music. Yet he is not simply reducing the composition. His "Maple Leaf" has a rhythmic drive that Joplin's lacks, not just because he emphasizes the syncopations but because he varies them and uses his simplifications of the melodic themes as occasions for both melodic and rhythmic improvisation; Morton replaces the intricacies of Joplin's harmonic counterpoint with an equally intricate "rhythmic counterpoint."

If we equate sophistication with European art music and its foregrounding (at least until recently) of melody and harmony, ragtime as Joplin composed and perhaps performed it is a more sophisticated form than its jazzed interpretations, even those played by someone as sophisticated as Morton. Yet it is no surprise that the oral, unwritten blues stylings continued to flourish in the bars and brothels and that composed ragtime—even though it borrowed from this oral tradition—had to be subsumed back into the dynamic of oral practice in order to have a role outside the parlors and concert halls. There are several clear and important reasons for this beyond the technical limitations (in respect to composed art music) of some of the musically illiterate bar and brothel pianists. One is rhythmic. In spite of its syncopations, composed ragtime is relatively static rhythmically, at least for the kinds of dancing favored in houses of ill repute. But there is also a fundamental "rhetorical" issue: with composed ragtime, the performer's job is to render the text, and that text, that composition, that work, is the point. For a whorehouse ivory-tickler, the composition (when there is one) is a means to an end rather than an end in itself; his job is to use his musical skills to interact with his audience and support their interaction with each other. His musical materials and mode of performance require a certain improvisational freedom if he is to play to and for his patrons. Even something as basic as duration is an issue here: when one is playing a text, the piece is over when it's over, but when one deploys materials improvisationally or semi-improvisationally, the piece can continue as long as there's a need.

Whether we prefer Joplin's composition or Morton's improvisational treatment of it is a matter of taste, but it seems clear that Morton, while able to render Joplin's text, was finally aiming at something else. His focus was less the composition as fixed and final text than the ways its elements could be redeployed and elaborated in the give-and-take of a specific situation. In his approach, text and work were not one and the same; the written material was material toward a series of performances, each related to the other, each specific to its occasion, each *a* work, and none *the* work. Morton's interest was the fluidity of performance, not the fixity of texts. For him, Joplin's ragtime was useful only if he could free it from the page and recast its themes and phrases. For all that he was himself a "composer" of a string of important jazz pieces (e.g., "King Porter Stomp," "The Pearls," some printed before he began recording) and an "arranger" of his music when he gathered small ensembles to record it, the pieces he wrote and the materials he borrowed, whether learned by eye or by ear, were to be elaborated in performances that were neither strictly limited to what was notated nor fully represented by what was notated. They were occasions for improvisational expression, and what was being expressed was not the text.

As it happens, Morton's responsiveness to the "oral" and performative in spite of his command of the written and textual can be heard in his performance of "Mamie's Blues," recorded for General Records on 16 December 1939. While he plays a simple blues figure, Morton comments: "This is the first blues I no doubt heard in my life. Mamie Desdumes, this was her favorite blues. She hardly could play anything else more, but she could really play this number. Of course to get in on it, to try to learn it, I made myself the can rusher."[6] A notated transcription of this piece would offer no more than a simple and basic figure coupled with a few relatively standard blues verses, but as Morton savors the figures—both those he plays and those he sings—he not only infuses the piece with his own presence but also projects something of what must have compelled him originally: not Desdumes's "composition" nor the text she probably could not have written, but her ability to use these few elements to perform her moods. What Morton seems to have learned from Desdumes and other figures who were—at least musically—of the folk world, was their stance, a stance that was part of his ability to coopt and transform the written texts of Joplin and others, and part of his ability to make something as formally threadbare as "Mamie's Blues" seem emotionally and musically resonant.

I Thought I Heard Buddy Bolden Say

Morton's ability to read and write music means that he is a somewhat tainted example for this discussion. More compelling would be, say, a turn-of-the-century recording of Mamie Desdumes herself playing her blues or trying out one of "Maple Leaf Rag's" strands by memory and ear. Unfortunately, we have little direct evidence of how the earliest jazz musicians approached their materials in performance. Such legendary figures as the trumpeter Buddy Bolden did not write the pieces (as Morton sometimes did) that he and his small band played at dances, and they probably couldn't write music in any case. Nor were these earliest performers recorded. When Bolden's group was the rage, cylinders and 78s were for more "polite" musics. African American musicians playing crude dance music in New Orleans were not candidates to record, and we "know" their work mostly through descriptions by those who heard it and the recordings of slightly later figures (King Oliver, Bunk Johnson) who were influenced by it. (A couple of Bolden's near contemporaries, such as Freddie Keppard, did record a few sides, but they were well past their prime when they did so, and by that time the newer styles of Louis Armstrong and others had somewhat altered the way jazz was played.) Like Homer, Bolden is beyond the textual horizon—legendary, foundational, and only partly knowable.

What we do know, though, suggests that early jazz was a music in which the performers drew on a stock of figures that were mostly learned by ear, or so transformed when gleaned from the written text that they quickly became part of the memorized pool of materials with an existence both separate and different from their original textual form, and that the performers elaborated this stock of figures in a collective and semi-improvisational manner as they responded to each other and their audience (usually an audience of dancers). It thus seems to have been a music where the process of the performance—and one's participation in it, whether as player, dancer, or listener—was primary; the songs and structures were scaffoldings for the real "work," which was performing and the participation it enabled. Although this early jazz was first and foremost an ensemble music, the logic of it somewhat parallels the practice of preliterate oral poets, whose art also seems to have been their ability to select elements from a memorized stock in the flow of performance and embellish them in response to a specific occasion and audience (jazz riffs as Homeric epithets?). The logic of this early jazz practice, though inferred and necessarily generalized, is enough for us to begin to identify the impact of recording on jazz—the effect, that is, of bringing the oral practice of early jazz within the textual horizon.

When record companies first began recording jazz extensively around 1923, the musicians seem to have been primarily attempting to play in the studio as they would have performed for an actual audience. A group like King Oliver's Creole Jazz Band would have had no reason to think of the recording process as anything other than a way to represent what they played live, since that had been their only experience of playing to that point. Yet no one has ever mistaken these early 78s for full and transparent representations of what Oliver's group played at dances. For one thing, before the introduction of the "electric" microphone, jazz drummers could not play as they normally would without popping the needle out of the wax platter that was the actual recording medium. Moreover, the size of the platter limited performances to about four minutes, and the sound captured by the horn into which the musicians played was thin. But even with these limitations and distortions, those first 78s of King Oliver's music are an infinitely richer record than we have of Bolden's.

Recording introduced a fundamentally new way to textualize a musical performance. Instead of having to represent the performing by abstracting it into some variety of code, either by describing it in written language or translating it into musical notation, a performer could inscribe the music directly on the wax (later acetate, then magnetic tape) as he played. King Oliver did not have to translate his performances into musical notation to produce texts of "Dipper Mouth Blues," "Snake Rag," and "Alligator Hop"; he wrote them with his trumpet, and this simultaneity of the performing and the inscribing minimizes the difference between performance and the representation of performance in a way that differs qualitatively from earlier textual modes.

This dynamic, this blurring between the process of performing and creating a representation of the performing, seems to suggest that jazz recordings would become an increasingly full and faithful representation of what musicians actually created in live performances as the fidelity of the recordings improved. In one sense, this is what happened. By the late 1920s, 78s could store a fuller image of the actual sound of the instruments. By the late 1930s, amateur recordings were being made of groups playing for actual audiences—or example, a complete 1940 dance the Duke Ellington Orchestra played in Fargo, North Dakota. Today's tape and CD world can leave us wondering whether it's Ella Fitzgerald or Memorex. We have, it seems, reached the point where recording reproduces performance so fully that a music like jazz could remain fully a praxis, a process, yet attain (or be given) the permanence and reproducibility of an artifact.

But this is not quite where we have ended up. Ironically, as recording technology improved and made it more possible to capture and transmit jazz as a practice, composition also became a more central feature; the music itself gradually became more of an artifact—and not just with self-conscious efforts like Paul Whiteman's to legitimize jazz as a concert music.

First, the collective improvisation of Oliver's generation gave way to the practice of individual musicians soloing in a predetermined order over a more or less composed accompaniment. Then, as ensembles grew in size and more jazz musicians could read music, written arrangements became common. By the late 1930s, only fifteen years after jazz recordings became common, jazz had developed from being essentially a folk practice—a process for generating performance—into a popular art, a commodity in which each performance of a piece by a musician or group was expected closely to resemble a previous performance of the piece, and had developed in some instances (Ellington, for example) even a composed art music.

The various socio-economic and biographical elements jazz histories cite to explain these developments were certainly factors, but so was the dynamic of textuality that recording added to jazz. It is all the more telling that this seems to have happened even though this textual technology enforced less abstraction than writing. That is, recording did more than just make it possible to store actual jazz performances, albeit in imperfect form, and thus allow them to be reproduced and transmitted. Recording—by making an artifact of performance out of actual performance—fundamentally shifted the performer's relationship to his materials and audience and thus to his practice. With the advent of recording, performance could be understood not only as a means and end in itself but also as a means to a specific end, the distillation of the recording; or it could take the form of a self-conscious recasting of a previously recorded performance that both performer and audience might already hold in mind as a model for what the piece was supposed to be.

Recording's impact is apparent as early as the young Louis Armstrong. There were few if any jazz musicians in the late 1920s who did not spin his Hot Fives and Hot Sevens over and over, and his bravura flights were carefully analyzed and imitated; and they could be—precisely because they were recorded. This mode of learning was quite different from standing next to the bandstand trying to catch and remember the details of a live performance or later talking over the performance, even with the performers. Textualizing the music, even with a medium as neutral and transparent as analogue recording, thus helped to create and then enforce and accelerate the move in jazz toward working from composed materials, toward more fully elaborated compositions, and toward the adoption of musically more and more complex and abstract materials. This shift is analogous to the shift that Ong and others contend occurred with the transition from orality to literacy: a transition that, like jazz's transition to textuality, inclines us to become more committed to the distillation of "finished" aesthetic objects than to the participation of praxis.

The analyses Ong and others offer of literacy help to explain why this might be so. The key element in the development of literacy (the intertwined technologies of writing and reading) is the capacity it provides to store verbal performance in a medium other than individual memory, along with the complementary capacity to derive an image of the performance by processing the stored visual marks. This capacity encourages a progressively greater awareness of our verbal performances as things in themselves rather than transitory, if powerful, gestures. Verbal performances become potentially created objects that have a fixity beyond the dynamic of performance. And like the shift to literacy, the shift to textuality encourages the sense that the records of various performative acts can be scrutinized, revised, manipulated, and perfected. It provides a necessary basis, and in part the impetus, for a folk art to evolve from a process or practice into a self-conscious art tradition that preserves the aesthetic objects produced within it.

If this is so, it suggests that two factors drive textuality's transformational capacity. One is the greater (as with writing) or lesser (as with tape recording) abstraction of the storage medium, which can gradually drop from view both for the practitioner and for the consumer as the practitioners learn to think primarily in terms of creating specifically for the medium, or as the medium becomes increasingly able to capture actual performance without diminishing its texture or resorting to abstract encoding. The other is the way textuality itself, of any sort, changes the practitioner's relationship to past gestures within the tradition by "storing" and foregrounding a particular array of works—by encouraging, that is, the view that the "art" is more a product than a process, and that these products can be copied or subjected to further refinement or extrapolation. The example of jazz suggests that this transformational dynamic is even more fundamental than the greater or lesser abstraction enforced by the particular medium of storage. That is, textuality seems to encourage—and certainly enables—a self-conscious mixing of styles and gestures that have been learned through the study of more or less stable artifacts, and practitioners of textualized arts thereby stand in a different relationship to their materials, their audience, and their tradition than do practitioners of arts that are not textual (if any still exist).

Dead Heads/Dead Ends

The apparent impact of the capacity for textuality on the development of jazz suggests that textuality enforces an increasing hegemony of the compositional that steadily eclipses the performative. If the focus here were literary, we might be inclined to consider such pieces as *The Waste Land* and *The Cantos* as projects where (triumphantly, to some) a textually supported aesthetic of composition and construction nearly effaces the personality of performance.[7] But just as the aggressively performative "Howl" demonstrated that the high modernist aesthetic was not the end of the story, part of the significance of jazz is the way its performative origins—its orality—exist in a still unresolved dialectic with the compositional capacity that the textuality of recording encourages. This dialectic between the impulse to value improvisation and the personal expression of performance yet to move toward the distillation of recorded composition is not just a way to clarify the evolution of jazz as a music; it may even be a key element of what jazz expresses, since the jazz creator often seems to be negotiating a liminal space between the performative and the textual and seeking out strategies that will either express both or (in some way and if only temporarily) resolve their potential dissonance. This is the space evoked by the old jazz joke about the musician who interviews for a job with a big band and, asked if he can dot (read the dots of a musical score), answers, "Yes, but not enough to hurt." The same bifurcation between the oral and the compositional can be found in the practice of John Coltrane, who, when handed a transcription of his famous solo on "Giant Steps" and asked to play it, replied that he couldn't play what was notated because it was too hard—in spite of his ability to sight-read and play intricate and demanding written exercises on his tenor saxophone.[8]

Thus, a look at the history and current array of practices in jazz seems not only to help clarify the nature of textuality and to argue that textuality's impact is fundamental and unavoidable once introduced; it also suggests that the emphasis on construction and composition that textuality supports does not (even over time) eliminate the emphasis on performance on which oral practices necessarily build, but instead leads to a situation where the performative and the compositional interact in varying ratios in the work of different individuals and traditions. These ratios, along with the interacting dynamics of different modalities of storage, transmission, and consumption, can be viewed as what we might call a rhetoric of textuality.

Battle of the Bands: *Anthem of the Sun* Meets *Somebody to Love*

Until fairly recently the textual rhetoric of most jazz recordings has actually been relatively simple. A Coltrane album is supposed to allow us to feel that we are participating in the spontaneity of an actual performance to an actual audience, minus the cigarette smoke, the clinking glasses, and the pretentious boor at the next table who thinks he's suave. At times this requires at least some distillation (studio performances tend to be shorter than those for a physically present audience), and at times what one hears on record has actually been honed in the studio across various takes. But even so, much of the recorded jazz legacy has involved musicians recording performances and then choosing which ones to release in a process that echoes King Oliver's "waxing" his notes. The reason for this is partly economic. Jazz records sell modestly compared to pop music; studio time costs money, and jazz records have typically had to be produced cheaply to be commercially viable. That both jazz musicians and patrons have wanted to continue to believe that the music's significance is that it is at root performative (expressive, improvisational) is also a factor; no matter how many times we might play Armstrong's "West End Blues" or Coleman's "Lonely Woman," we still want to believe the lines are being invented right then for us as we listen. These factors may explain why textuality's impact on jazz has tended to be more on the way the music is performed and what is written for performance (with recording as transparent as the technology permits) than on experimenting with the ways recording can itself be used to construct compositions. Even when tape matured to the point that it allowed for multi-tracking and building a "performance" from pieces spliced from different takes and partial takes, the jazz recordings actually released continued to be typically integral performances with an occasional chorus or two snipped out for reasons of length or structure, or they were carefully managed to convey the illusion of an integral performance.[9]

With pop music, though, the sense that recording was actually a way to construct a product rather than to preserve and circulate a performance took hold more quickly and completely—at least with the producers and executives pitching 45s to the teen market and looking for a hit. These producers were not simply constructing pieces of music to sell but constructing the performers into marketable commodities as well. As Bill Parsons (a.k.a. Bobby Barc) has it in "All American Boy," a ditty cut right after Elvis got drafted: "Come here cat, I'm gonna make you a star." The tendency to see Phil Spector, not the ostensible performer, as the star of the 45s he produced exists not just because he had the ego to claim he was a musical genius. The textual rhetoric of the pop 45, then, is about as straightforward as the one governing most mainstream jazz recordings—but happens to be its opposite.

Yet as the example of the Grateful Dead (to round at last toward the beginning) suggests, not all textual rhetorics are as direct as those of mainstream jazz and 1950s rock and roll. Of the 1960s San Francisco bands, the Dead proved not only the longest-lived but also the most committed to the improvisation and experiment of live performance. Their allegiance to praxis, their decision to emphasize the participatory give-and-take of the moment, meant that each dance concert could and did involve substantially different renderings of the musical skeletons on which they wove their performances. Those of us who trekked to the ballrooms for the group's amalgam of jug band, blues, and bluegrass came to accept that the price of sporadic stunning and revelatory flights were stretches when the music was (to be kind) amorphous and meandering. At issue here, though, is not so much what the Grateful Dead was like in its early years for the Fillmore and Avalon audiences, but rather what happened when the band came to record—when its emphasis on praxis collided with Warner Brothers' goal of recasting that praxis as saleable records.

When Warner Brothers signed the Grateful Dead (in part because the media had proclaimed that a "San Francisco Sound" might be the next market trend), AM radio was the main way record companies marketed their product (FM "underground" radio was not yet a factor much beyond big cities). Radio listeners bought the 45s that caught their ear and sometimes albums that included these songs, and radio programmers expected songs to be no more than about three minutes: longer songs left too little time for commercials. It is thus no surprise that *The Grateful Dead* (1967), recorded in three days, has six songs less than three minutes long, and that only the ninth and final track, the ten-minute "Viola Lee Blues," is long enough for the improvisational elaboration that typified the group's performances (another track, "Good Morning, Little School Girl," fades just as the band begins to modulate from the basic song into improvisational territory).[10] Producer Dave Hassinger's goal seems to have been to pull some brisk pieces from the band's repertory and distill them into something with a chance of radio play, thereby creating a market for the album. But though brief and upbeat, "The Golden Road (to Unlimited Devotion)" was too strange, ragged, and swirlingly kinetic to pass as a pop object. It wasn't "Good Vibrations" or "Mickey's Monkey," each in its own way perfectly constructed AM pop; it wasn't even "White Rabbit" or "Somebody to Love," the two instances where a 1960s Bay Area band successfully constructed something for the pop marketplace. The only region where either "The Golden Road" or *The Grateful Dead* sold even modestly was, not surprisingly, San Francisco.

In the months after this first encounter with the recording industry, the group became even less marketable. Adding a second drummer brought complex polyrhythms to the mix and rendered the songs themselves even more secondary, and the commitment to improvisation increased, with pieces stretching out until a single improvisation might fill an entire two- or three-hour set. The Dead had thus become even less recordable, and at one point the band declared that their first album would be their only one, and that they would henceforth focus exclusively on performing. Yet in 1968 the band and Warner Brothers released *Anthem of the Sun*.[11]

On the first album, the group's improvisational performing had been secondary to the company's agenda of recasting its "songs" as AM product. *Anthem of the Sun,* however, was constructed as if the AM market didn't exist. Instead of short pieces, it presents what are essentially two compositions, each taking a whole side of the album, one a medley of three "songs" and the other of two, and fashioned by splicing and layering units recorded in concert (the cover lists the fourteen performances as sources) with units generated in the studio, including pieces of "Electronic Tape" influenced by the experiments in electronic music and electronically manipulated sound then current in classical music. The way these discrete units have been amalgamated resembles the way a filmmaker might use film stock generated at different points under different circumstances to fashion the illusion of continuous action. Ironically, the result of all this assembly is an album that more fully evokes the band's improvisational performing practice in this period than does the first album and actually projects something of its sound at full rumble—even as one registers the electronic effects and the splices where pieces from different taped performances butt against each other; in fact, *Anthem of the Sun*'s manipulated material probably sounds more like the band in concert than do the unmanipulated concert recordings of the band's fourth album, *Live Dead*.

Anthem of the Sun's two sides are thus meticulously constructed yet seem to unfold as performances; they are—paradoxically—compositional representations of the group's improvisational aesthetic, and as such they reflect an intriguing attempt to use the long-playing album to mediate the compositional and performative. *Anthem of the Sun* derives from concert material and evokes a concert, but it is not a concert. It mimes the band's performance practice in the way it incrementally modulates and elaborates the rudimentary materials of the "songs," but it has a compositional density, a kind of architecture, and a clearer sense of form than an actual performance. In performance, the music is invented in real time as played and is meant to be heard/experienced once; on the album, the music has been chosen, shaped, revised, and reconsidered and is meant to be listened to over and over. For all that the album conveys the spontaneity of improvisation, it neither rambles nor detours. It might be termed a "composed performance" as opposed to a performed composition. It is this hybridity that is finally significant—though this is not an attempt to canonize *Anthem of the Sun* as a crucial post–World War II musical episode.

Without textuality, we have only performance. When textuality enforces considerable abstraction—as do both the alphabetic representation of spoken language and the notation of music as dots and lines on a page when they recast transitory sound as more permanent visual codes—it seems to drive an emphasis on construction and composition. More transparent textual technologies like tape recording, however, tend to blur these two capacities by promoting a compositional consciousness in oral performers and a fascination with the oral mode among at least some whose primary reference has been the compositional realm that abstract notation supports and helps enforce. (It would perhaps be worthwhile in this context to consider the quite different experimental agendas of such composers as Harry

Partch, John Cage, Morton Feldman, Lou Harrison, George Crumb, and recent minimalists.)

A Coda of Sorts: One Man's Ceiling Is Another Man's Floor; or, Have You Ever Been to Electric Textland

In spite of some fine Garcia solos and stirring kazoo cadenzas, the Grateful Dead's attempt to be both live and "Memorex" on *Anthem of the Sun* was a commercial flop, which may be one reason why the group never tried this hybrid mode again. Some later albums, like *Aoxomoxoa* and *Working Man's Dead,* use the studio to render songs; others are compilations of recordings of live performances (*Live Dead, Europe '72*). Thus, for the Dead the solution to the polarity of pop artifact and oral performance was finally to treat the polarity as a given and to explore its two possibilities separately. The band's communal aesthetic, a sort of tie-dyed update on the bluegrass festivals Garcia fondly remembered, may have encouraged them to see recording and the marketing of recordings as a complement to performing. One made music because one enjoyed the process of making music and enjoyed drawing in those who came to listen—to participate. Recordings were another outlet for the music, but they weren't the music. Recordings could be treated as secondary.

In part, the Dead's resolution of the polarity depended on the willingness of those in the group not to be pop stars (that Garcia had become a kind of folk icon even before his death complicates but does not contradict this) and to work out their own sub-economy on the margins of the pop music industry. For a figure like Jimi Hendrix whose ambition was to be a pop star, however, the challenge was to confront the polarity between pop artifact and oral performance, to do so within the context of commercial music, and—if one was to be fully an "artist" as opposed to a pop product—to do so in such a way that one somehow altered or mastered it. For all his experience as a blues, rhythm and blues, and rock performer, his flamboyance as a performer, and his improvisational energy, Hendrix seems to have sensed that this synthesis had to be through, by, and of the recording studio.

A radio documentary on Hendrix, later marketed as a set of CDs, offers a gloss on this that can stand as a sort of coda to this blurring of composition and performance and of work and text. At the end of the second disc, Eddie Kramer, a recording engineer who worked with Hendrix on *Electric Ladyland,* describes the mixing of "1983 . . . (A Merman I Should Turn to Be)":

It [*Electric Ladyland*] was a double album and Jimi had much more time to develop his ideas. One of the songs that sticks out in my mind would be "1984 a Mermaid I Should Be" [*sic*] which I worked on with him for about eighteen hours straight. And we mixed the entire thing—the entire side of the record—in one go with no interruptions, so it was a complete piece. It was like a performance, and Jimi and I mixed it together, where he would grab his vocals and some of his guitar effects and I would do the drums and his other guitar effects and generally hold on to the whole thing so it didn't fall apart. And we'd be flying around the board like lost flies. It was wonderful. It was the a creation of a piece of music in addition to what had already been recorded.[12]

The "board" is the mixing board through which Hendrix and Kramer could simultaneously play the various taped pieces of vocals, rhythm tracks, guitar solos, and sound effects that had previously been recorded for the piece.

Unlike *Anthem of the Sun,* none of the taped material for "1983" derives from an actual performance for an audience, though the strands were by the musicians; this suggests that "1983" is primarily, inherently compositional: Hendrix started with an idea of what he wanted to construct; he and his colleagues generated "tracks" of tape toward this end; and he and his engineer then selected the tracks to mix into the final recording and, as the final compositional step, mixed them. But in describing this final step, Kramer stresses that they mixed the piece "with no interruptions" in what seemed "like a performance." To Kramer, it seemed that he and Hendrix were actually performing a piece of music using the mixing board and taped tracks as their shared instrument. Their decisions about which tracks to bring in and the level and tonal qualities of these tracks were responses to the unfolding piece, to each other, and to what they were discovering as they went, and these were real-time reactions made without stopping to deliberate and plan. The notes to the CD identify the version of "1983" that follows Kramer's comment as "an alternate mix of a song that appeared on *Electric Ladyland*" and characterize it as "one of a series of experimental mixes—each totally unique."

With a piece like "1983 . . . (A Merman I Should Turn to Be)," the studio becomes both an instrument for performing (albeit to an absent audience) and a tool for producing a compositional record, and the process of producing the piece finally involves a different logic than the process for producing *Anthem of the Sun.* For "1983," Hendrix and Kramer—having previously created the material to be used—"performed" a series of mixes, of compositions, then chose one for the album. The sides of *Anthem,* in contrast, seem each to have been composed and constructed as a single mix; that is, the mix was deliberated step by step. The difference is like the difference between performing a sketch and constructing a collage. The mixes of "1983" are a series of closely related sketches, whereas each side of *Anthem* is a collage. In the Dead's experiment, acts of performance become the themes and elements of the composition, and the results might be termed a composed improvisation in which the raw tracks—both those derived from concert performances and those constructed or played in the studio—have been used to represent a performance that never occurred and would never occur in quite this fashion. With "1983" and Hendrix, however, the distinction between performance and composition blurs even more and is even more problematic. The mixes of "1983" are two things: the only record of a "composition" that exists as a series of realized, stored, reproducible, and transmittable "texts"; and performances of that composition, one of which Hendrix has privileged over the others by choosing it for the album. The track on the album represents neither a possible performance of "1983" nor a composition called "1983" that others might perform; it is simply "1983," in much the way that a painting is simply itself. One man's composition is another man's performance, and vice versa, and both and neither may be texts.

Although neither Garcia nor Hendrix (nor Buddy Bolden) saw himself as a textual theorist, the encounters with the dynamic of recording that their examples highlight suggest that recording (especially audio tape and its attendant technologies) has a capacity to fuse performance, composition, and text into a single phenomenon in a way that the code of written language does not. If so, the models of textual rhetoric we will need to guide the textual analysis and editing of recorded material will be different from the ones we have developed out of and in response to written and printed material. If this is the case, it at least raises the possibility that "text," "work," and "performance" are more fluid phenomena than we may have realized, and that these terms are less names for stable categories and qualities than markers whose meaning is historically contingent and is shaped by the differing dynamics of the various textual media. Although this is not the place or time to launch a deconstructive reading of the famous "Is it live or is it Memorex?" commercial featuring Ella Fitzgerald, that could be a worthwhile effort to which the answer might also be "both" and "neither."

Notes

1. See *The Grateful Dead,* Warner Brothers WS 1689 (1967); *Anthem of the Sun,* Warner Brothers WS 1749 (1968); *Aoxomoxoa,* Warner Brothers WS 1790 (1969); and *Live/Dead,* Warner Brothers 2WS 1830 (1969). Also, see below for a discussion of these issues in the first two of these albums.

2. For a systematic survey of these issues and summaries of relevant research, see Walter J. Ong, *Orality and Literacy: The Technologizing of the Word* (New York: Methuen, 1982). See also Khosrow Jahandarie, *Spoken and Written Discourse: A Multi-disciplinary Perspective* (Stamford, Conn.: Ablex Publishing Corporation, 1999).

3. Eric Havelock's recasting and extension of the work of Milman Parry and Albert B. Lord provides a sustained examination of this process and its cultural and social impact in the context of Homeric and Classical Greece. Havelock's *The Muse*

Learns to Write (New Haven: Yale University Press, 1986) both summarizes and extends the analyses he developed in such studies as *Preface to Plato* (1963; reprint, Cambridge, Mass.: Belknap Press of Harvard University Press, 1987) and *The Greek Concept of Justice: From Its Shadow in Homer to Its Substance in Plato* (Cambridge, Mass.: Harvard University Press, 1978).

4. The British rockers frequently note their interest in the blues and rhythm and blues of the 1950s and early 1960s in various interviews and fanzine stories. In the notes to the recent CD compilation *Dave Van Ronk, The Folkways Years: 1959–61* (Smithsonian/Folkways SF 40041 [1991]), Van Ronk recalls the impact of Harry Smith's *Anthology of American Folk Music* (three double-record sets from the early 1950s that gathered some of the key blues and country 78 recordings of the 1920s and 1930s): "The scope of this collection [Smith's anthology] was panoramic: Uncle Dave Macon, Mississippi John Hurt, Blind Willie Johnson, Buell Kazee, Lemon Jefferson, the list goes on and on. *The Anthology* was our bible. We [the performers of the urban folk revival] knew every word of every song on it, including the ones we hated. They say that in the 19th century British Parliament, when a member would begin to quote a classical author in Latin the entire House would rise in a body and finish the quote along with him. It was like that."

5. Morton's spring 1938 Library of Congress sessions have been released commercially several times and are available on CD. His illustrations of "Maple Leaf Rag" are part of the selection "Discourse on Jazz," *Jelly Roll Morton: The Library of Congress Recordings, Volume Eight,* Swaggie Records S1318 (n.d.).

6. Morton's sides for General were later acquired by Commodore Records and have been reissued several times; they are available on CD. See Jelly Roll Morton, *New Orleans Memories Plus Two,* Commodore Records XFL 14942 (1979).

7. It is certainly true that these poems can be read aloud (both Eliot and Pound "performed" them for audiences), but Eliot's insistence on the impersonality of art and his various strategies for suppressing narrative and deflecting any identification of the poem's language with a stable "voice," especially his own, suggest the extent to which his "performances" were distinctly secondary to the poem's status as composed and fixed artifact. Similarly, Pound's role in helping Eliot distill *The Waste Land* and his decision to discard the "ur-Cantos"—which feature a sort of narrative voice, a persona in which we are invited to take a dramatic interest—suggest his rejection of the oral and performative, in spite of his fascination with pre-technological culture.

8. Sometime in my years of reading album liner notes, articles in *Down Beat* and the like, and books on jazz, I ran across this anecdote, but I cannot remember its source.

9. Some of the tracks on Charles Mingus's *Mingus Ah Um,* Columbia CL 1370 (1959), for instance, have had material deleted (a solo or two here, a bridge or chorus there), and it is not clear who decided to snip these pieces out, or why (because of length? to improve structure? something else?). What is clear is that the listener is expected to listen to this processed performance as if it were simply an unprocessed performance. Unedited versions of these tunes were released after Mingus's death in *Nostalgia on Times Square,* Columbia JG35717 (1979). The pieces on Miles Davis's *Miles Ahead,* Columbia CL 1041 (1957), are the result of even more radical

manipulation, yet here too, for the listener these constructions—a complex pastiche of spliced takes and overdubs—play as if they were integral performances. Phil Schaap's painstaking analysis of the construction of these tracks is included in the booklet accompanying the Mosaic Records LP version (MQ11-164) of the Sony/Columbia CD set, *Miles Davis/Gil Evans: The Complete Columbia Studio Recordings* (1996).

10. *The Grateful Dead,* Warner Brothers WS 1689 (1967).
11. *Anthem of the Sun,* Warner Brothers WS 1749 (1968).
12. *Lifelines: The Jimi Hendrix Story,* Reprise 9 26435-2 (1990).

Henry Schwarz

From Text to Work
Postcolonial Textuality

Textuality

In a famous essay written in 1971, Roland Barthes asked us to consider the transformation "from work to text" that had taken place "over the last few years." By recalling this essay in my title, I do not want merely to reverse its claim as a simple opposition but rather to continue probing into the necessary relation between these two terms. Work does not pass definitively into text in Barthes's essay, as if superseded by the author's urbane modernity. Instead, by reconsidering Barthes and the poststructuralist milieu of the French 1970s, I hope to open a conceptual space between European textual theory and cultural practice in postcolonial India. My essay will also touch on issues of value, labor, production, and performance.

In the ancient history of 1972, Fredric Jameson commented on the relationship between Marxism and the emerging structuralist method then sweeping French intellectual life. Far from the antagonism and mutual incomprehension we see between such camps today, Jameson noted, "The French Structuralists . . . are the beneficiaries of a Marxist culture, if only in the sense that they are no longer free to ignore the theoretical problems raised by the Marxist tradition: indeed, they know Marx so well as to seem constantly on the point of translating him into something else."[1] In seven terse formulations, Barthes asserted that since the last century—Marx and Freud being the iconic instigators—"we" have not been living in history but in repetition, the "infinite deferment of the signified."[2] The epistemological break inaugurated by Marx and Freud had relativized the relationship between reader and critic, and thus the stability of the signified formerly implicit in works had given way to the infinite playing of the signifier that characterizes texts. Older canonical works are transformed by this new "relativity of the frames of reference" (Barthes, 156) and are opened to signification in ways that radically rearrange their contents. Newer texts and their readers exhibit a *"stereographic plurality* of its weave of signifiers" (emphasis in original); what the reader perceives is "multiple, irreducible, coming from a disconnected, heterogeneous variety of substances and perspectives.... So the Text: it can be it only in its difference" (159).

What has this passage into repetition done to the body of the work, the corpus? Textuality, we find, is in fact the work of the body: "It is bound to *jouissance,* that is to a pleasure without separation" (164). Far from displacing the material solidity of the work onto the ineffable, transient text that can be interpreted variously and without limits, Barthes hypermaterializes the text, making it literally a tissue of networked fibers, each linked to the body's tactile receptors. The older spiritual authority of the work is loosened and broken up by this operation of the body, and in this breaking, the particulate fragments of the textual organism become newly conceivable *as matter* in opposition to the older appearance of wholeness, and thus to the weighty and forbidding gravity they had previously been seen to possess.

Ever eclectic and resolutely contemporary, Barthes reminds us, inter alia, that this modern sense of signifying repetition as textuality derives from—or opposes itself to—the then-reigning structural Marxism of Louis Althusser, to which so much subsequent postmodernist theory owes its inspiration. Barthes's formulations regarding the body rely, from a then hotly debated motif of Marx's, on the essential human capacity for labor, or praxis. Barthes writes, *"the Text is experienced only in an activity of production"* (157, emphasis in original). Equally, Barthes claims for his project the radical chic of another Althusserian slogan, "theoretical practice," when he writes that the goal of intellectual labor must be socially transformative: "The theory of the Text can coincide only with a *practice* of writing" (164, my emphasis). Although Barthes titled his essay "From Work to Text," the transitive force of *work*—as productive human labor—is actually enhanced in the movement from signified to signifier. Work as *praxis*—something produced by the critic in the laborious act of interpretation—replaces work as *opus,* something fixed, finished, and stable, a totality conceived a posteriori to the labor that produced it. To be sure, Barthes found in the work of textual productivity or interpretation not the sublime production of machine labor but the tactile pleasure of love's labor, the ceaseless interstitching and overlapping of contiguous articulation. And while one would not easily label Barthes a Marxist, at least since *Mythologies* (1957), and would respect his oppositional stance to the policing of cultural correctness by the French Communist Party in the late 1960s, the category of production he retained from Marx (as much as the productive forces of the unconscious in Freud) plays a crucial role in the disseminative motion of his textuality.

At the same time, common to the intellectual backgrounds of both Barthes and Althusser, there existed in Paris a Nietzschean–Heideggerian anti-humanist trend which, when applied to Marxist thought, would attack the supposed anthropological essence of the human subject identified in the "early" Marx: the bearer of labor-power. For Althusser, the subject was not defined by its ability to produce, measured as abstract labor-power, but was rather decisively "decentered" by the structural relations in dominance of the social totality. Far from the workerist humanism to which Marx's value theory could give rise, Althusser's functionalism led to a theory of ideology in which subjects were constituted by the social totality that made them possible and in turn structured their consciousness. The constitution of subjectivity was seen not to reside in a human essence, labor-power, made conscious by its creative action on the objects of nature, but was an interested construction of the state which produced "subject-effects" in order to provide an illusion of individuality in its members that was necessary for reproducing the relations of production in the capitalist economy. Individuals thus subjected provided the most effective units of production, consumption, and reproduction; their supposedly unique capacities were appealed to in order to stimulate production, their idiosyncratic tastes dictated consumption, and their presumed individual autonomy prevented mass organization and resistance. Althusser's theoretical anti-humanism was designed to undermine the Fordist ideology of compromise between labor and management by revealing such humanism as ideological coercion. Related theoretical developments in the context of humanistic study could lead as well to questioning the authority of the European cultural tradition. Such questioning may have seemed radical at the time, but by the mid-1970s it would be misunderstood in this context as a full-scale reaction against the supposedly totalizing and determinist constraints of Marxism *tout court*.

Unfortunate for Althusser and his followers were the actual texts of Marx. *The Economic and Philosophic Manuscripts of 1844* had been published only in the early 1930s, and their humanist conceptions of "alienation" and "reification" had been used politically, as in eastern Europe, against the rigid and determinist forms of communist orthodoxy that had developed under Stalin. As China denounced the "right-wing revisionism" of Krushchev's liberalization of the Union of Soviet Socialist Republics in the early 1960s, and as the French Communist Party followed Russia's policies of "peaceful coexistence" and "nonviolent transition to socialism," theoretical anti-humanism was seen by Althusser as a politically necessary correction to the bourgeois "cult of man" once again breaking out in Europe.[3] Ironically, the semi-autonomous level of social and literary theory would break from any notion of determination in the last instance, and the next generation of Parisian Nietzscheans of *la pensée 68*—notably Foucault, Derrida, and Lyotard—would embrace this anti-humanism even as they divorced themselves from communist politics.[4]

For Althusser and Barthes alike, even in their divergent constituencies, the notion of a productive subject held particular political significance. For the former, the epistemological centrality of *Capital* within Marxian science was at stake, while for the latter, the question of the body and its capacities posed a serious challenge to intellectual orthodoxy. As Barthes veered further away from organized politics, the ambivalence of the body seemed to sanction increasingly subversive behavior; as for Althusser, the attack on humanist essentialism led him to a purer left-wing communism. For both thinkers, questioning Marx's labor theory opened onto political projects, but their journeys terminated at different destinations.

Althusser posited a break between the "early" humanistic Marx of the *1844 Manuscripts* and the "mature" Marx of *Capital,* volume 1. This allowed him to reject the notion of a producing subject, available in the young Marx, in accordance with the later, scientific Marx, who was interpreted to have rejected such a conception of the subject's preexisting its determination by the social totality. The labor theory was cast as essentialist and thus unnecessary to a more accurate epistemology. In opposing Stalin in the name of Marx, Krushchev's return to humanism would be a return to bourgeois ideology. For Althusser and his followers, Marxian science demanded an objectivity unencumbered by bourgeois sentimentalism, and the search for human essences such as labor-power only replaced the latter with the former—sentimentalism for science.

The theoretical question posed by *Capital* could be phrased this way: Did human labor bring capitalism into existence, and would it thus lead to capital's surpassing (Marx's early position); or did capitalism bring into existence the necessity of positing a laboring subject as a condition for capitalism's possibility (Marx's later position, according to Althusser)? Was the notion of labor merely the afterimage of capitalism, a retrospective construction made necessary, and necessarily limited by, the social conditions that structured the epistemological field? This was not a mere rhetorical exercise. Althusser's premise was that Marx was the first to understand the true nature of capitalism, in the manner of a scientific breakthrough, to be the limit event that rewrote all previous understandings of human society. In other words, capitalism had created—and *Capital* conceptualized—the conditions whereby man could finally glimpse his true nature scientifically: that he had no "true nature," that human "nature" was in fact an illusion produced by social arrangements determined in the last instance by the forces and relations of production. This "immense theoretical revolution," understood only by the mature Marx of the 1860s, undercut the foundations of the earlier labor theory and argued in favor of the empty or decentered subject overdetermined by social relations contemporaneously embraced by poststructuralist thinkers of textuality—but without acknowledging that debt.

What the social relations of capitalism seemed to indicate for individual subjects was the imperative to produce under its conditions. This social imperative had been misunderstood previously as an innate, essential component of human identity. However, the scientific study of capital—enabled most of all by capital's achieving sufficient spread and density to allow it to be studied scientifically—revealed a contrary truth. For the Althusserians, the famous inverted world described by Marx in the *German Ideology,* seen as through a camera obscura, becomes righted only in *Capital.* Capitalism forces humans to produce, to sell their labor-power, in order to survive. Modern capitalism requires, for the first time in human history, a comprehensive system of exchange to bring humans the goods they need for this new, fragmented existence. Thus, one must have something to exchange in order to survive within the system. Barring great reserves of wealth, the subject must enter the system through labor, the object that capital can extract from the subject to drive its machines. In this sense, capitalism actually produces labor rather than vice versa; the system of exchange unleashed by commodity production, which organizes all the functions of society around its perpetuation, forces humans to produce. Labor-power is not an innate human trait that progressively builds capital, and it is not exercised universally as an invariant "fact" of humanity. Instead, social relations based on exchange look to classify humans as they do commodities, and they find that the labor of a human is one—most abstract—way of quantifying his value. All labor is not equal. As Bruce Roberts states succinctly in a recent essay: "Value is not determined separately from, prior to, or independent of its forms."[5]

As Barthes argued with regard to texts, and indeed other signifying systems such as fashion and photography, the products of labor must appear within the exchange relation in order to be registered as value. In Barthesian terms, this work acquires value only when textualized, when it enters into circulation within the system of signs. One cannot posit an origin—human labor, artistic genius—and then logically deduce from it the varied appearances of the world. Rather, it is the system itself in all its appearances that offers hints as to the laws of its creation. But these laws apply only in describing that state of the system, not its origins. Only *after* commodities are accorded value through their exchange can one work backward to the value of the labor that created them, retroactively producing a concept, labor, that had not been registered prior to the conditions of existence of the system. The commodity, as Marx explained through his obsession with ghosts, actually makes its producing subject disappear.

Recent theorists reread the texts of Marx with an eye for this peculiar oscillation between being and non-being in the formulations on labor and nature. Derrida describes as "spectrality" this barely perceptible slide between the ontology of a producing subject, possessing its labor as being or substance, and the haunting of that material being by the textual processes that simultaneously render its materiality intelligible within the system of exchange and its immediate producer ghostly, absent.[6] Similarly, Slavoj Zizek discovers an "unconscious" hiding behind the secret of the commodity-form. Labor-power is not merely the answer to this secret, its revealed truth; according to Zizek, "The unmasking of the secret is not sufficient. . . . What is not yet explained is simply its form, the process by means of which the hidden meaning disguised itself in such a form."[7] What the discovery of labor-power cannot explain about the commodity is how and why the commodity takes particular varieties of forms and values. That answer can be provided only by the system in all its complexity at historically determinate moments of its unfolding.

This is a question we could well address to Barthesian textuality. If the text is a production and its theory is always bound up with an act of writing, then who produces it? Not an author, an entity that is merely an invention of the bourgeois capitalist era with its convenient reverence for the ownership of property and "the human person" (Barthes, 143). Writing, instead, is the work of a body that not so much assists, as is made possible by language: "Language knows a 'subject,' not a 'person,' and this subject, empty outside of the very enunciation which defines it, suffices to make language 'hold together,' suffices, that is to say, to exhaust it" (145). The body does not know meaning as such but acts as a transport and a limit for the passing on of language; language's structure, its grammatical rules, syntax, and phonology, create subject-positions which must be inhabited, however briefly, for utterances to "hold together." In Althusserian language, the subject is essentially empty, but it allows ideology to be reproduced by performing the labor structurally required of it. The two processes are not symmetrical, but they occupy a similar moment of intellectual history in which a literary hedonist and a communist philosopher could find each other mutually illuminating. Yet the "aleatory materialism" resulting from these formulations has distinct resonances with other forms of textual productivity beyond Europe.[8]

Postcolonial"ity"

It is instructive to compare Barthes's description of the new textuality with an ensemble of actual textual practices in the postcolonial world. The question is not really so new (Barthes ascribes it to "the last few years," but that is rather a sign of avant-gardism), and not so local as Paris. Nor is it an aridly theoretical issue in much of the decolonizing world, where Marxism was prominent as theory and practice for most of the twentieth century, and where the relations of text and production—and if somewhat less so, literary theory—pose vital questions for urban intellectuals attempting to communicate with differently literate, rural audiences. Before describing this relationship, however, it is necessary to place postcoloniality on our theoretical map, as much in an attempt to continue the dialogue between Marxism and poststructuralism as to situate the relevance—or rather, the forms of appearance and their value—of postcolonial textuality within the current craze of American academia.

In a recent essay exploring the uses and abuses of the term "postcolonial," Stuart Hall outlines three horizons for its productive employment.[9] In order to begin constructing a genealogy of postcolonial textuality, I will summarize and reformulate his conclusions. Hall contrasts the denatured postcolonial"ism" that has been widely criticized in the United States with the continuing productive engagement with the contexts of decolonization worldwide in order to describe this engagement. Following Gayatri Spivak and others, Hall opts for the difficult term "postcoloniality" precisely because it challenges the homogenization of power relations—implied by older practices such as Orientalism—that are residual in the "ism" of "postcolonialism." If we are to use the term "postcolonial" at all, we must resist recasting the world in the flattened images inherited from Europe's colonial adventures. The very inelegance of "postcoloniality" causes it to stick in the mouth a bit longer, allowing us a moment to reflect before applying it uncritically to the rest of the world.

As a historical and sociological description, says Hall, the term "postcolonial" designates the common condition of having endured colonization and having gradually, through either internal pressure or external forbearance, attained decolonization or independence. This condition, though obviously insufficient by itself to define as similar the varied histories and lived experiences of the colonized world, would just as obviously apply to the colonizing countries themselves as to their colonial subjects. Scores of newly decolonized states entered the world stage between the 1950s and 1980s; many, such as India, China, Egypt, and Indonesia, avowed strong socialist principles and equally strong national autonomy, wishing to remain nonaligned with the two reigning superpowers. Their common membership in a Third World community, as formulated in the 1955 Bandung Conference, led Neil Larsen to term this historical conjuncture the Bandung Era.[10]

Tracking colonial conditions across time and around the world indicates that the conditions of inclusion in a common postcolonial project were neither unequivocally post capitalist exploitation nor homogeneous in all decolonized regions. Indeed, regional situations were remarkably varied and distinct, despite the fact of foreign rule that marked all for inclusion in this category. The differences between Japanese colonization in East Asia and British colonization in South Asia practically outweigh the similarities. An unimaginably heterogeneous collection was produced by local patterns of indigenous capitalist growth, continued neocolonial exploitation by home countries and by the world system, and the patterns of governance and dependency transferred to local elites, along with the distinctive cultures, classes, and types of colonial rule and decolonizing activity practiced within them; thus, many scholars have argued against considering them together on this basis. The question of how to treat Australia, South Africa, Israel, Ireland, and the Americas, where colonizing migrants are still in place, is much discussed. Equally, the continuation of certain forms of colonial domination, such as unfair trade links and the imposition of legal and political structures invented by the colonizers, provokes questioning of the historical distance the postcolonial has traveled from colonial in many locations. Hall claims the unifying rubric of postcolonial as describing the very persistence of foreign dominance within the newly independent territories: the "displacement from the colonizer/ colonized axis to [its] internalization within the decolonized society itself" (248). I prefer Gayatri Spivak's continual reminders that this internalization is not shared by great numbers of the colonized population, for whom independent national elites are as much a problem as empire ever was.[11] Thus, although we can usefully employ the postcolonial framework to make certain generalizations about world power, the description practically implies a scrupulous commitment to differences.

Hall's second horizon is theoretico-philosophical and concerns the ways in which colonized societies attempted to think through their external and internal domination and to arrive at new ways of conceptualizing and realizing their freedom. Hall terms this theorizing "thinking at the limit," a phrase he borrows from Jacques Derrida. In the colonial setting (although substantial battles occur in the tranquil halls of European philosophy), this thinking of limits confronts previous traditions of liberation—Marxist, feminist, and European revolutionary liberal—and finds them wanting in the drive for local autonomy. Thus Franz Fanon writes, "Marxist analysis should always be slightly stretched every time we have to do with the colonial situation";[12] to him, the masses of colonized subjects worldwide do not constitute a global proletariat, as was sometimes claimed in communist circles. Five years earlier, Fanon had rejected similar totalizing strains of the Sartrean dialectic then ascendant in Europe, whereby the black colonial subject of *négritude* could be seen as the necessary antithesis of colonialist white racism, and their clash as paving the way toward a nonracial, global *Aufhebung*.[13] Similarly, women's movements—as did Indian women reformers at the turn of the twentieth century, or Algerian women during their war of independence in the early 1960s—can reject the "prostitution" of Western liberal feminism in a radically different social structure that is itself distorted by the alienating claims of Western individuality and "freedom." This same individual freedom, much touted by earlier liberal reformers who would rescue degenerate natives from the slavery of their superstitions, becomes a dubious watchword when it is the official ideology of the ruler. Thinking at the limit means forging, in thought and practice, practical solutions to the unprecedented contradictions of colonial existence, objective circumstances that must be theorized and acted on without reliable guides. It is in this region of hybrid philosophy that the theory of value elaborated above becomes pertinent. "Every postcolonial liberation is a first," records Fanon, even as the materials of liberation are derived at least partially "from the master's house." Revolutionary traditions developed in one location do not necessarily travel well. The social, cultural, and historical specificity of these solutions presents a strong case for refusing the "ism."

This insistence on plurality, hybridity, cultural specificity, and uniqueness has provided rich soil for some of the themes of poststructuralist theory to flourish in when applied to postcolonial locations. Early in the twentieth century, Chinese modernism produced such a hybrid form in the radical literature of the May Fourth Movement, when the techniques of European aesthetics were introduced into the imperialized and feudal social structures of the East. *Négritude* was another improper adaptation of the hegemonic, liberal self-image of Europe (the "Universal Cultural Society") when applied to heterogeneous black populations of Africa, the Caribbean, and the United States. The form of the novel, of European origin, has now been practiced almost everywhere in the world and has been transformed in each local application into something distinct from its European tradition. World cinema requires its own unique vocabulary, history, and formalist nomenclature, as argued by the editors of *Questions of Third Cinema*.[14] Such dislocations and reappropriations of world culture, called "misplaced ideas" by the Brazilian critic Roberto Schwarz, require new lenses for cultural observation.[15] Despite the minute attention to local situations necessitated by these hybridized forms, there is still some logic in referring to the era and the practice of "thinking at the limit" as postcolonial, if only to imply that we need to look more closely at them.

We surely cannot separate colonial intellectuals from recent developments in European intellectual history, claiming one side for practice and the other for theory. Indeed, as Robert Young suggestively notes, many of the leading French poststructuralist theorists come from colonial roots (Derrida, Cixous, Althusser, and Bourdieu in Algeria; Barthes taught in Egypt; Lévi-Strauss worked in Brazil).[16] The vast majority of colonial intellectuals who have become visible to European observers were themselves educated in European systems, if not physically in Europe, and it was often European traditions of resistance and revolution that they were reconfiguring for colonial contexts. Barthes's materialist textuality provides an appropriate metaphor for postcolonial thinking at the limit. From the authority of the original "work," decolonizing practice reconfigures, recontextualizes—"reworks"—the limits of that authority, producing disjointed "texts" in places where the former work of authority applies only ambivalently.

Homi Bhabha has shown this process at work in an essay on the English book which shows how the Bible, the very bedrock of divine authority in the West, is literally shredded by its reception among proselytized natives in India. "And what is the significance of the Bible?" Bhabha asks. "Who knows?" The uses to which the English Bible is put in its new location literally dismembers it. A tired missionary complains, "Still everyone would gladly receive a Bible. And why? That he may store it up as a curiosity; sell it for a few pice; or use it for waste paper."[17] Such shreddings and rewritings—"waste paper"—comprise the necessary remodeling of works at the limit before they can become useful texts in their new locations. Hall describes this appropriation and transformation as what Spivak calls "affirmative deconstruction": criticizing a structure that one inhabits intimately, while knowing that the possibility of criticism is itself predicated on that structure. Hall puts it this way: European ideas "have been subjected to a deep and thoroughgoing critique, exposing their assumptions as a set of foundational effects. But this deconstruction does not abolish them, in the classic movement of supersession. . . . It leaves them as the only conceptual instruments and tools with which to think about the present—but only if they are employed in their deconstructed form" (255).

Beyond the traces of Western concepts "in abeyance" (255), postcolonial audiences deal in local works much more frequently than in imported ones, and the authority of these documents, often from modalities of reception widely different from those of European import, stake a far greater claim to authenticity on the local imagination. Just as Mohandas Gandhi, the London-trained barrister, could spin cloth from an ancient *charkha* to drive Manchester textiles out of India, the symbolic authority of the Indian epics, the *Ramayana* and *Mahabharata*—themselves documents of an older colonization—were frequently stretched to their limits to legitimate anticolonial activity. Mahasweta Devi's short story "Draupadi" evokes the epic topos of Draupadi's miraculous rescue by Krishna in the *Mahabharata* to underwrite the revolutionary struggle of agricultural laborers in the 1970s.[18] Fanon brilliantly described the transformations in traditional material during anticolonial struggle as a "zone of occult instability." It is the zone of limits, of radical reworkings and new imaginings that call into question all received ideas, and in which foreign influences and local practices combine in whatever mixture necessary to produce that unimaginable thing: liberation.

The third horizon of postcoloniality is institutional and disciplinary; it concerns the ways students and scholars approach culture in a world indelibly marked by colonization. By the time of World War I, or the "First Imperialist War," 85 percent of the earth's surface was claimed by European governments. This should give us pause when we consider, for example, European literature of the period: How could it *not* be marked by this phenomenon? According to the economist A. K. Bagchi, the very possibility of Britain's industrial revolution resided in the colonization of India as the supplier of its raw materials and the consumer of its mass-produced goods. Bagchi calculates that the 8 percent annual drain of Indian wealth during the years 1813–57, when invested in England, produced the economic "miracle" of modem industrial capitalism.[19] The question of what would have happened had those sums been invested in India is too painful to ask. How can the "industrial novel," the making of the English working class, or even the Victorian era be studied apart from the exploitation of the colonial world?

Sticking more comfortably to the question of literature: at the time of World War I, English literature was barely taught in the greatest English universities: it was considered beneath dignity as serious scholarly material. As Terry Eagleton put it, English literature as a discipline "rode to power on the back of wartime nationalism."[20] But the fact that the English literary curriculum was actually invented in India one hundred years earlier, and used there as a "mask of conquest,"[21] is surely a story that students of English need to know. More radically, employing the concept of postcoloniality to rethink the objects and methods of cultural study could result in vast redefinitions of history, regions, and textual objects—an approach that has been particularly fruitful in Latin America, for example. Just as the currency of Latin American literature in the North illustrates the exhilarating range of cultural hybridity between margin and center, the very fact that Latin America is not decolonized (if perhaps it is in some sense postcolonial) reminds us to qualify our descriptions of "colonial" in every case. One need not go as far as Enrique Dussell—who has claimed that the silver mine at Potosí financed the European Renaissance, and thus that the history of modern Europe is in reality the history of colonial Bolivia—to recognize the tremendous contributions to both Spanish literature and South American politics of the early colonial writers, as has Doris Sommer, or to perceive the spectacular challenges to textuality posed by Walter Mignolo's studies of Native American orality, pictography, and cartography.[22] In Hall's reckoning, the postcolonial era begins in 1492. This makes it practically coterminous with European capitalist modernity. If postcolonial studies were to become the organizing rubric for departments, as have cultural studies and modern studies in some places, reorienting humanistic study in this way would force a convergence between studying European culture and studying the cultures Europe dominated over the past five hundred years.[23] If this is a movement toward textualization, it is even more surely one toward material reality.

Conclusion

As the empire of signs replaces the signs of empire, at least three permutations of the "work" into the "text" become visible. Postcolonial textuality can be characterized by at least these three interlocking phenomena of colonial rule and postcolonial independence:

1. In the colonial period, there was a simultaneous legitimation and delegitimation of textual authority. European elites erected scriptural representations of supposedly ancient societies which they deemed inferior to modern European civilization. These scriptural representations were often gross caricatures of local knowledge. Nonetheless, the images stuck, and postcolonial authority often borrows on colonial modes of textuality to legitimate its own claims to authority. So-called religious fundamentalisms can be attributed in part to this dubious legitimization of Oriental authority.

2. During decolonization, a delegitimizing and textualization of European authority takes place. Barthesian textuality continues its work. "All that is solid melts into air." Europe is overthrown for Africa and Asia. Yet the structure of the interstate system persists in place, and the independent nation gradually accedes to the demands of the international system.

3. After independence, there is a popular rediscovery of Carnival license. Both national rulers and national elites can be defied. With the announcement of freedom from colonial oppression, the formerly colonized enact a textualization of all ideologies of rule. The most cynical are reincorporated into strategies of legitimation (such as the interstate system). However, a new regime of signification overlaps the old, based partly in history, partly in myth, and partly in the memory of colonial autocracy. In this space the subaltern subject arises. Neither proletarian nor peasant exactly, the subaltern represents the work that postcolonial textuality has yet to define.

Notes

This essay has aired in several places, and I am grateful for the comments offered by those audiences. One section of it was presented to the conference on Commonwealth and Postcolonial Literature at Georgia Southern University, April 1997; another to the concurrent conference of PSA/COPRED, Georgetown University, June 1997; and further considerations were presented to the Marxist Literary Group-Institute on Culture and Society, University of Illinois at Chicago, June 1997. I also wish to thank the participants in the George Washington University Seminar on South Asia who generously criticized a later version in October 1997. Particular thanks are due Alf Hiltebeital, Judith Plotz, Cynthia Leenarts, and Mustapha Kamal Pasha. The writing of this work has been supported by a fellowship from the National Endowment for the Humanities, an independent federal agency.

1. Fredric Jameson, *The Prisonhouse of Language: A Critical Account of Russian Formalism and French Structuralism* (Princeton: Princeton University Press, 1972), 102.
2. Roland Barthes, *Image Music Text,* trans. Stephen Heath (New York: Hill and Wang, 1977), 158.
3. Gregory Elliott, *Althusser: The Detour of Theory* (New York: Verso, 1987).
4. Alex Callinicos, "What Is Living and What Is Dead in the Philosophy of Althusser," in *The Althusserian Legacy,* ed. E. Ann Kaplan and Michael Sprinker (New York: Verso, 1993), 40.
5. Bruce Roberts, "The Visible and the Measurable: Althusser and the Marxian Theory of Value," in *Postmodern Materialism and the Future of Marxist Theory,* ed. Antonio Callari and David Ruccio (Hanover, N.H., and London: Wesleyan University Press, 1996), 192–211.
6. Jacques Derrida, *Specters of Marx: The State of the Debt, the Work of Mourning, and the New International,* trans. Peggy Kamuf (New York: Routledge, 1994), 127.
7. Slavoj Zizek, *For They Know Not What They Do: Enjoyment as a Political Factor* (New York: Verso, 1991), 15.
8. The phrase is from Louis Althusser, "Matérialisme aléatoire," in *Écrits philosophiques et politique,* vol. 1, ed. François Matheron (Paris: STOCK/ IMEC, 1994).
9. Stuart Hall, "When was the 'Post-Colonial'?: Thinking at the Limit," in *The Post-Colonial Question: Common Skies, Divided Horizons,* ed. Iain Chambers and Lydia Curti (New York: Routledge, 1996), 242–60.
10. Neil Larsen, presentation at conference on cultures of theory, University of Maryland, April 1996.
11. Gayatri Chakravorty Spivak, *Outside in the Teaching Machine* (New York: Routledge, 1993), 77–78.
12. Franz Fanon, *The Wretched of the Earth,* trans. Constance Farrington (New York: Grove, 1968), 40.
13. Franz Fanon, *Black Skin, White Masks,* trans. Richard Markham (New York: Grove, 1967).

14. Jim Pines and Paul Willemen, *Questions of Third Cinema* (London: British Film Institute, 1989).

15. Roberto Schwarz, *Misplaced Ideas* (New York: Verso, 1992).

16. Robert Young, *White Mythologies: Writing History and the West* (New York: Routledge, 1990).

17. Homi Bhabha, "Signs Taken for Wonders: Questions of Ambivalence and Authority under a Tree Outside Delhi, May 1817," in *"Race," Writing and Difference,* ed. Henry Louis Gates, Jr. (Chicago: University of Chicago Press, 1986), 121–22.

18. Mahasweta Devi's short story "Draupadi," in *In Other Worlds,* trans. Gayatri Chakravorty Spivak (New York: Methuen, 1987).

19. Amiya Kumar Bagchi, *The Political Economy of Underdevelopment* (New York: Cambridge University Press, 1982).

20. Terry Eagleton, *Literary Theory: An Introduction* (Minneapolis: University of Minnesota Press, 1983), 30.

21. Gauri Viswanathan, *Masks of Conquest: Literary Studies and British Rule in India* (New York: Columbia University Press, 1989).

22. Enrique Dussell, presentation at conference on globalization, Duke University, November 1995; Doris Sommer, *Foundational Fictions: The National Romances of Latin America* (Berkeley: University of California Press, 1991); Walter Mignolo, "Misunderstanding and Colonization: The Reconfiguration of Memory and Space," *South Atlantic Quarterly* 92, no. 2 (spring 1993): 219–60.

23. See Henry Schwarz and Sangeeta Ray, eds., *A Companion to Postcolonial Studies* (Malden, Mass.: Blackwell, 2000).

Stuart Moulthrop

Testing the Wires

If one takes the claims of textual theory at their most radical—as a serious challenge to the regime of print, conventional literacy, and logocentrism—then it is hard to write any further in this line without a sense of false consciousness. The problem is both philosophical and practical, or artifactual. John Mowitt noticed several years ago: "Either the text's relation to the book has been inadequately theorized (you are, after all, holding a book in your hands), or . . . the text's theorization is unfinished—hence the prolongation of the era of the book."[1] Mowitt's words certainly apply to the present essay as much as to his own more ambitious work. Both reflect a certain compulsion, not to say compulsiveness. In a better possible world, Mowitt apologizes, you would not have to read my apology—a statement that bears repeating here. What is the point of this? Textual theory sometimes seems like the eschatological naming of God. Once the final term is enunciated, we come to the end of the story; but the final utterance or "theorization" eludes us, and so we go back to our books, trying once again to locate ourselves in what Jay Bolter provocatively calls "the late age of print."[2]

Bolter goes Mowitt one better (or worse, as the case may be): we must now consider not only the vicissitudes of poststructuralist theory, but all manner of technical inventions as well—not just Barthes's or Foucault's *reseaux* of intertextual relations but also actual electronic networks such as the Internet and the many strange forms that propagate there. We pass from theorization to praxis, or, more accurately, we find our ideas inevitably caught up in things. In this situation there is more to deal with than the deferred closure of textual theory. As often happens when closure does not arrive, there are other stories to tell.

That much seemed abundantly clear one morning while I was writing this essay, when the *New York Times* presented two highly relevant items below the front-page fold. The first was headlined "On Prison Computer, Files to Make Parents Shiver." The story in the next column was headed "Profit Squeeze for Publishers Makes Tenure More Elusive."[3] The first report concerns information about schoolchildren possibly compiled for pedophiles. The files were found on a computer run by inmates at a Minnesota prison, who also used the machine for a successful programming and marketing business. The second story discusses the reluctance of university presses to publish certain scholarly books. With production costs rising and libraries buying fewer volumes, some editors have apparently declined to review work in narrowly specialized areas. The article quotes senior professors who speculate that tenure requirements may have to be reconsidered because of economic barriers to publication.

Even without their clear proximity on the morning's front page, the mutual resonance of these articles would have been hard to miss. Both concern the status and implications of texts—fictional and nonfictional, legitimate and criminal, commercial and academic, verbal and graphic; both deal with limits on expression and institutional boundaries for texts; and both are stories about information technologies, old and new. One might even say that both stories deal with computing, the Internet, and electronic communication in general, though that claim needs explaining. It would be more accurate to say that the first story seems to be about electronic texts, while the second appears to center on print, though in fact the first is not primarily concerned with computers, and the second probably should be. It is almost as if these stories are fragments of a single narrative cut apart and scrambled, mismatched and contradictory fragments of a missing account.

Although the headline and lead of the first story point to a "prison computer" as the chief menace, the bulk of the report, buried in the Metro section, significantly complicates this claim. The suspect in the case may have secreted information about children on a personal computer, but the information itself came originally from a community yearbook excerpted in a prison newspaper—both print sources. The suspect had evidently kept other ominous notebooks with pen and paper before he went on line. These facts are noted, but they do not seem to register. As the *Times* account allows in its penultimate paragraph: "The prison computer list was apparently created as much from parochial newsprint as from global computer power. But that was no comfort" (B11). Neither is an apparently positive application of electronic technology. Evidently the suspect's postings to Usenet newsgroups, recorded in electronic archives, have been obtained by investigators as possible evidence of a criminal interest in children, but this too lends no comfort. This is not a story about complex interactions of technologies, or about the dual capabilities of electronic networks for good and ill. It is a story "to make parents shiver," representative of much recent scare reporting about the Internet.

In its way, the second story is also disturbing because it attempts to avoid any engagement with newer technologies. Although it may seem strange to announce a crisis in academic publishing without more than cursory mention of on-line alternatives, here is all the *Times* sees fit to print: "One possibility is the rise of electronic publishing to the point that manuscripts could just be distributed and reviewed over the Internet rather than published in book form. But while electronic publishing is growing, few think the Internet is likely to replace books" (B11). In support of this alleged consensus, the author invokes two sources: the director of a notably conservative university press, and a senior professor from an Ivy League university. Despite their impressive credentials, these witnesses are hardly unimpeachable. One may wonder about their grasp of broader institutional realities, just as one can point out that electronic circulation does not necessarily "replace books"—but such objections are essentially moot. The newspaper of record has run its piece, which remains fixed on the page, beyond appeal. As Socrates memorably complained, we can harangue a piece of writing all we want, but it will not change its story.

The operative story on that particular morning in the late age of print was an alert about the unsuitable and dangerous qualities of new media. To be sure, these were only two notes in a complex chorus: in its business pages, the *Times* regularly offers more balanced analyses by John Markoff, Diane Caruso, Peter Lewis, Steve Lohr, and others, and the newspaper maintains a substantial presence on the World Wide Web. But pride of place, on this morning at least, belonged to the skeptics. Print, the front page assured us, is the only proper mode for serious thinking. Computers will not replace books or even prison newspapers (except in scare stories), and even though computers may help us identify dangerous sex offenders, they open up uncontrolled channels for communication—and, not incidentally, for commerce. In these articles, users of computers are suspect individuals subject to exposure and dismissive critique. The Internet aids pederasts even as it earns the justified scorn of top men at Princeton and Columbia. Read on, dear reader, but do not feel obliged to read on line.

This is ideology talking, of course, and when that happens we can expect contradictions. By presenting these stories in tandem, the *Times* invoked a fundamental division between serious, dignified, but unprofitable discourse (academic writing) and the lawless chatter of the Internet, which is deeply *promiscuous* in the general sense of that term: "to promote mixing or disregard boundaries." Yet the very anxiousness of these stories, evident in their strange contortions of the facts, belies this and similar distinctions. As the *Times*'s ambitious Web operation attests, the peculiar textuality of the Internet has already become a major influence in the communications industry, among others. The Internet may not be poised to replace books, but neither will it soon go away. People who care about communication should be thinking seriously about the nature and implications of electronic networks. *Pace* Mowitt, theory and practice must converge.

This convergence thesis is most clearly identified with George Landow, one of the most fervent believers in a post-print textuality. Landow jointly invokes poststructuralist theorists and information technologists, naming Jacques Derrida in the same space as Theodor Nelson and setting Roland Barthes alongside Andries Van Dam.[4] These figures, Landow points out, are intellectual explorers whose lines of flight crossed in the noösphere some time back, and whose intersecting vapor trails now weave for us the sign of the Net (2). One apparent product of these overflights is hypertext, a type of associative writing that shares a conceptual framework with "threads" in discussion groups, "links" on the World Wide Web, and the general notion of "navigating" in virtual space. In Landow's account, hypertext differs in many respects from the textuality of print. Its products are fluid and fundamentally permutable, less written than writeable, inviting not deconstruction so much as recombination. According to Landow, they promote an erosion of authorial autonomy and even of readerly "self," leading to a flattening of hierarchies and radical "democracy" of expression (100).

Landow duly notes the evident connection between these effects and poststructuralist textual theory, at times implying that hypertext fulfills prescriptions of Barthes, Foucault, Kristeva, and Derrida. The closeness of these affiliations is open to dispute, but they are only part of Landow's thesis—in the long run, perhaps the least important part. To suggest a parallel between literary philosophy and information science is mildly interesting. To claim that both fields reflect an emerging cultural dominant seems more revealing, though it raises suspicions of technological determinism. But Landow makes a significant move beyond both these positions. Theory is only the starting point, he argues. From theory flow rhetoric and actual, applied writing: "Hypertext intervenes at the level of discursive practice" (184). Though we may begin with literature or informatics, any committed engagement with electronic text leads out of the laboratory or the library and on to classrooms, businesses, and markets. What goes on in these places does not spring from any simplistic causality. "What is perhaps most interesting about hypertext," Landow tellingly observes, "is not that it may fulfill certain claims of structuralist and poststructuralist criticism but that it provides a rich means of testing them" (11). So much for determinism: in any proper test, the outcome is not known in advance. Landow suggests we may be entering a period of testing and experiment. This would, of course, leave us in radical uncertainty about what comes next. What might be the fate of writing, or the social practice of textuality, when the late age of print finally comes to an end?

Like all works that wander between the regime of print and the new order of signs that uneasily succeeds it, the present essay is concerned with conditions of probation. As someone says every few weeks on the radio, apropos of suspended endings, *this is a test.* And the reader might wonder, "Is it *only* a test?" And that is just the first of many questions. In what sense can we practically evaluate ideas from contemporary criticism? Which concepts are to be tested? By what standards will outcomes be judged? Or, to raise the most important issue of all: What would it mean to pass this test, and what would it mean to fail?

Not surprisingly, the negative outcome is easier to define. We can imagine in some detail how poststructuralist textuality might be tried outside the realm of theory and found wanting. A few years ago, the science fiction writer Bruce Sterling delivered a notably pessimistic picture of civil society in the early twenty-first century in his novel *Heavy Weather* (1994).[5] Sterling includes some choice remarks about electronic (or, as he prefers, "electric") writing. His main character, suffering through the not-so-long disease of a life, sometimes amuses himself with a digitized, full-text version of the Library of Congress:

He'd hammered away in the Library on occasion when absolutely sick of cable television, but the way he figured it, the big heap of electric text was way overrated. There were derelicts around who could fit all their material possessions in a paper bag, but they'd have a cheap laptop and some big chunk of the Library, and they'd crouch under a culvert with it, and peck around on it and fly around in it and read stuff and annotate and hypertext it, and then they'd come up with some pathetic, shattered, crank, loony, paranoid theory as to what the hell had happened to them and their planet. . . . It almost beat drugs for turning smart people into human wreckage. (74)

To be sure, this is all an especially bad dream. Sterling's novel is a sort of inverse *Wizard of Oz* where tornadoes are not magical transportation but signs of environmental collapse, and where the man behind the curtain looks less like Professor Marvel than like Doctor Strangelove. But Sterling's glancing dismissal of hypertext makes some sense. Considering certain recent trends, this passage seems increasingly compelling, if not portentous. Even without imagining anarchy in the United States or super-twisters venting the atmosphere to space, there are ways that electronic textuality could produce "human wreckage"—and no matter what the *Times* says, not all involve outlaws and sex offenders.

In contrast to Sterling's dystopia, consider what might happen in a somewhat better possible world. By 2010, the obsequies for the late age of print are finally over. Featherweight, portable touchscreens have become ubiquitous, making it possible to read electronic texts al fresco or in bed, winning over the most dour Gutenberg elegists. As happens with ideas whose time has safely gone, interest in electronic writing becomes intense among certain elites. After two or three decades in denial, academics and other knowledge workers suddenly embrace the technologies they once refused to take seriously, and they do it with the great fervor of fresh converts. The World Wide Web, all but abandoned in the "push technology" revival of '04, becomes the de facto preserve of research faculty. The census of Web pages, which peaked above a billion but fell to half that number after the shift to on-line "channels," begins to edge up again. More telling, the ratio of hypertext links per page, which has always hovered around four to one, suddenly jumps into double digits.

In late 2011 the World Wide Web Consortium and Modern Language Association jointly release the first major revision of hypertext markup language since the turn of the century. The new standard formalizes seven categories of hypertext reference and redefines references as first-class objects, meaning that authors can now create links to links, links to links to links, and so on. The new markup tools are eagerly adopted by disciples of "fabrication," an insurgent critical method that regards primary texts as "frames" upon which generations of *fabricateurs* "excorporate" the text by weaving hypertextual tissues of connection and commentary. Cryptic remarks in the movement's anonymous manifesto hint that the object of these "fashionings" is a sign system so densely imbricated that its full comprehension demands a "post-human" intelligence. (Some say the manifesto itself is machine-generated.)

Meanwhile, frustrated doctoral candidates at major universities begin petitioning to submit their dissertations off-line, using only antique "analog" footnotes. Their pleas fall on deaf ears. Enrollments in divinity schools surge.

This sketch may be only slightly less outlandish than Sterling's, but it aims at a similar point. Both scenarios identify a dangerous outcome for electronic text: its development in a purely esoteric or inward direction. The post-apocalyptic derelict and the post-millennial "fabricator" both pursue a kind of godless kabbalism, a devotion to textuality as very nearly an end in itself. This danger comes inevitably with inventions like hypertext and networked communication, which deny the closure of a unified work and thus create the possibility of endless complication even as they offer the consoling possibility of a strictly annotative discourse. Electronic textuality, whether in stand-alone hypertext or the distributed Web, could indeed be bad news for smart people. But it is worth keeping in mind that any such ill effects would be symptoms as well as causes. The fault is not solely in textual practices, nor indeed in theory per se. The root problem lies more fundamentally in social institutions, as Mark Taylor and Esa Saarinen make clear: "Expert language is a prison for knowledge and understanding. A prison for intellectually significant relationships. It is time to move beyond the institutional practices of triviledge, toward networks and surfaces, toward the play of superficiality, toward interstanding."[6]

It is interesting how these remarks conflate the two halves of the *Times*'s anti-Net diptych. For Taylor and Saarinen, prison and academy are not moral antipodes but one and the same. More important, this critique sheds valuable light on the cultural matrix where any "testing" of textuality must take place. The neologism "triviledge" puts a number of terms into play: triviality, *trivium,* knowledge, and privilege. As Taylor and Saarinen develop it, this word indicates the privileging of trivial knowledge in self-referring, self-promoting "expert language" born of a culture of expertise—or, as we might also call it, the corporate-academic complex. It is worth remembering that the post–Cold War Internet sprang from just such institutional roots.[7] It is also worth noting that the culture of expertise tends to breed true. Used as an instrument of triviledge, electronic textuality might well become a "prison for intellectually significant relationships"—or a prison built of such relationships. One possible "test" of textuality in the age of electronic networks might be the ability to avoid this outcome.

Taylor and Saarinen mark the alternative to triviledge with another portmanteau word, "interstanding," meaning a mode of discourse in which "to comprehend is no longer to grasp what lies beneath but to glimpse what lies between" ("Interstanding," 1). Arguably, interstanding might offer a way to avoid the imprisoning sentence of esotericism by emphasizing the extensive over the intensive, replacing annotation with excursus. For Taylor and Saarinen, this involves a particular kind of "superficiality." A text of interstanding would presumably concern itself less with the ground of textual authority than with potential figures that might be overlaid as responsive and responsible lines of flight. Or perhaps (extending the original terms somewhat) interstanding implies a keener grasp of figure and ground that allows these polar identities the possibility of reversal—something like Landow's textual "democracy" or Bolter's "network culture" (231–33). But this is all theory, and theory alone will not suffice. In essence, the testing will have to be practical.

This seems particularly true for Taylor and Saarinen's project of "media philosophy." Presumably this is not just a series of slogans but the program for an actual break with expertise, essentialism, and other trappings of disciplinary culture. Chief among these are print publication and the academic book. "To attempt to resurrect history or reopen the book," Taylor and Saarinen announce at one point, "is to try to put the brakes on the speed that has become our milieu" ("Speed," 9). To which one wants to say, *wait—not so fast.* To recall Mowitt, "You are, after all, holding a book in your hands": this book, that book; their book, my book, our book. Why should we believe claims about "Ending the Academy" (another of Taylor and Saarinen's chapter titles) that come packaged as a monograph—even one whose graphic designs are also available as Marimekko table coverings? How can "interstanding" help us break away from triviledge when it remains instantiated in the book?

Clearly this criticism has to begin at home. You hold in your hand a book about books about books. Hypertext is hardly alone in its potential for esoteric absorption. At best, one can try to be clear-headed about the implications of one's medium, and in this Taylor and Saarinen set an example. They recognize that they are at least one step away from any putative revolution. "If an electronic text can be published in printed form," they ask, "is it really electronic?"

The alternative would be to give up print and publish an electronic text. But the technology necessary for accessing electronic texts is still rather limited. Furthermore, most of the people we want to reach remain committed to print. There is no sense in preaching to the converted. Our dilemma is that we are living at the moment of transition from print to electronic culture. It is too late for printed books and too early for electronic texts. Along this boundary we must write our work. ("Telewriting," 5)

The years that have passed since Taylor and Saarinen delivered this opinion have been most eventful, especially for the World Wide Web, which in early 1993 contained something less than two million documents, but by century's end held more than a billion. The Web now regularly figures in political campaigns, advertising strategies, and even academic and cultural life. In its sheer scope and activity, it tends to belie Taylor and Saarinen's claim that the time for electronic texts is not yet. Though it seems strange to have reached this point so quickly, we clearly need to reconsider our putative "dilemma." It is easy enough to walk the line, musing on the new world powerless to be born; but that is something less than theory, and as we keep noting, our needs are increasingly practical.

To speak pragmatically, then: Does the World Wide Web prove anything? In its short time on the cultural scene, has it made even a small difference in the way people construct and circulate information, or texts? If the Web represents the most realistic hope for an ex-poststructuralist fusion of theory and praxis, can it pass the test of social application?

Though we do not yet have definitive answers for these questions, early indications seem negative. Theodor Nelson, the man who invented the word "hypertext" in the mid-1960s, has been heard to dismiss the Web as "a labyrinth of ever-changing shop windows," a very far cry from the universal library and egalitarian publishing system he outlined in *Literary Machines*.[8] The point is well taken. Commercial interests were bound to dominate the Internet, and this dominance has predictable consequences. Drawing on the experience of information services like Compuserve, Prodigy, and America Online, businesses have approached the Web less as a venue for innovative communication than as an extension of existing markets. Web "content" is increasingly seen as a way to lure users to advertising banners and on-line buying opportunities. In other words, the World Wide Web is poised to become a scaled-up, slightly more sophisticated version of cable television.

In clear confirmation of this trend, operators of pay television systems have begun to offer their own version of Internet access via cable modems, devices that offer vastly increased bandwidth and hence the ability to transfer much more information in a short timespan than was previously possible.[9] Not surprisingly, promoters commonly demonstrate this promised power by displaying World Wide Web pages containing multiple windows of "streaming" (in effect, broadcast) video. As one cable engineer told me, "We're selling speed." One could also say they are selling television. Now, as we wander the labyrinth of shop windows, we can keep up with all our favorite shows. More to the point, as we gaze through the inset frame at another episode of *Seinfeld* or *The X-Files*, we can use the vast interactive powers of the Internet to make impulse purchases. *Agent Mulder, what's that aftershave you're wearing?*

Product tie-ins and marketing-as-entertainment are very old ploys, of course, but they are not inscribed within the laws of media. The Internet has a way of confounding commercial expectations. Perhaps this technology will not be so easily forced into stale variations of the familiar. For one thing, the quantitative differences between old and new media are enormous. Cable television gives its viewers at most a few hundred choices at any given time. In theory at least, the Web offers many billions. Even though most Web surfers couldn't care less about this galaxy of mainly irrelevant data, its vast unseen mass provides a conceptual background for any selections they make. The Web is nothing as definite as a channel grid. One never knows quite what is out there. Though it is easy enough to find links that lead to uninteresting material, or that lead in circles, there is always the potential for undiscovered content and new offerings. In this respect, electronic textuality is indeed something like Barthesian or Foucauldian *texte:* a teeming network of possibilities in which the evidence of the particular both excludes the general and testifies to its fecundity.

It may be argued that this quantitative shift from work to (hyper)text also brings a significant qualitative change, suggesting that television as passive entertainment may not work in the new paradigm. To return to the case of cable modems, consider the recent popularity of simple digital video cameras, now priced under $100, as well as inexpensive audio-visual cards that digitize input from consumer camcorders. The widespread availability of these devices suggests that part of the new bandwidth could be taken up with something other than regularly scheduled programming: tours of the local toxic dump, footage of police brutality, unpaid political announcements, a million amateur clips from basement bands, mime theater, paranoid rants, folk dancing, crop circle reports, America's phoniest home videos—and of course, all the carnal possibilities of exhibitionism, mate-swapping, and other forms of sexual exploitation so popular on the bit-mapped screen.

There is a catch, though. Since cable companies control the hardware, they can severely restrict subscribers' transmission capacity. Design of these new networks becomes less a matter of topology than of topography, or the clever manipulation of technological gravity. In the most likely scenarios, torrents flow from the reservoir on high while consumers are able to pump only a minimal trickle back up the line. In some schemes currently in use, reception is measured in hundreds of millions of bits per second, a rate appropriate for video, while transmission is held to hundreds of bits, allowing only for encoded responses: *access this Web page, download that image, charge the aftershave to VISA.* Given the fact that current Internet technologies are, as always, near the limit of their carrying capacity,[10] system designers have a strong motivation to reserve bandwidth for themselves. Such systems, offering anything but a level playing field, might well make the Internet safe for television and other familiar tools of consumerism.

All of this is indeed practical, even technical and commercial, but it seems to take us a very long way from the usual concerns of textual theory, which in the first place have mainly to do with literary or philosophical discourse, and chiefly with formal writings, not popular entertainment. What can cable modems and commercial websites have to do with *S/Z, The Post Card, The Telephone Book,* or even with Greg Ulmer's pedagogic, post-Gutenberg "mystories" (1991).[11] Perhaps the threatened collapse of the World Wide Web into cable television suggests a second way poststructuralism might fail Landow's test of practical application. The outcome might well be negative unless we use theory to engage, and thus to transform, the matrix of assumptions about semiotic production and consumption that Mark Poster calls the "mode of information."[12]

To some, the high probability of failure here might argue for disengagement. Aside from e-mail and certain auxiliary forms of electronic publication, why should thinking people have anything to do with the Internet? Our prejudices run the other way. Let scholarship be scholarship; popular culture ye will always have with you. Keen observers like Poster, Ulmer, and Fredric Jameson make it clear that serious engagement with information technology cannot come easily. Jameson points out that there is something unrepresentable in contemporary technology, which offers to our examination "not the turbine, nor even Sheeler's grain elevators or smokestacks, not the baroque elaboration of pipes and conveyor belts, nor even the streamlined profile of the railroad train—all vehicles of speed still concentrated at rest—but rather the computer, whose outer shell has no emblematic or visual power, or even the casings of the various media themselves, as with that home appliance called television which articulates nothing but rather implodes, carrying its flattened image surface within itself."[13] Does the widespread nostalgia for the book proceed in part from the computer's failure to signify, from its refusal to be (ostensibly) anything but a mirror of other media?

Indeed, the current situation is even worse than this. After television and computer (or out of their miscegenation) comes the Internet, whose ways and means are even harder to know. No wonder we can no longer speak of "revolution," now that we dwell in the solid state surrounded by invisible logic instead of moving parts. Yet according to one speculative scenario, this new crisis of representation might actually prove the turning point for third-stage capitalism. Here are two characters in Neal Stephenson's novel *The Diamond Age* (1995), discussing a twenty-first-century offshoot of today's "cyberspace":

" . . . our media system no longer works like the old system—dedicated wires passing through a central switchboard. It works like that." Carl pointed to the traffic on the street. . . .

"So each person on the street is like an object?"

"Possibly, but a better analogy is that the objects are people like us, sitting in various buildings that front the street. Suppose that we want to send a message to someone over in Pudong. We write the message down on a piece of paper, and we go to the door and hand it to the first person who goes by and say, 'Take this to Mr. Gu in Pudong.' And he skates down the street for a while and runs into someone on a bicycle who looks like he might be headed for Pudong, and says, 'Take this to a pedestrian who can negotiate the snarl a little better,' and so on and so on, until eventually it reaches Mr. Gu. When Mr. Gu wants to respond, he sends us a message in the same way."

"So there's no way to trace the path taken by the message."

"Right. And the real situation is even more complicated. The media net was designed from the ground up to provide privacy and security, so that people could use it to transfer money. That's one reason the nation-states collapsed—as soon as the media grid was up and running, financial transactions could no longer be monitored by governments, and the tax collection systems got fubared."[14]

"Fubar" is an evocative piece of hacker slang, an acronym like "snafu," where f and u represent the familiar verbal phrase and the last three letters stand for "beyond all repair." In Stephenson's future, gone past recall is the old world order with its stable, traceable system of messages and referents. Gone too is the mass market that was, with its clear and monolithic demographics. This is in every sense of the word a much more *cryptic* situation. Stephenson's "media net" is a chaotic, self-configuring system that depends on fortuitous and promiscuous linkages. That is, it is actually and formally what the poststructuralist text is theoretically: a structure for the production of unanticipated and perhaps unsanctioned connections.

If such a system were actually created, there might indeed be a way for poststructuralist textuality to pass Landow's test of application; but of course, Stephenson's scenario is fiction. Nothing like the "media net" now exists, and it is hard to see how it could come about. In fact, it is hard to *see* anything relating to information technology. As Jameson, Poster, De Landa, and others point out, postmodern capitalism is even more than its predecessors an invisible regime, a domain of software, demographics, marketing strategies—which is to say, semiotic and textual practices. Perhaps these practices could be shaped and articulated to produce a future closer to Neal Stephenson's than to Bruce Sterling's (or the cable companies'). Indeed, Jameson himself calls for "a pedagogical political culture which seeks to endow the individual subject with some new heightened sense of its place in the global system" (54). But this supposed enlightenment requires a clear agenda for practical intervention.

It is beyond the scope of this essay, and its author's abilities, to take on Jameson's "cognitive mapping" in anything like suitable detail. However, a recent critique provides an important starting point for that project, and thus possibly a way past the ineffability of information technology. In an essay about the rhetoric of technological promotion, Martin Spinelli contrasts claims made about the Internet with equivalent productions in the early days of radio, drawing on the work of Hans Magnus Enzensberger:

Enzensberger would not have us see in emergent media a panacea or a pacifier for the disenfranchised, but the power to "mobilize." This mobilization is not the virtual movement of telnetting from San Francisco to Milan, nor is it access to the Library of Congress at affordable prices. It is the mobilization of production—*that is, a public identified as producers, not consumers.* Any democratic potential in an emergent medium must lie in its ability to facilitate the organization of non-virtual politics, not in vacuuming political action into itself.[15]

It is undeniably radical to suggest that people in the developed world, to say nothing for the moment of the poor and nonwired, could become producers as well as consumers of informational value. It is not, however, implausible. Henry Jenkins and others in cultural studies have described thriving fan subcultures that on occasion challenge the creative authority of studios, networks, and conglomerates.[16] Sherry Turkle documents the emergence of a new aesthetic of simulation, experiment, and manipulation of identity that seems a long way from the passive role-modeling offered by television and the movies.[17] Certain alternatives to mass marketing and passive consumption have received widespread exposure. For all its technological, social, and political limitations, the World Wide Web has introduced basic concepts of electronic textuality to several million people. The convention of the "home page" may be fading from the scene (to be replaced, one supposes, by "the You channel"), but whatever ensues, this genre did lay a fundamentally individual, production-centered groundwork for initial engagement.[18]

Spinelli's thesis about production and consumption asks us to recognize the fundamental conflict of interest underlying development of the Internet, and indeed of any information technology. As tools of information production become more widely available and distribution networks improve, a gulf appears between material production, which depends on enduring patterns of scarcity, and information production, where value can be generated quickly at many points in the system.[19] To call for an end to passive consumerism and a conflation of production and consumption is to begin the first lesson in Jameson's political pedagogy. At least as far as immaterial goods are concerned, this means disturbing the foundations of monopoly capitalism.

Spinelli calls for actual change, rejecting any esoteric rhetoric that "vacuum[s] political action into itself." Taking this charge seriously, is there any way to realize the convergence of information production and consumption in plausible practice? Some would say there is. Nelson's first outline for a global hypertext system, the yet-unrealized "Xanadu," contained a scheme for micro-payment of royalties based on the actual amount of content acquired by users. Operators of the system would take a percentage, but since they would not be bothered with printing, warehousing, shipping, retailing—or, in the sublime fiction of theory, by industrial-capitalist greed—fee structures would favor authors much more strongly than in print publication or broadcasting. In essence, Xanadu would transfer to producers of information a much larger share in the means of dissemination. This might be a crucial step toward the convergence of information consumption and production. The consequences could be significant if played out over a long enough scale. This will not happen any time soon, however. Not surprisingly, corporate interests have not rushed to implement Nelson's schemes.

Despite this lack of major capitalist enthusiasm, several speculative ventures have been launched on the World Wide Web that offer access to content for small or infinitesimal fees.[20] These operations differ markedly from commercial on-line services, which of course also charge for access to content. The new "nano-economic" ventures stake their hopes on the emergence of self-organizing and self-validating information markets where the distinction between receiver and provider is not sharply marked—markets that are, in fact, more like communities. By contrast, the on-line services mainly seek to increase connection time and regard the information they deliver as a means to that end. They promote their own interest as media managers at the expense of content providers, dictating the nature of information content according to competitive strategies and advertising campaigns. Like the conglomerates they emulate, on-line services favor traditional information commodities (investment guides, parenthood tips, sports coverage, games) and take on eccentric or niche markets mainly as an afterthought. At the moment, it remains unclear whether the nano-marketers will offer a distinct and viable alternative, or whether they will survive only by reproducing the old order.

In other words, the era of the book (or the pop song, the sitcom, the nightly news broadcast, the feature film, the sports event, the video game) is far from over. Though far advanced in theory, we have barely begun Landow's "testing" of poststructuralist ideas in the postmodern marketplace, and we seem unlikely to go far with that project until we better understand the convergence of production and consumption in genuinely decentered networks. Theory does play an important role here. Mowitt's critical assessment of textualism helps frame the problem, Ulmer's recent 1994 work on post-print invention suggests a productive focus for future work, and David Kolb's experiments with hypertextual analysis represent a crucial move into praxis.[21] Yet for the most part, even these far-seeing contributions remain, like what you are reading now, shadowed by the dreamy penumbra of the late age of print.

Real progress demands the opening of alternatives in both media and cultural institutions. It requires that we set a limit on our belatedness and step off the borderline between production and consumption, theory and praxis, print and its alternatives. It may ask us indeed to visualize the unrepresentable, which is less a case of gazing into the solid-state machine than of seeing through the apparent solidity of monopolistic, mass-market infrastructures, at least where the mode of information is concerned. This may ask us to do things that do not come naturally to children of triviledge, such as reading and writing business plans, facing the realities of competition, or understanding and renegotiating the forms of intellectual property. We can, as we have done here, relate these matters to changes in technology or textuality, but they belong in fact to larger developments: the continuing decentering of information, the countervailing attenuation of economic power, the current vacuum in political theory and practice, and perhaps even the demise of the taxpayer state. Though our textual lives are inevitably connected to this matrix of forces, it will take some effort to work out the articulations. *This is, indeed, a test.*

Notes

1. John Mowitt, *Text: The Genealogy of an Antidisciplinary Object* (Durham: Duke University Press, 1992), 1.

2. Jay Bolter, *Writing Space: The Computer, Hypertext, and the History of Writing* (Hillsdale, N.J.: Lawrence Erlbaum, 1991), 3.

3. Nina Bernstein, "On Prison Computer, Files to Make Parents Shiver," *New York Times,* 18 November 1996, A1, B11; Peter Applebome, "Profit Squeeze for Publishers Makes Tenure More Elusive," *New York Times,* 18 November 1996, A1, B11.

4. George Landow, *Hypertext: The Convergence of Contemporary Critical Theory and Technology* (Baltimore: Johns Hopkins University Press, 1992).

5. Bruce Sterling, *Heavy Weather* (New York: Bantam Books, 1994).

6. Mark Taylor and Esa Saarinen, "Communicative Practices," in their *Imagologies: Media Philosophy* (New York: Routledge, 1993), 9. This work consists of several named sections with individual pagination. Citations by section and page number are included in the text.

7. Manuel De Landa, *War in the Age of Intelligent Machines* (New York: Zone, 1991), 218–24.

8. Theodor Nelson, *Literary Machines* (Sausalito, Calif.: Mindful Press, 1990).

9. Mark Landler, "Where on Line Is on Cable," *New York Times,* 31 January 1996, D1, D4.

10. W. Wayt Gibbs, "Snap, Crunch or GigaPOP?" *Scientific American* 275, no. 6 (December 1986): 38–39.

11. Greg Ulmer, *Teletheory: Grammatology in the Age of Video* (New York: Routledge, 1991).

12. Mark Poster, *The Mode of Information: Poststructuralism and Social Context* (Chicago: University of Chicago Press, 1990).

13. Fredric Jameson, *Postmodernism, or the Cultural Logic of Late Capitalism* (Durham: Duke University Press, 1991), 36–37.

14. Neal Stephenson, *The Diamond Age, or, A Young Lady's Illustrated Primer* (New York: Bantam Books, 1995), 246.

15. Martin Spinelli, "Radio Lessons for the Internet," *Postmodern Culture* 6, no. 2 (1996): 35; emphasis added.

16. Henry Jenkins, *Textual Poachers: Television Fans and Participatory Culture* (New York: Routledge, 1992).

17. Sherry Turkle, *Life on the Screen: Identity in the Age of the Internet* (New York: Simon and Schuster, 1995).

18. Richard Furuta and Catherine Marshall, "Genre as Reflection of Technology in the World-Wide Web," in *Proceedings of the International Workshop on Hypermedia Design* (Berlin: Springer, 1995), 203–14.

19. William Mitchell, *City of Bits: Space, Place, and the Infobahn* (Cambridge, Mass.: MIT Press, 1995).

20. Tom Steinert-Threlkeld, "The Buck Starts Here," *Wired* 4, no. 8 (August 1996): 132–35, 194–95, 197.

21. For Ulmer's work on post-print invention, see his *Heuretics: The Logic of Invention* (Baltimore: Johns Hopkins University Press, 1994); see also David Kolb's hypertext *Socrates in the Labyrinth* (Cambridge, Mass.: Eastgate Systems, 1995).

Gregory L. Ulmer

Response
Text Culture Grammatology

The Textual Study of Culture

This section of the volume has delivered what the plan promised: a placement of the text/theory problematic in a context of the cultural studies movement. A list of primary ingredients—topics given substantive treatment—for the section would include at least the following categories:

- Theory: Havelock and Ong (orality and literacy); Bolter and Landow (hypermedia); Barthes and Althusser (structuralism/poststructuralism).
- Object of study: Literature—Bruce Sterling (science fiction), Mahasweta Devi (Bengali fiction); Music—Scott Joplin, Jerry Garcia, Jimi Hendrix.
- Frames of reference: Technology (sound recording, computing, the internet); institutions (literacy, disciplinarity, popular culture); cultural politics (postcoloniality).

From this diverse range of materials, the authors have produced several challenging questions that indicate a new direction for textual-critical research. The challenge to scholarly work covers media (Hunt: "The models of textual rhetoric we will need to guide the textual analysis and editing of recorded material will be different from the ones we have developed from and in response to written and printed material"); mode of production (Moulthrop: "If the Web represents the most realistic hope for an expoststructuralist fusion of theory and praxis, can it pass the test of social application?"); and discipline formation (Schwarz asks if the European model of literary purity can accommodate the quite different textuality of non-Western practices).

A retrospective glance over the cumulative argument of this volume reveals an attempt to imagine the language disciplines in general, or even English in particular, as they might exist in a postliterate era. There is no doubt that our expertise has central relevance for this new era, but it is less clear that the institutionalization of this expertise is sufficiently flexible to support the kind of bootstrapping operation that is needed to meet the new challenges. Thinking about the evolution of my own department makes me appreciate how my great-grandmother must have felt when she watched the televised landing of men on the moon and recalled her own arrival in North Dakota by covered wagon. In fact, Grandma went to her grave believing that the moon landing was a hoax (a view shared by a not insignificant percentage of Americans). The changes I have witnessed in my department over twenty-five years have been similarly profound, and some of the participants remain as unconvinced about our "progress" as was my great-grandmother about the moon landing.

The problematic of this collection could be restated to foreground the question of graduate study—the training of the next generation of specialists in our disciplines. The question might be stated as follows: Is this profession impossible? When I was in graduate school, it was still assumed that it was reasonable to "cover" English. A comprehensive exam at the end of course work tested the apprentices' knowledge of the history of English literature from its beginnings to the present. If the apprentices were expected to have read the canon, as writers they were trained to be subspecialist experts—again a coverage model, in that the production of original scholarship assumed mastery of the entire bibliography on the topic. Methodologies included formalist close reading, historical scholarship, and some interpretive work (allegoresis). No one was taught to address the range of topics covered in *Reimagining Textuality*.

The history of relations between textual scholarship and literary theory was marked in the 1970s by rivalry and even mutual exclusivity, to judge by what happened in my department. In the mid-1970s, the graduate studies committee voted to replace the bibliography course (which until then had been the methods course, emphasizing textual skills in the Anglo-American sense of the term) with a course in critical theory, an introduction to Continental theories of structuralism and poststructuralism. Theory became the new force of coherence in our program, replacing history and textual study. Textualist training in its old form disappeared almost completely owing to lack of interest among the students. At another level, however, textual study reemerged in critical theory in a new form. That is, structuralism represented a new alliance between linguistics—concerned with the micro-scale operations of language within the sentence—and literary study, concerned with the macro-scale of complex unstable entities beyond the sentence. Structuralists within many fields of the human sciences (Lévi-Strauss in anthropology, Lacan in psychoanalysis, and Althusser in Marxism, to name only a few) redescribed their objects of study and their methodologies by using linguistic models. From this synthesis of linguistics and epistemology emerged *text* in the new, expanded sense. Now everything and anything could be understood in terms of textuality, from biology to international relations. These developments have been called the "linguistic turn" in our disciplines.

This new-found methodological power emerged simultaneously with political and ethical concerns that motivated the opening of the canon. The coherence once provided for the discipline by means of historical coverage broke down under the weight of expanded information produced by multiculturalism and postcoloniality. If coverage was already something of a heuristic fiction within the confines of a national literature, it became an absurdity when the field opened its borders to global culture, including not only works of high culture in world literature but the other arts as well; not only the arts, for that matter, but all other institutions and artifacts had to be taken into account in the expanded field. Fortunately, a new heuristic fiction was available: that this complex global multiplicity of cultures and their products functioned in a textual manner.

Indeed, one of the directions for further work proposed by the present section concerns just this symbiosis between poststructuralist theory (beyond structuralism) and the expanded object of study (beyond literature), suggesting that the shift to theory in the humanities constituted just-in-time learning. The "aleatory materialism" of Barthes and Althusser, Schwarz observes, "has distinct resonances with other forms of textual production beyond Europe," especially in the decolonizing world. Moulthrop notes a similar fit between poststructural theory and the technological properties of interactive computing. The implication is that our disciplines today have arrived at the beginning of a new plateau similar to the one confronted a century ago as the field shifted from classics to the modern languages and literatures. This new mutation is well under way, and it is time to acknowledge it explicitly in our curriculum and pedagogy at all levels. My purpose here is to place this mutation in a broader context of world-historical changes.

The Pictorial Turn

Reimagining Textuality marks another turning point in the relations between text and theory that may have an even greater impact on our disciplines than did the linguistic turn. The enabling fiction that carried literate study from a national literature to global culture—the theoretical proposition that the world is a text—has been put into crisis by the increasingly obvious fact that the world is a text and a picture (to retain this reductive shorthand). Actually, it is a text and a picture and a sound track. Pity the poor graduate student whose department still operates with the tools of coverage and specialization (as most still do, no doubt)! And just when the disciplines believed that they had weathered the storm of theory, along came another phenomenon—the computer—to reinitiate the cycle of the fortunate fall.

The cycle of events that surfaced in the 1970s—the turn to theory and the opening of the canon—is beginning again in the 1990s in relation to computing. Exactly two decades after it replaced the bibliography course with critical theory, my department began teaching writing in a computer lab called the Networked Writing Environment (NWE). The introduction of computing has been accompanied by many of the same dynamics associated with the introduction of theory, dynamics that could be characterized as another battle of the ancients and the moderns. Moulthrop calls attention to the hinge between *Reimagining Textuality* and this latest turn in the profession when he reflects on the limitations of the book as a medium and a form for dealing with the current state of textuality. My own publications about "electracy" (electracy is to computing what literacy is to print) have been criticized for still being books, after all. Indeed, the apparent ease with which the academic article is able to describe recording technologies, popular culture, and non-Western states of mind tends to give rise to the same kind of response that my great-grandmother had to the moon landing; she had seen more convincing representations of space technology in the mode of fiction. This book is the television in my analogy: it communicates the new reality, but in a way that does not distinguish it from the old one. It creates the illusion that new recording technologies, visual culture, and non-Western arts are just some new themes calling for still more subspecializations in the smorgasbord curriculum.

What are the alternatives to the "prison house" of the book? I say that the computer makes possible another fortunate fall because, like theory before it, it provides a just-in-time answer to the crisis confronting our culture. That the pictorial turn has been experienced as a crisis by the discipline, if not by the society at large, may be seen in a series that Bill Moyers made for public television, *The Public Mind* (1989). "This series," according to the brochure circulated by Films for the Humanities and Sciences, "explores the impact on democracy of a mass culture whose basic information comes from image-making, the media, public opinion polls, public relations, and propaganda." Moyers interviews a large number of academic critics across the spectrum from uptight to hip (from Neil Postman to Mark Crispin Miller) who make a case for media literacy on the grounds that the society now does its business in a new discourse whose essence is pictorial, and which functions according to an emotional process immune to the critical tools of conceptual logic, with advertising as the prime exhibit. Following the rules of literate argument, the opposing side is represented in the form of the editorial staff of *Self* magazine. The choice is not arbitrary; the academics claim that one of the chief effects of the new media on our society is the destruction of selfhood as it has been constituted within the literate tradition. Replacing selfhood in the era of media is "the look," the desire to be an image. The women editors of *Self* defend "the look" and everything it takes to achieve it, from fashion to plastic surgery, using the literate assumptions of an autonomous critical intelligence making informed choices about what is in one's own best interest. The readers of *Self* simply "want" more luscious lips for very good reasons, the editors contend.

Unfortunately, Moyers does not seem to realize that *The Public Mind* is self-refuting, in that it argues that the new discourse of images is immune to literate logic, but at the same time the series proposes media literacy as a response to the dangers of the new mentality of "the look." Media literacy makes sense when our only tool is the book. The strategy is in the terms themselves: impose book models on the alien forms and practices emerging within the new media. The computer, however, opens the way to a completely new strategy, which is to continue the tradition of invention preserved in the heritage of our discipline. It is useful, even inspiring, to remember that one of the founding works of our profession—Aristotle's *Rhetoric*, whose influence is obvious in the handbooks still used in our general education writing courses—is a response to the alphabetic turn in Greek civilization. The institutions of orality had lost control of the new medium, and a new practice was needed to operate within writing in its own terms. To call for "media literacy" is similar to Aristotle's calling for alphabetic orality. Perhaps the *Rhetoric* is a kind of literate orality, but it includes a new logic specific to alphabetic technology. Desktop computing, augmented by the Internet, has brought about the conditions in which it is possible for the general population not just to "consume images" (the title of the first program in Moyers's series is "Consuming Images") but to produce them as well: to become electrate. But how is this to be done? If ever our society needed its textual theorists, now is the time.

Grammatology

The same force that motivated me to teach the theory course in 1974 put me in the NWE computer lab in 1994: the force of literate reasoning (for the invention of electracy is a bootstrapping operation). Perhaps there is no better occasion for a reiteration of the lessons of grammatology than this conclusion to *Reimagining Textuality,* since grammatology provides the means to reimagine the project of our profession. Let me propose in the space that remains at least one direction that follows from the cumulative argument of the preceding essays. The history of literacy recorded in works by Havelock, Goody, and Ong, among others, offers an analogy for understanding the issues of electracy: the elements of the shift from orality to literacy may be accepted as at least a relay, if not a poetics or even a model, for the invention of electracy.

Orality, literacy, and electracy are apparatuses or social machines organizing the language of an epoch. An apparatus in this sense is a matrix that includes a technology, institutional practices, and individual identity formation. The factors of change come as much from the social elements as from the technological, so the explanation of technological determinism does not fit these conditions. Rather, the apparatus is a matrix in which each dimension (materiality, society, psychology) contributes equally to the whole effect. The aspect of the matrix most immediately relevant here is the fact that Greek literacy included not only the assimilation of the alphabet but also the establishment of a new institution (Plato's Academy, school) and the emergence of a new experience of identity (individual selfhood). From our vantage point, it is possible to understand, logically if not causally, the past two millennia as the dissemination of conceptual categorization made possible by literacy through every scale of individual and social organization.

W. J. T. Mitchell's *Picture Theory* shows that this working out of the potentials of the concept took place within an ideological binary hierarchy that privileged reason over emotion, mind over body, and text over image. The prejudice against images is deeply ingrained within the Western tradition. In his explicit discussion of the pictorial turn, Mitchell makes clear how difficult it is going to be to make the shift from literacy to electracy. The brilliant insight of his book is the folding of the formal relationship between text and picture together with the ideological hierarchy of master and slave as it is registered through all the categories of identity (race, sexuality, gender, nation, religion, ethnicity, and the like). With such studies in mind, we are better prepared for what is actually at stake when we accept the challenge of inventing the institutional practice demanded by digital technologies. The machines in the NWE support graphics as easily as text. How natural it seems to want to embellish our argumentative essays with the ornaments of desktop publishing—layout, diagrams, color, and illustrations of all kinds! When we pose this possibility as a research question, however, and apply to it a more systematic methodology that demands to know the full extent of what is involved in this new environment, we catch a glimpse of an epochal transformation—already well advanced—that has been sweeping us along willy-nilly.

An application of the grammatological schema to the pictorial turn construed as a disaster in Moyers's TV series produces a different understanding of what is happening. The schema predicts that the technological changes—the sequence of inventions from photography to the World Wide Web—is only the most visible part of a mutating apparatus. We should expect also to find the emergence of a new institution within which the practices needed to work with the technology are evolving, along with new individual behaviors associated with these practices that in turn give rise to a new experience of subjectivation (identity construction). Once one gets past the literate point of view that frames the argument, much as the Church Fathers wrote about heresy, the Moyers series turns out to be a useful inventory of some features of the emerging apparatus. The more neutral or even sympathetic view proposed by grammatology would describe "the look" as the subjectivation that follows from the new recording technologies. Eric A. Havelock has described in great detail the impact of writing as the recording of the spoken word. The concept as a unit of reason was discovered/invented over several hundred years; the visualization of the Greek epics in writing allowed the scriptors to notice a pattern in the words that had gone unobserved in the ordering structure of narrative that provided coherence in orality. Clustered around the actions of the epic heroes was a whole series of terms concerning the quality of "justice."

When Plato completed the invention of the concept by authoring a dialogue devoted to justice in its own right, as an abstract category distinct from the actions of any given protagonist, philosophy was born, and with it the institutional practice of method. The grammatologist must ask, then: What is the equivalent of this discovery for electracy? I want to introduce this question now as a point of departure for further work. We do not have the luxury of the slow pace of history that characterized the ancient world. We need to understand now what unit of reasoning is associated with the body when it is recorded that we did not notice when it was named in our concepts (even while we responded to its effects), and so we could not "write" or teach it. If writing down the epics made visible and ultimately controllable a dimension of meaning called "concept," what new categorizing formation is emerging in the filming of our novels? The schema suggests that this unit will appear as a pattern already at work in the material, but that it must be isolated, defined, synthesized, abstracted, and sublated into its own form and genre. I have suggested elsewhere that this unit is "mood" or "atmosphere," and that it is carried by the props of object, dress, and setting.

Related to this audio-visual categorical unit is a new experience of identity, in the same way that selfhood and conceptual thinking are part of the literate matrix. Our recording technologies do for the human body in particular, and for the materiality of the world in general, what the alphabet did for the spoken or sung word. Now that we can and do record the body with all its nonverbal gestures, sounds, and manners, translating nearly all of our literature into audio-visual media, it comes as no surprise (at least in the grammatological schema) that people who consume forty-plus hours a week of recorded bodies would internalize this effect to the point of having an experience of identity different from that produced within literacy. This new experience is what was condemned in the Moyers series as "the look." The experience of being an individual self—of having an interior depth separate from the social and natural world in which one found oneself—arose from the behavior of reading. Now the behavior of viewing audio-visual recording is creating a different subject. Again, we must pose this problematic as a question in need of research. Theory has already addressed this problematic in terms of identity politics.

Syncretism

The grammatological schema further suggests that the institution that has emerged with the new recording technologies, and that is the place creating the practices needed to generalize the use of the technology across the civilization, is entertainment: entertainment is to electracy what school is to literacy. The struggles for the hearts and minds of the population that took place between the church and the academy throughout the epoch of literacy seem likely to be repeated between school and entertainment in the epoch of electracy. The history of these institutions is quite complex, and I am speaking here in grossly reductive terms in order to outline a direction for further research. In fact, the scenario of alternating conflict and truce will become triangular, with entertainment added to the ongoing conflict between religion and education.

What is the grammatological understanding of entertainment? To answer this question requires an inventory of the elements at work in the matrix of electracy. Any apparatus is a kind of push-me-pull-you dialectical process among technologies, institutionalization, and subjectivation over time and space. Literate methodologies, being linear and analytical, have difficulty grasping phenomena at this epochal and holistic scale of emergence. Still, the move from literacy to electracy is a bootstrapping process, and an analysis of the modern period leads to the following conclusion: entertainment is the site of a new syncretism. The last epochal syncretism is associated with the career of Saint Augustine, whose work is described by historians as a fusion or synthesis of the Greco-Roman and Judeo-Christian worldviews, traditions, collective states of mind, or epistemes. That this syncretism is again on our minds may be inferred from Michel Foucault's *History of Sexuality* and its concern with "technologies of the self," and especially volume 3, *The Care of the Self,* which deals explicitly with Augustine and his moment. Foucault tells the story of the passage from the Greek technique of the self, which included the male love of boys, to the Christian restrictions on pleasure of all kinds and the condemnation of homosexual love. Foucault associates his methodology with Nietzsche's *Genealogy of Morals,* which also addresses the consequences of Greco-Roman/Judeo-Christian syncretism.

Within the frame of grammatology, the genealogies of Nietzsche and Foucault look somewhat different than they do strictly within the disciplinary debates of critical theory. The important points grammatologically are not only the shift from one attitude to the body to another, for example, but also the fusion of features between what we might characterize as Western and Eastern civilizations. The assimilation of this fusion produced an extraordinary culture, for better or worse, and established in principle that syncretism is a legitimate potential within our tradition. This process of fusing radically different epistemes is happening again in our own time as a result of the entire history of colonialism. The short version of the story is that the Western tradition is syncretizing with the Black Atlantic (to use Paul Gilroy's convenient term for the African diaspora). Although it remains to be seen if he holds his place in history, Elvis Presley is a good candidate for the figure to hold a place for the new Saint Augustine. All the features of the electrate apparatus are at work in Elvis's story—the new recording technologies, entertainment as an institution, and the syncretism of African (or African American) culture with European culture in the forms of music. Not least in importance is the new attitude toward the body manifested by Elvis in particular and by rock and roll in general.

The new body is "funky" in the fullest sense of the word, and the emergent experience of this body is as different from the Christian techniques of the self as the Christian techniques were from the Greek. One does not think of the Greeks any more than of the Christians, however, as being inclined to shake their booty. If we borrow from Nietzsche's hostile account to name the state of mind that resulted from the Christian synthesis—*ressentiment*—then we could fill in the pattern by identifying the state of mind emerging in the Black Atlantic synthesis as "cool." The Western tradition must now be characterized as having not two pillars, as I was taught in my college humanities course, but three: Greco-Roman, Judeo-Christian, and Black Atlantic. Once identified, the pattern of the Augustinian syncretism is easily recognized in the Elvisian one: Roman colonization of the Judeo-Christian world, domination and enslavement of the Semitic peoples, led to eventual assimilation and ultimately conversion to a Christian Rome; its equivalent lies in the European colonialism in Africa and the New World, followed by the whole process of the transvaluation of values described in *The Genealogy of Morals*. President Clinton playing blues or jazz saxophone in the White House might serve as a parallel with Constantine's conversion to Christianity.

Africa has entered Western culture and the academic disciplines under both negative and positive signs: negative for critical theory, whose evolution could be told entirely in terms of the history of "fetishism," and positive for the arts, whose embracing of that same fetishism as an alternative to European norms constitutes the history of the avant-garde. This familiarity with the practices of African culture within academic research and production is a major resource for the grammatological project of inventing electracy. This project requires us to set aside the inflections and rationales that have legitimated our fetishism within literacy, and to rediscover our theories and productions as an expertise directly relevant to our three-pillared syncretic civilization. The grammatological schema indicates that the Internet is the academy of entertainment, and fetishism is its dialectic. Nothing is guaranteed in these conditions, nothing determined in advance. Literacy is capable of describing these new conditions, but not of thinking them, nor of fitting them into a book.

Let us imagine, then, a postliterate image-textual picture theory. This re-imagining will require the support of the prostheses or augmentations available in hypermedia arts practices. We need to move this discussion on line, for the same reasons of magnitude that chaos theory requires a computerized environment. The most we can expect of the academy—or that I can hope for myself—is that it may become virtually funky (and that should suffice).

Contributors
Index

Contributors

CHARLES BERNSTEIN's most recent books are *My Way: Speeches and Poems* (1999) and *Republics of Reality: 1975–1995* (2000). He is executive editor of the Electronic Poetry Center (http://epc.buffalo.edu) and is director of the Poetics Program at the University at Buffalo, where he is David Gray Professor of Poetry and Letters.

MARY ANN CAWS is distinguished professor of English, French, and comparative literature at the Graduate School, City University of New York. She is the author of many books, including *The Art of Interference: Stressed Readings in Visual and Verbal Texts* (1988), *Robert Motherwell: What Art Holds* (1995), *The Surrealist Look: An Erotics of Encounter* (1997), *Picasso's Weeping Woman: The Life and Art of Dora Maar* (2000), and *Manifesto: A Century of Isms* (2001), and the editor of *Surrealist Painters and Poets* (2001).

JOHANNA DRUCKER is Robertson Chair of Media Studies and professor of English at the University of Virginia. She is author of *Theorizing Modernism* (1994), *The Visible Word: Experimental Typography and Modern Art* (1994), *The Alphabetic Labyrinth* (1995), *The Century of Artists' Books* (1995), and *Figuring the Word* (1998), a collection of essays. In addition to her scholarly work, Drucker is internationally known as a book artist and experimental, visual poet. Recent titles include *Narratology* (1994), *Prove before Laying* (1997), *The Word Made Flesh* (1989; 1995), and *The History of the/My Wor(l)d* (1990; 1994). She is currently at work on a scholarly book about art and/as information and has recently completed two artists' books in collaboration with Brad Freeman, *Nova Reperata* (2000), a response to the seventeenth-century prints of Johannes Stradanus, and *Emerging Sentience* (2001).

RACHEL BLAU DUPLESSIS's *Genders, Races and Religious Cultures in Modern American Poetry, 1908–1934* (2001) joins her earlier critical works *Writing beyond the Ending: Narrative Strategies of Twentieth-Century Women*

Writers (1985), *H.D.: The Career of that Struggle* (1986), and her book of innovative essays, *The Pink Guitar: Writing as Feminist Practice* (1990). She is also known for her ongoing long poem; *Drafts 1–38, Toll* will be published in 2001. DuPlessis edited *The Selected Letters of George Oppen* (1990), and has coedited three anthologies: *The Feminist Memoir Project: Voices from Women's Liberation* with Ann Snitow (1998), *The Objectivist Nexus: Essays in Cultural Poetics* with Peter Quartermain (1999), and *Signets: Reading H.D.* with Susan Stanford Friedman (1990). DuPlessis is professor of English at Temple University.

MORRIS EAVES, professor of English at the University of Rochester, is working on *Posterity,* a study of the posthumous authority of readers and spectators. He is author of *Blake's Theory of Art* (1982) and *The Counter-Arts Conspiracy* (1992) and editor of several volumes, including *The Cambridge Companion to William Blake* (2002). He is coeditor of the William Blake Archive (http://www.blakearchive.org) and of *Blake/An Illustrated Quarterly.*

DANIEL FERRER is director of research at the Institut des Textes et Manuscrits Modernes (ITEM-CNRS, Paris) and editor of the journal *Genesis.* The books he has written or (co)edited include *Post-Structuralist Joyce: Essays from the French, L'Écriture et ses doubles: Genèse et variation textuelle, Ulysse à l'article: Joyce aux marges du roman, Genèses du roman contemporain: Incipit et entrée en écriture, Writing Its Own Wrunes for Ever: Essais de génétique joycienne / Essays in Joycean Genetics, Pourquoi la critique génétique?: Méthodes, theories, Bibliothèques d'écrivains,* and *Virginia Woolf and the Madness of Language.* He is now editing Joyce's *Finnegans Wake* notebooks, writing on the theory of genetic criticism, and working on the problems of hypertextual representation of drafts.

NEIL FRAISTAT is professor of English at the University of Maryland and a founder and general editor of the Romantic Circles website. He has published widely on literature of the Romantic period and on textual scholarship in such journals as *PMLA, JEGP, Studies in Romanticism,* and the *Keats–Shelley Journal,* as well as in such books as *The Poem and the Book, Poems in Their Place,* and *The "Prometheus Unbound" Notebooks.* Most recently, he has coedited with Susan S. Lanser Helen Maria Williams's *Letters Written in France* and with Donald H. Reiman *The Complete Poetry of Percy Bysshe Shelley* and the Norton Critical Edition of *Shelley's Poetry and Prose.* Fraistat is the recipient of the Society for Textual Scholarship's Fredson Bowers Memorial Prize, the Keats–Shelley Association Prize, and the Keats–Shelley Association's Distinguished Scholar Award.

Contributors

DAVID GREETHAM is distinguished professor of English and interdisciplinary studies at the Graduate School, City University of New York, and founder and past president of the Society for Textual Scholarship. His latest books are *Textual Transgressions: Essays toward a Biobibliography* and *Theories of the Text*. He is currently working on an electronic database of citation, copyright, and digital morphing in the arts.

JOSEPH GRIGELY is an artist and critical theorist, and associate professor of art at the University of Michigan. His recent exhibitions include shows at the Whitney Museum of American Art in New York City, the Museum of Contemporary Art in Los Angeles, Portikus in Frankfurt, the Victoria and Albert Museum in London, and the Musée d'Art Moderne in Paris. He has also participated in the Berlin, Venice, Istanbul, and Sydney biennials. His recent publications include *Conversation Pieces* (1998) and *Textualterity: Art, Theory, and Textual Criticism* (1995).

TIM HUNT, professor of English at Washington State University, is the editor of the five-volume Stanford University Press edition of *The Collected Poetry of Robinson Jeffers*. His work also includes a critical study of Jack Kerouac, a collection of poems, and articles and essays in *American Literature, American Poetry,* and *TEXT*.

ELIZABETH BERGMANN LOIZEAUX, associate professor of English at the University of Maryland, is author of *Yeats and the Visual Arts* (1986) and essays on verbal-visual studies in such journals as *Word & Image* and *Yeats: An Annual*. She is currently working on a study of modern poetic ekphrasis.

JEROME J. MCGANN is the John Stewart Bryan University Professor, University of Virginia, and the Thomas Holloway Professor of Victorian Media and Culture, Royal Holloway, University of London. He is the general editor of the Complete Writings and Pictures of Dante Gabriel Rossetti: A Hypermedia Research Archive. His most recent books are *Dante Gabriel Rossetti and the Game That Must Be Lost* (2000) and *Radiant Textuality: Literary Studies after W3* (2001).

STUART MOULTHROP is professor of communications design at the University of Baltimore. He is editor emeritus of the on-line journal *Postmodern Culture,* serves on the Board of Directors of the Electronic Literature Organization, and has published several widely discussed works of electronic fiction including *Victory Garden* (1991), "Hegirascope" (1995–97), and "Reagan Library" (1999), as well as numerous technical and critical articles.

HENRY SCHWARZ is associate professor of English at Georgetown University. He is author of *Writing Cultural History in Colonial and Postcolonial India* and has recently coedited Blackwell's *Companion to Postcolonial Studies.*

GREGORY L. ULMER, professor of English and media studies at the University of Florida in Gainesville, is the author of *Applied Grammatology* (1985), *Teletheory* (1989), and *Heuretics: The Logic of Invention* (1994). Ulmer is coordinator of the Florida Research Ensemble, whose current project is a choragraphy of Miami, entitled *MIAMI MIAUTRE: CAPITAL OF VIRTUAL AMERICA.* His book in progress is entitled *Electracy: What to Do with the Internet.*

Index

Aarseth, Espen, 7
Abelard, Peter, 36, 39, 45*n24*
Ackroyd, Peter, 114–16
Adorno, Theodor, 36, 45*n25*
Akeley, Carl, 75
Althusser, Louis, 13, 41, 211, 212, 213–14, 220, 241, 243
Anglicus, Bartholomaeus, 44*n23*
Appian, 34
Aquinas, Thomas, 39
Arakawa, Shusaku, 11, 12, 126–45, 146, 147, 148, 179, 183–84; *The Mechanism of Meaning* (Arakawa and Gins), 11, 126–43, 148
Aristotle, 86, 173, 245
Armstrong, Louis, 198, 200, 203
Artaud, Antonin, 150*n9*
Auden, W. H., 92
Augustine (Saint), 248, 249
Augustine, Jane, 94*n2*

Bach, J. S., 87
Bagchi, A. K., 221
Balin, Marty, 190
Barnes, Djuna, 87, 94*n2*
Barthes, Roland, 5, 12–13, 34–35, 211–13, 214, 215, 216, 217, 220, 225, 228, 241, 243; "From Work to Text" 12–13, 211–12; *Mythologies,* 213; *S/Z,* 234
Baudelaire, Charles, 182
Beach Boys, 190
Benjamin, Walter, 119*n1*
Bentley, G. E., Jr., 114, 116, 122*n29*
Bergson, Henri, 150
Bernstein, Charles, 12, 15*n2,* 125, 163, 165–66, 167, 168
Bhabha, Homi, 220

Bible, 101, 191, 220
Birkerts, Sven, 181
Blair, Robert, 116
Blake, Catherine, 115
Blake, William, 7, 11, 12, 99, 102–16, 119*nn4, 5,* 10, 11, 120*nn12, 14, 20,* 121*nn24, 25,* 122*n29,* 178, 179, 181–83, 184; *The Book of Urizen,* 106; "Illuminated Books," 105; *Jerusalem,* 105, 106, 114, 178; *The Marriage of Heaven and Hell,* 105, 113; *Songs of Innocence and of Experience,* 105, 106, 107, 109, 111
Blake Archive, 24, 117
Bloom, Harold, 182
Bolden, Buddy, 198, 199, 208
Bolter, Jay, 225, 231, 241
Boole, George, 170
Bornstein, George, 15*nn2, 4*
Boswell, James, 120*n16*
Bourdieu, Pierre, 220
Bowdler, Thomas, 71, 77–78
Bowers, Fredson, 9, 38, 44*n20,* 46*nn34, 36,* 57*n1,* 120*n19*
Boydell, John, 101
Building Sensoriums, 1973–1990, 143
Bunting, Basil, 180
Buñuel, Luis, 24
Burke, Edmund, 109
Butts, Thomas, 105

Cage, John, 184, 206
Cameron, Sharon, 88
Camille, Michael, 15*n4*
Carnap, Rudolf, 170
Caruso, Diane, 227
Caws, Mary Ann, 11, 12, 13, 183
Cézanne, Paul, 138

Chapman, Dinos and Jake, 66
Châteaubriand, François-René de, 52
Chaucer, Geoffrey, 52
Chomsky, Noam, 171, 175$n3$
Chopin, Frédéric, 195
Cixous, Hélène, 220
Clint, George, 70
Clinton, William Jefferson, 3, 250
Cockram, Patricia, 47$n45$
Coleman, Ornette, 203
Coltrane, John, 202
Crouwel, Wim, 159
Crumb, George, 206
Cunningham, Allan, 106
Curran, Amelia, 70
Curran, Stuart, 88

Darwin, Charles, 63
Davidson, Donald, 150$n1$
Davie, Oliver, 75
Davis, Miles, 209$n9$
de Biasi, Pierre-Marc, 88, 89
DeJarnette, Joseph, 63
De Landa, Manuel, 236
della Rovere, Cardinal, 34
de Man, Paul, 36, 44$n20$
Dennett, Daniel, 150$n1$
Derrida, Jacques, 5, 32, 41, 42$n1$, 173, 175$n6$, 214, 216, 218, 220, 228; *Glas*, 41; *The Post Card*, 234
Descartes, René, 124
Desdumes, Mamie, 197, 198
Devi, Mahasweta, 221, 241
Dickinson, Emily, 88, 183
Diderot, Denis, 66, 148
Dorfman, Deborah, 120$n14$
Drucker, Johanna, 11, 12, 15$n2$, 179–80
Duchamp, Marcel, 126, 128, 184
Duggan, Hoyt, 20
DuPlessis, Rachel Blau, 10, 11, 13, 14
Dussell, Enrique, 221
Dylan, Bob, 193, 194

Eagleton, Terry, 221
Eaves, Morris, 7, 11, 15$n2$, 179, 181–82
Eco, Umberto, 36, 40, 44$n21$, 124
Eisenstein, Elizabeth, 120$n17$
Eliot, T. S., 62, 94$n2$, 120$n16$, 201, 209$n7$
Ellington, Duke, 199, 200
Emerson, Ralph Waldo, 124

Enzensberger, Hans Magnus, 236
Erdman, David V., 114

Fanon, Franz, 218–19, 221
Feldman, Morton, 206
Ferguson, Joanne, 94
Ferrer, Daniel, 10, 11, 85, 86, 88, 90, 92
Fitzgerald, Ella, 199, 208
Flanders, Julia, 18, 19, 20, 21
Flaubert, Gustave, 50, 51, 52, 54, 59$n21$, 92
Foucault, Michel, 42$n1$, 214, 225, 228, 249
Fraistat, Neil, 16$n9$
Frege, Gottlob, 170
Freud, Sigmund, 90, 128, 211–12, 213
Froger, Dom, 53
Frost, Robert, 18

Gabler, Hans Walter, 51, 56, 75
Gandhi, Mohandas, 220
Garcia, Jerry, 189, 190, 193, 194, 206, 208, 241
Gaydos, Tim, 70, 73
Gilchrist, Alexander, 103, 107–8, 109, 110, 115
Gilroy, Paul, 249
Gins, Madeline, 11, 12, 126–43, 146, 147, 148, 179, 183–84; *Helen Keller, or Arakawa*, 148; *The Mechanism of Meaning* (Arakawa and Gins), 11, 126–43, 148; *To Not to Die*, 147, 148
Ginzburg, Carlo, 53, 58$n13$
Glazier, Loss Pequeño, 15$n2$, 163, 164, 166
Godard, Jean-Luc, 4
Goffman, Erving, 68
Goodman, Nelson, 51–52
Graham, Bill, 189
Grateful Dead, 12, 189, 191, 203–5, 206; *Anthem of the Sun*, 204–5, 206, 207; *Aoxomoxoa*, 206; "The Golden Road (to Unlimited Devotion)," 204; "Good Morning, Little School Girl," 204; *The Grateful Dead*, 204; *Live Dead*, 205; "Viola Lee Blues," 204; *Working Man's Dead*, 206
Greenberg, Clement, 15$n2$
Greetham, David, 9, 10, 11, 12, 15$n2$, 85, 86–87, 89, 90, 150$nn2$, 5
Greg, W. W., 9, 38, 44$n20$, 46$nn34$, 36
Grigely, Joseph, 9, 10, 11, 12, 14, 40, 85, 86, 90
Grimm, Brothers, 191, 192

Index

Grumbrich-Simitis, Ilse, 90
Gutenberg, 230
Györgi, Ladislao Pablo, 169

Habermas, Jürgen, 31, 32, 36, 42*n5*
Hall, Stuart, 217, 218, 220
Hall, Walter Mignolo, 222
Handel, George Frideric, 104
Haraway, Donna, 62, 79
Harrison, Lou, 206
Hassinger, Dave, 204
Havelock, Eric A., 192, 208*n3*, 241, 246, 247; *The Greek Concept of Justice*, 209*n3*; *The Muse Learns to Write*, 208*n3*; *Preface to Plato*, 209*n3*
Hawthorne, Nathanial, 120*n19*
Haxthausen, Charles W., 145–46; *Reversible Destiny*, 126, 128, 145–46, 147, 148, 149, 183, 184; "The Road to Critical Resemblances House: Report of a Mapping," 145–46
Hayley, William, 102, 104, 105
H.D. (Hilda Doolitle), 87, 90, 94*n2*; *The Gift*, 87, 88, 94*n2*; *Helen in Egypt*, 90
Hegel, G. W. F., 37
Heidegger, Martin, 42*n1*
Hendrix, Jimmy, 206–8, 241
Heydt, Erich, 90
Hill, W. Speed, 37
Hirsch, E. D., 42*n1*
Hofstadter, Douglas, 158
Homer, 115, 120*n16*, 192, 198; *The Iliad*, 191, 192, 193
Hooker, John Lee, 189
Hooker, Richard, 37
Howard-Hill, Trevor H., 45*n30*
Howe, Susan, 88
Hugo, Victor, 92
Hume, David, 101
Humphry, Ozias, 119*n11*
Hunt, Tim, 12, 14, 241
Hurt, Mississippi John, 194, 209*n4*
Husserl, Edmund, 42*n1*, 173, 175*n6*, 179

Iser, Wolfgang, 129
Isidore (Saint), 36, 39, 44*n22*

Jagger, Mick, 193
James, Henry, 92
James, William, 57*n1*

Jameson, Fredric, 211, 235, 236, 237
Jarmusch, Jim, 101–2, 116
Jauss, Hans-Robert, 41, 129
Jefferson, Lemon, 194, 209*n4*
Jefferson Airplane, 189
Jenkins, Henry, 237
Johnson, Blind Willie, 209*n4*
Johnson, Bunk, 198
Jones, Karen Sparck, 175*n3*
Jones, Steven E., 16*n9*
Joplin, Scott, 195, 196, 197
Joseph, Gerhard, 34, 35
Joyce, James, 50, 51, 52, 54, 92; *Ulysses*, 50, 51, 75

Kac, Eduardo, 169
Kafka, Franz, 52
Kant, Immanuel, 21
Kay, Martin, 175*n3*
Kazee, Buell, 209*n4*
Keats, John, 62
Keeler, Mary, 22
Kenney, E. J., 46*n31*
Keppard, Freddie, 198
Keynes, Geoffrey, 114
Kidd, John, 75
Kircher, Athanasius, 160, 161
Kirschenbaum, Matthew, 24, 171
Knesl, John, 143
Knuth, Donald, 156, 158, 176*n9*
Kolb, David, 238
Kramer, Eddie, 206–7
Krieger, Murray, 6
Kristeller, Paul Oskar, 46*n37*
Kristeva, Julia, 228
Krushchev, Nikita, 213, 214

Labrie, Jean, 75, 76
Lacan, Jacques, 243
Lamb, Charles, 71
Landow, George, 228–29, 231, 234, 236, 238, 241
Lang, Cecil, 103, 104
Larson, Neil, 218
Lateef, Yusef, 189
Leibniz, Gottfried, 169, 170
Leisman, Antonio, 70
Lennon, John, 193
Leonardo da Vinci, 128, 148
Lessing, Gotthold, 11, 117

Lévi-Strauss, Claude, 220, 243
Lewis, Peter, 227
Lifton, Robert Jay, 118*n1*
Linnell, John, 115
Lipking, Lawrence, 85
Livingston, Ira, 62
Lohr, Steve, 227
Love, Harold, 41
Lyotard, Jean-François, 32, 214

Maas, Paul, 53
Macdonald, Dwight, 119*n1*
Machan, Tim William, 42*n2*
MacLagan, Eric Robert Dalrymple, 121*n24*
Macon, Uncle Dave, 194, 209*n4*
Mahabharata, 220–21
Mallarmé, Stéphane, 52, 184
Manilow, Barry, 192
Mantegna, Andrea, 128
Markoff, John, 227
Marotti, Arthur, 41
Marshall, Madame J. W., 80, 81
Marx, Karl, 37, 40, 211–15, 216; *Capital*, 214, 215; *The Economic and Philosophic Manuscripts of 1844*, 213, 214; *German Ideology*, 215
McCartney, Paul, 193
McCarty, Willard, 20
McGann, Jerome J., 5–6, 7, 9, 11, 14, 15*nn2, 3*, 38, 40, 45*nn27, 30*, 47*n44*, 62, 85, 117, 119*n10*
McKenzie, D. F., 5, 8, 40, 41, 45*n30*
McLeod, Randall, 38
Melchoir, Claus, 51
Melville, Herman, 103
Mènard, Pierre, 50
Mendel, Gregor, 63
Michelangelo, 39, 104
Migne, Jacques-Paul, 45*n24*
Miller, Mark Crispin, 245
Milton, John, 101, 107, 111, 192
Mingus, Charles, 209*n9*
Mitchell, W. J. T., 6, 13, 246
Monroe, Bill, 190
Moore, Marianne, 89
More, Paul Elmer, 120*n14*
Moreau, René, 172, 176*n10*
Morris, William, 40
Morton, Jelly Roll, 12, 195, 196, 197, 198, 209*nn5, 6*

Moulthrop, Stuart, 13, 241, 243, 244
Mowitt, John, 225, 228, 232, 238
Moyers, Bill, 244–45, 247, 248
Mumford, Lewis, 119*n1*
Murch, Walter, 3–4

Negroponte, Nicholas, 117, 118
Nelson, Theodor, 228, 233, 237–38
Newton, Issac, 37
Niedecker, Lorine, 93
Nietzsche, Friedrich, 42*n1*, 249, 250

O'Hara, Frank, 18, 93
Oliver, King, 198, 199, 200, 203
Olson, Charles, 93
Ong, Walter, 192, 200, 241, 246
Oppen, George, 92, 93

Paré, Ambroise, 74–75
Parry, Milman, 192
Parsons, Bill (Bobby Bare), 203
Partch, Harry, 205–6
Pascal, Blaise, 170
Patmore, Coventry, 120*n14*
Patterson, Lee, 45*nn27, 30*
Peacock, Thomas Love, 70
Pearson, Norman Holmes, 90, 114
Perkins, Maxwell, 106
Plato, 86, 148, 246, 247
Pollard, Alfred, 44*n20*
Pope, Alexander, 120*n16*
Poster, Mark, 235, 236
Postman, Neil, 245
Pound, Ezra, 15*n2*, 47*n45*, 201, 209*n7*
Powers, Richard, 177*n19*
Presley, Elvis, 203, 249
Proust, Marcel, 54

Rainey, Lawrence, 32
Ramayana, 220
Reed, Jimmie, 189
Reiman, Donald H., 70, 71, 73
Reynolds, Joshua, 102
Reznikoff, Charles, 93
Richards, Keith, 193
Richmond, George, 115
Rifkin, Libbie, 91
Roberts, Bruce, 215
Robinson, Peter, 20
Rockman, Alexis, 69, 70

Index

Rorty, Richard, 32, 150*nn1, 2*
Rosa, Guimaraes, 54
Rosenberg, Jim, 15*n2*, 163, 164–65, 166
Rossetti, Dante Gabriel, 23–24, 25, 26*n7*, 40; *The Blessed Damozel*, 25; *Poems*, 26*n7*
Rossetti, William Michael, 114, 121*nn24, 25, 26*
Rossetti Archive, 18, 20, 22, 23, 24, 25, 26*n2*, 38, 117
Rousseau, Jean-Jacques, 52, 148
Ruskin, John, 149
Russell, Archibald George Blomefield, 121*n24*
Ryle, Gilbert, 150*n1*

Saarinen, Esa, 13, 231–32
Samuels, Lisa, 25
Sassari, Ritta and Christina, 66, 67, 68
Schaap, Phil, 210*n9*
Schwarz, Henry, 12–13, 242, 243
Schwarz, Roberto, 219
Shakespeare, William, 62, 71, 78, 92, 101, 111, 115; *King Lear*, 51
Shelley, Mary W., 70
Shelley, Percy Bysshe, 70
Sherry, James, 180
Slick, Grace, 190
Smith, Adam, 37
Smith, Charlotte, 10, 88
Smith, Harry, 209*n4*
Smith, J. T., 119*n11*
Smith, Martha Nell, 88
Socrates, 227
Sommer, Doris, 222
Spector, Phil, 203
Spinelli, Martin, 13, 236, 237
Spivak, Gayatri, 217, 218, 220
Stafford, Barbara, 69
Stahmer, Carl, 16*n9*
Stalin, Josef, 213, 214
Stanleys, 190
Starr, Kenneth, 3
Stein, Gertrude, 89
Stendhal (Henri Beyle), 52, 54
Stephenson, Neal, 235–36
Steppe, Wolfhard, 51
Sterling, Bruce, 229–30, 236, 241
Sterne, Laurence, 41
Suarès, André, 148
Sutherland, Kathryn, 8

Suvakovic, Misko, 184
Swinburne, Algernon Charles, 11, 103, 104, 105, 108–14, 121*n24*, 182, 183; *Critical Essay*, 182, 183; *William Blake, a Critical Study*, 108, 121*n24*

Tanselle, G. Thomas, 35, 39, 41, 46*nn34, 36*, 62, 117, 118, 179
Tatham, Frederick, 106, 115
Taylor, Gary, 71
Taylor, Mark, 13, 231–32
Tennyson, Alfred, 34, 35, 40
Thompson, Francis, 120*n14*
Thomson, James, 108
Timpanaro, Sebastiano, 53, 58*n14*
Tinkle, Theresa, 15*n4*
Toklas, Alice B., 89
Tory, Geofroy, 156, 157
Toulmin, Stephen, 31
Trevisa, John, 45*n23*
Truffaut, François, 4
Turing, Alan, 170
Turkle, Sherry, 33, 34, 46*n40*, 237
Turner, Dawson, 105–6, 119*n11*
Twain, Mark, 41

Ulmer, Gregory L., 8, 13, 14, 62, 234, 235, 238
Unsworth, John, 181

Valéry, Paul, 92, 148
Van Dam, Andries, 228
Van Ronk, Dave, 209*n4*
Vermeer, Jan, 138
Vickery, Ann, 91
Vinci, Leonardo da. *See* Leonardo da Vinci
Virgil, 52, 107, 110
Von Neumann, John, 170

Ward, Aileen, 116, 122*n29*
Waters, Muddy, 194
Watten, Barrett, 91
Welles, Orson, 3–4; *Touch of Evil*, 3–4
Whiteman, Paul, 199
Whitman, Walt, 182
Wilkins, Bishop John, 160
Williams, Edward E., 70
Wittgenstein, Ludwig, 20, 22, 150*n1*
Wizard of Oz, The, 229

Wordsworth, William, 106; *The Prelude*, 120*n16*

Yeats, William Butler, 15*n2*, 92
Young, Robert, 220

Zizek, Slovoj, 216
Zukofsky, Louis, 93